Actual Innocence

Jim Dwyer
Peter Neufeld
Barry Scheck

Doubleday

New York London Toronto Sydney Auckland

Actual Innocence

Five Days to Execution and Other Dispatches from the Wrongly Convicted

PUBLISHED BY DOUBLEDAY
a division of Random House, Inc.
1540 Broadway, New York, New York 10036

DOUBLEDAY and the portrayal of an anchor with a dolphin
are trademarks of Doubleday, a division of
Random House, Inc.

Book design by Maria Carella

Library of Congress Cataloging-in-Publication Data

Scheck, Barry
Actual innocence: five days to execution and other dispatches from the wrongly
convicted / by Barry Scheck, Peter Neufeld & Jim Dwyer.—1st ed.
p. cm.
1. Judicial error—United States. I. Title. II. Neufeld, Peter (Peter J.)
III. Dwyer, Jim.
KF9756 .D98   2000
347.73´1221—dc21   99-045876
CIP

Printed in the United States of America

February 2000

First Edition

1   3   5   7   9   10   8   6   4   2

Contents

Authors' Note

This is a work of nonfiction. Our descriptions of events are based on interviews, the personal experiences of one or more of the authors, court transcripts, and legal filings. We also relied on works of legal and social science scholarship, which are enumerated. We used no anonymous sources.

Following the convention of American journalism, we have not named the living victims of sexual assault, other than those who have chosen to speak in public. These are pseudonyms: Irma Lopez (Chapter One), Faye Treatser (Chapter Three), Jeannie (Chapter Five), Molly M. (Chapter Seven), Louise Lewis (Chapter Ten).

Other than in this note, we refer to ourselves in the third person, one at a time, as Barry, Peter, and Jim.

Jim Dwyer, Peter Neufeld, Barry Scheck
New York City, August 2, 1999

Preface

Wrong Numbers

The thing is, you don't have many suspects who are innocent of a crime. That's contradictory. If a person is innocent of crime, then he is not a suspect.

Edwin Meese, Attorney General
of the United States, 1986

The phone rings. His mother and aunt have gone to bed. Dennis Fritz stares at a movie, though he doesn't know its name or plot, and is ready for sleep, just as soon as he can hoist himself from couch to bed. It is a spring night in Kansas City, and the windows of Lister Avenue are open to the cool air, and curtains skip along the breeze. A jangling phone at that hour, in this house, could only be a wrong number.

"Hello," says a woman. "Is Dennis Fritz there?"

"Yes," says Fritz.

"Is this Dennis Fritz?" she asks.

"Yes, it is," he says, and his soft, western-accented voice is answered by a dial tone. The woman had hung up.

A wrong number, he thinks for an instant, then realizes that made no sense. Dennis Fritz walks back to the sofa and plops again in front of the television. He is thirty-seven years old, a handsome man, his hair neatly trimmed and piled back. This gives a clear view of his finely featured face, unlined skin, and the blue eyes that seem intelligent and generous. His compact body probably would be fit even if he did not work at construction and home repair in southeastern Oklahoma. This week, he has come to Kansas City to do a paint job for his mother and aunt. At night, the history of the day can be read in his muscles, a mild fatigue written by eight hours with brushes and cans, rollers and masking tape, ladders and drop cloths. Slowly, the house is taking on a fresher look, but he knows a few coats of paint will not transform it. When he finishes, his mom's home still would look pretty much like every other one on the street, a fifty-year-old, two-story house that happened to be smack in the middle of the country, a home for people who could have been anyone.

The promotions for that night's TV news are playing, but nothing grabs Dennis. He stands, stretches, yawns, and then hears the car doors. He glances past the curtains and sees a small army of police officers fanning across his yard and taking up combat positions. They must have rolled up silently. Dressed in sniper and SWAT team gear, they focus, for some reason, on his mother's house. He opens the door and steps across the threshold. Two men in plainclothes materialize from the shadows.

"Dennis Fritz," said one, and now Fritz could make him out, placing the face of a detective from the little town where he had lived, Ada, Oklahoma. Whatever in the world was he doing in Kansas City?

"Yes," says Dennis.

"Raise your hands. We have a warrant for your arrest."

"What?" asks Fritz.

"You are charged with murder in the first degree and rape in the death of Debra Sue Carter," says the detective.

As he feels them cuffing him behind his back and sees the snipers uncoil from their firing position, the name of Debra Carter moves through his mind. The girl had been killed, it must have been four or five years earlier in Ada, and half the men in town had been questioned at the time, Dennis included. It had been an unpleasant episode, but a necessary one, he had supposed at the time, and he had thought little about it in the years since. Now, the police had emerged from a spring night to accuse him of murder. A moment before, he had been ready for bed, stretching his arms. Now he had fallen into an unreal dream.

He left his mother's home in handcuffs on that spring night in 1987. He would not return until the spring of 1999. Before he took up construction, Dennis Fritz had been a high school science teacher, a single parent, an amateur musician, a thoughtful man. Nothing about him suggested that he would be plucked from a home in the middle of the country, singled out as a murderer who carried out his gruesome business in especially hideous fashion, and sent to prison for the rest of his life. Dennis Fritz looked like he could have been any one of hundreds of millions of ordinary American citizens. In fact, he was. He, too, was an innocent man.

———————

On another spring evening, twelve years later, the matter of Dennis Fritz crossed the desk of a senior executive at a major television network. The network's prime time newsmagazine show had been collecting footage on Fritz for nearly a year, as it grew more likely that he would be set free. The executive was called by Fritz's lawyer in early April 1999.

"Dennis is getting out a week from Wednesday," said the attorney.

"We're going to pass," said the executive.

"After all you've put into it?" asked the lawyer.

"I'm really sorry, but my bosses think there are too many of these stories going around," said the newsman. "He's just another one of these innocent guys getting out."

Not long ago, to claim that an innocent person had been imprisoned was audacious, even risky, a proposition that was close to unprovable. In 1992, Barry and Peter dropped legal papers with an editor at a New York City newspaper. They said they had proof that a Long Island, New York, truck driver had done eleven years hard time for rapes that he did not commit. New tests, not available at the time of his trial, showed that the rapist had one kind of DNA and the prisoner another. The papers landed with Jim, who did not know Barry or Peter, but knew that no sane lawyer would try to bluff such a story.

Nine months later, that man walked free from a courtroom on Long Island. And word of this new DNA test moved from cell to cell block, from tier to prison yard, from the weekend visiting room to the chartered bus rides home, from cities to states, coast to coast. Innocent people in jails lunged at this story. They wrote to Barry and Peter and asked them to make it happen again. Other defense lawyers called to ask for help. So did mothers and fathers, brothers and sisters.

As the letters and requests piled up, Barry and Peter decided to give this paper pyramid a name. They called it the Innocence Project. And in two out of every three cases where the old evidence could be found, the Innocence Project clients were exonerated.

A grave digger in West Virginia was freed from a life sentence. Then a rich man's son in Tulsa, Oklahoma, was sprung from a three-thousand-year term. A marine corporal in Orange County, California, doing twenty-five years. A boiler repairman in Virginia, locked up for forty-five years at the age of twenty. A Chicago drifter, sentenced to die. That truck driver on Long Island, serving twenty years. The former science teacher Dennis Fritz, arrested in his mother's home in Kansas City and sent away forever.

As of this writing in August 1999, DNA testing has provided stone-cold proof that sixty-seven people were sent to prison and death row for crimes they did not commit. The number grows every month, as the Innocence Project and other advocates file new cases. Stories of innocent people liberated from prison by DNA tests have flickered onto the evening news shows across the country, almost faster than the eye can follow, certainly before any reasonable person would have a chance to think about what they mean.

The newly freed men hug their families at prison gates. They talk on TV about how they are looking forward to that first bite of pizza, or sip of beer, or long hot bath. They say they feel no anger or bitterness. They do wonder why it took so long for anyone to hear their cries of innocence. Officials vow to find the true perpetrators. They say that if they had to do it all over, they would change nothing. By the start of the next news cycle, the babble of trivia is spent—long before the question of what went wrong is answered, or even asked.

A moment of rare enlightenment is at hand. For generations, American lawyers and crusaders have fought to overturn the convictions of people they believed innocent. Until recently, they had to rely on witnesses to recant or for the real perpetrators to confess. In what seems like a flash, DNA tests performed during the last decade of the century not only have freed sixty-four individuals but have exposed a system of law that has been far too complacent about its fairness and accuracy. What matters most is not how these people got out of jail but how they got into it.

Now the fabric of false guilt is laid bare, and the same vivid threads bind a wealthy Oklahoma businessman and a Maryland fisherman: Sometimes eyewitnesses make mistakes. Snitches tell lies. Confessions are coerced or fabricated. Racism trumps the truth. Lab tests are rigged. Defense lawyers sleep. Prosecutors lie. DNA testing is to justice what the telescope is for the stars: not a lesson in biochemistry, not a display of the wonders of magnifying optical glass, but a way to see things as they really are. It is a revelation machine. And the evidence says that most likely, thousands of innocent people are in prison, beyond the reach of the revelation machine, just as there are more stars beyond the sight of the most powerful telescope. Most crimes, after all, do not involve biological evidence—blood, semen, hair, skin, other tissue—which means there is no genetic material to test.

Beyond the vista of the wrongly convicted looms another phenomenon, barely noticed but of vast importance. Today, DNA tests are used before trial. Of the first eighteen thousand results at the FBI and other crime laboratories, at least five thousand prime suspects were excluded *before* their cases were tried. Overall, more than 25 percent of the prime suspects could not be implicated because many, if not most, were innocent. For this unseen legion of innocent suspects, only the genetic tests halted their forced march from wrongly accused to wrongly convicted. How many other innocent people, charged with crimes that involve no biological evidence, were chained and led at gunpoint into prison? Thousands, these tests suggest, far more than the most jaded jurists or cynical scholars ever envisioned.

Preface

The emphatic belief of witnesses, police, and prosecutors in the correctness of their accusations—even in the face of undeniable evidence of innocence—drills into issues at the marrow of humanity. A woman in California, to this day, maintains that her ex-husband raped and beat her into a coma, even though a serial killer confessed to the crime and was proven to have been her attacker.

The powerful human drive to right a wrong, the instinct to improve a personal narrative that has taken a turn for the worse, cannot be denied. Neither can this fact: Eyewitness error remains the single most important cause of wrongful imprisonment. The face of a suspect is pressed into the soft putty of memory. Then it hardens into a shape. History is made. And the histories formed by mistaken identifications are buttressed by every level of society.

"Juries seem disposed more readily to credit the veracity and reliability of the victims of an outrage than any amount of contrary evidence," Prof. Edwin Borchard wrote in his 1932 classic, *Convicting the Innocent.*

After a violent crime, both the damaged victim and society seek the equilibrium of prosecution, as relentlessly as ice will melt and boiled water will cool. To disturb this balance by suggesting the wrong person has been punished borders on heresy. In nearly half the sixty-four exonerations, local prosecutors refused to release crime evidence for DNA tests until litigation was threatened or filed. These officials argue that as much as a convict might hope to prove his innocence, he has no absolute right to do so after a trial. He is not an innocent person but a convicted criminal, one who had been given his day in court. Society, they say, has a greater interest in the finality of judgment.

So an innocent person's hope of getting access to the evidence for testing is a crap shoot, dependent on the state, the county, the judge, even the clerk. "The execution of a legally and factually innocent person would be a constitutionally intolerable event," wrote Justice Sandra Day O'Connor in 1993, a sentiment shared by most, but not all, members of the Supreme Court. Chief Justice William Rehnquist, for one, cited precedents suggesting that "a claim of actual innocence is not itself a constitutional claim." He ducked the question of whether a "truly persuasive" showing of innocence, by itself, was enough to render a conviction unconstitutional.

Some six thousand people have been sent to death row since 1976. As of this writing, eighty of them have been cleared through a variety of means, including DNA tests. "Some people think that an error rate of one percent is acceptable for the death penalty," notes Kevin Doyle, the capital defender for the state of New York. "But if you went to the FAA and asked them to approve an airplane, and you said, oh, by the way, on every one hundredth landing, it causes or almost causes fatalities, people would say you were nuts."

The courts can minimize the risks of persecuting the innocent without undermining, and actually improving, the prosecution of the guilty. But that requires a rigorous inquiry into the mistakes revealed by DNA tests.

"Our procedure," wrote Justice Learned Hand in 1923, "has always been haunted by the ghost of the innocent man convicted. It is an unreal dream."

Today, those ghosts walk the land. But Hand's unreal dream is costing little sleep. The innocent neither count nor are they counted. Every unit of government, from the smallest locality to the U.S. Justice Department, totes crimes, complaints, warrants, arrests, indictments, pleas, dispositions, trials, jury trials, judge trials, verdicts, sentences, paroles, appeals, opinions. An entire division of the federal government tracks the quantity of felonies. Many states have similar machinery. Statistics are kept by the gigabyte and the shelf-full.

Yet not one number is assigned to represent the distinct matter of the innocent person. No one has the job of figuring out what went wrong, or who did wrong. No account is taken of the innocent person, wrongly convicted, ultimately exonerated. The moment has come to do so.

Actual Innocence

1

An Innocence Project

Trapped in a wilderness of wrong places, Inmate 85A6097 howled, body and soul. His skin erupted. His teeth rotted. His feet grew warts too big for his shoes. His lungs flooded with pneumonia. His scalp dried to sand, his hemorrhoids burned so hot that only a surgeon's knife could cool them. He was often cranky and defiant with the prison staff, so whatever time he did not pass at sick call or in a hospital usually was spent in a disciplinary program.

Marion Coakley had been a young man when he entered prison to serve a fifteen-year sentence for rape, and everyone who met him agreed that he was a simple soul and a difficult convict. "Marion is mentally retarded and a very angry individual," wrote a prison psychologist, one of many to use those words after meeting Coakley. "He has little insight into his behavior." The one bright note in his record was sounded by a prison teacher, who said that even though Marion understood little, he tried hard. She awarded him a certificate of merit for successfully memorizing the multiplication tables from zero to nine. He was thirty-two years old.

At ten minutes to five on September 3, 1987, Marion rose from the cafeteria table in the Fishkill penitentiary where he had been resolutely chewing every last bite. He was alone. Moments before, his unit had been ordered to leave the dining area. It was two years to the week since he had arrived in prison, and he certainly knew the rules required him to leave the table promptly when ordered. But Marion continued munching until he was good and ready.

He pushed back his chair and strolled over to a trash can to dump his tray. At the doorway, Corrections Officer T. Hodge waited.

"When the unit officer calls your unit to leave the mess hall, you have to leave," said Hodge.

"I wasn't finished," said Coakley.

"Doesn't matter, you had your time to eat," said Hodge. "When you're called, you're supposed to leave."

"I'm a man," roared Coakley. "I'll leave when I am done eating. And nobody's gonna tell me what to do!"

A supervisor, a corrections sergeant, walked over to serve as a human blanket on the fuss. The inmates ate in shifts, and a new cohort was waiting at the doors. The officers wanted to move Coakley out of the way quickly and quietly, before any sympathetic rumble could gather force.

"I ain't gonna leave till I'm finished," yelled Coakley, whirling his arms. "Now I'm finished, so I'm leaving."

"Please keep your arms at your side," said the sergeant.

"I ain't doing nothing, finishing my dinner," said Coakley, palms up, a shrug that did not mean surrender.

"This is a direct order: Keep your arms at your side," said the sergeant. Coakley dropped his arms.

"Give me your ID card," said Officer Hodge.

"Don't have it," said Coakley, an automatic infraction.

Another sergeant arrived, and the three officers quickly pinioned Coakley's arms to his side and rushed him away. He was put under immediate "keep-lock," an on-the-spot discipline administered to prisoners who pose threats to the order of the institution. He was confined to Cell 20.

As soon as the door closed behind the guards, Marion knew what he was facing, because already he had passed four months under keep-lock and related disciplines. He would lose his commissary privileges, his phone call privileges, and his package privileges. Visitors, too, most likely. He would not be allowed to leave his cell for much of the day because he would have no prison job to go to.

"This ain't right," he screamed. "This ain't right."

Then he did to his cell what his body had done to him during his two years of confinement. He slowly, solitarily wrecked the place.

The bedding was first to go. He hated the bed that owned too much of his nights and days. "I do not like to laying up doing noetin," he had written a few months earlier, asking to be released from an earlier keep-lock regimen. Now he hurled the mattress and blanket to the floor. He slammed the bed frame into the door, pounding away until it fractured. With a bar broken from the bed, he pulverized the sink. And with anything he could grab— paper, pillowcases, clothes—he stuffed the toilet bowl, where he had bled from his tortured hemorrhoids.

A small group of corrections officers gathered outside the cell, listening to the destruction. They saw water flowing under the door from the clogged toilet and busted plumbing. When the racket had settled for a minute, one of the guards shouted at Coakley to knock it off.

Marion responded by using the bed frame to batter the metal screen of the observation window in the door. The window screen buckled at the assault; then the glass shattered, flying into the courtyard of the cell block. "I want to see the warden," howled Coakley. "I don't belong here."

Spent, he collapsed in the flooded cell. Three hours after the start of his one-man, one-cell rampage, he was coaxed out by a prison chaplain. Marion was escorted to an empty cell, where he whistled and shrieked into the block. No one could sleep. The next morning, a prison psychiatrist was called to assess the inmate. A man could lose it one night, but Marion Coakley's over-all record was dreadful. From the day he shuffled his manacled feet into the prison system's reception center, Coakley showed "persistently negative adjustment" and had "performed less than satisfactorily in work placement." He refused to "accept staff direction," and showed "limited intelligence, little insight into his problems and current dilemma." He had been kept on antipsychotic medicine. The measure of its futility could be seen in the remains of Cell 20.

Less than twenty-four hours after Marion Coakley destroyed a very sturdy cell with his bare hands, the psychiatrist with the Department of Corrections concluded, unsurprisingly, that Marion Coakley remained an angry man. The Fishkill psychiatrist had the solution: Make him another prison's problem. "Psychiatrist recommended immediate placement in a more structured and secure environment," stated an evaluation written by the staff after the night of destruction. "Subject transferred at direction of the first deputy superintendent."

The subject had started his sentence two years earlier, on August 25, 1985, at the Bronx House of Detention. From there, he had gone on a tour of the New York State prisons: Fishkill, Sing Sing, Clinton, Franklin, Attica, Fishkill again.

Now he was going to Greenhaven, his eighth correctional facility in twenty-four months. At that rate, the state of New York would run out of prisons very quickly, and Coakley had many more years to serve. But he would take a reminder of his Fishkill tantrum with him, in a sentence of 150 more days in keep-lock. Plus, this episode had cost him six months of "good-time" credit toward a reduction of his sentence. He was losing good-time faster than he could earn it. Finally, he would have to pay the state of New York for the cell he destroyed. The bill came to $2,220.

"He feels," noted the evaluation report, "he was railroaded into prison."

————

On a fall afternoon in 1986, Barry and Peter fell in with the riptide of New Yorkers stepping down First Avenue, near the Midtown Tunnel. This was their first big legal conference in the matter of the *People v. Marion Coakley,* and by talking at the precise pitch audible only to each other, a crowded Manhattan sidewalk could be as private as a plush board room.

Barry and Peter walked past the grand lobby of New York University Medical Center, looking for a certain address, then found 520 First Avenue.

On its brightest day, the Milton M. Helprin Institute of Forensic Medicine was a dismal pile. The building facade was tiled in tones of municipal blue, all muted banality, giving away nothing, like the face of an undertaker. The Helprin Institute was constructed to have no visible character, certainly none that would disclose the grim function of the place. The design was a success. It sits virtually unnoticed in a two-mile stretch of grandiose hospitals and medical research centers, a biomedical alley of internationally renowned doctors, scientists, and technology. The proximity of powerhouse researchers did not benefit the Helprin Institute. During the mid-1980s, fifteen thousand autopsies were performed there annually under conditions that would not be tolerated in any respectable cattle slaughterhouse. Occasionally, word of some fresh atrocity visited upon the dead clientele would make it into the newspapers—lost brains, mistagged corpses, vanished limbs—leaving the city's chief medical examiner to serve under a state of siege so chronic that at times it was hard to tell if he worked there, or was merely another of the poor souls being worked upon.

If Barry and Peter had been shy about disaster scenes, if their legal apprenticeship had been served in any of the hundreds of white-shoe law firms in the city, the two lawyers would not have been at the Helprin Institute. Nor would they have been working on the Coakley case. But they were delegates from a world that paralleled the medical examiner's office.

Barry and Peter had started their careers a decade earlier as Legal Aid lawyers, which involved leaping, happily and headfirst, into that fierce cauldron of human affairs, the Bronx Courthouse. The Bronx in the 1970s produced catastrophes too numerous to catalogue, although the court calendar was a decent place to start; see Tom Wolfe's classic novel of manners, *Bonfire of the Vanities*. The borough was an urban mirror image of the tropical rain forests: it was depopulating, deindustrializing, and reforesting. And burning like crazy. The Legal Aid Society, the city's law firm for the poor, was just up the street from Yankee Stadium. During the 1977 World Series, a television blimp drifted away from the stadium to broadcast pictures of intentionally set fires that were devouring thousands of apartments in the Bronx. And over in the courthouse, justice was practiced in every known manner—from turnstile, to assembly line, to rough.

By the mid-1970s, Bronx Legal Aid had absorbed the energy and talents of politically active young lawyers who, as students, had protested the Vietnam War and marched for civil rights. The lawyers worked late. They fell in love. They quarreled. They were young, underpaid, and having the time of their lives.

Peter and Barry had been best friends, one would like to say almost from the moment they met nine years earlier in the shambling Bronx Legal Aid office. In fact, two minutes after they met, Barry was trying to have Peter fired.

On Peter's very first week in the office in 1977, a few lawyers were preparing the defense of a mugging case by conducting a mock trial. Legal Aid colleagues were enlisted as jurors and witnesses. The trial attorneys would work out their lines of questioning on these surrogates.

Peter served as a potential juror, who would be examined by the defense lawyer tooling his jury selection technique.

He was questioned by Barry, who already had served a year in the Bronx courts. He and Peter had never spoken until Peter was seated as a candidate for the jury in the simulated trial.

"Now, Mr. Neufeld," said Barry. "You understand that a real trial is not like the shows on television. You understand that this trial is not going to be the same as TV."

"Yes," said Peter.

"Would you expect me, in the way I present my case, to be like the lawyers you see on television?" asked Barry.

"No," said Peter.

"Wouldn't you agree," said Barry, "that the police you will see come to court and testify are not all going to be Kojacks?"

"Kojacks?" said Peter. "What is a Kojack?"

"The TV show about the bald police detective," shouted Barry. "*Kojack.*"

"I don't know what a Kojack is," confessed Peter.

"You're not serious," said Barry. "Are you?"

"I don't watch much TV," confessed Peter.

Barry was angry. He turned to the supervisor. Not only was this new guy unsuitable as a juror in the mock trial, he would never work as a lawyer. "Anyone so elitist, so out of touch with mass culture and entertainment, will never be able to relate to juries," Barry declared. He suggested, then and there, that Peter be fired. The supervisor declined. That seemed to leave no choice but the formation of a close and complicated friendship.

After they left Legal Aid, they worked as partners, but not in traditional business terms. Barry ran a legal clinic at the Cardozo School of Law.

Peter had his own private practice, across from the courts in Manhattan. They took on cases together. They dabbled in screenplay writing. Both settled with their families near the Brooklyn Bridge. Often, they would slip away from work in the afternoon for a movie.

One was a child of popular culture, the other, a bred-in-the-bone political activist. For Barry, celebrities were just people his father worked with. George Scheck, a former tap dancer, was the personal manager for Connie Francis, Bobby Darin, Mary Wells, and a swarm of lesser entertainers. As a boy, Barry became the Eloise of nightclubs. He would see his father for dinner at 1:00 in the morning at the Copacabana, the classic New York hangout of its day for mobsters and entertainers. In school, he became a debater, ferocious and charming, once arguing that the student draft exemption should be ended. The elite of American society would not tolerate a war that put their own sons at risk, he assured his high school classmates, some of whom were decidedly unsettled by his remedy. At Yale, he managed to get high-honor grades while working in a dizzying string of political causes, including the Dump Johnson movement, the McCarthy and Kennedy campaigns, the National Student Strike after the shootings at Kent State, and jury research for the trial of Black Panther Bobby Seale in New Haven.

While Barry was absorbing the fine and gross points of the entertainment world, Peter was collecting books for church-run Freedom schools in segregated southern school districts. His mother—Muriel Neufeld—had been a leader in the Ethical Culture movement, a left-leaning group of secular humanists. His older brother, Russell, was a national leader with SDS—Students for a Democratic Society—the primary militant student organization in the late 1960s that opposed the Vietnam War and racial discrimination. Peter did not have to be pushed into taking hard stands. At age fourteen, he was impeached as eighth-grade class president for organizing a petition drive against compulsory recitation of the Pledge of Allegiance. In high school, he spent a summer working with community organizers in Appalachia as part of the Encampment for Citizenship, a group founded by Eleanor Roosevelt. He was suspended in eleventh grade at West Hempstead High School for antiwar protests. As a freshman at the University of Wisconsin, he blocked a leader of the conservative Young Americans for Freedom who tried to cross a picket line. A CBS news crew filmed the scene. That got him thrown out of college for a semester.

If they were ever to try escaping from a jail, Peter would drive a high-powered truck through the wall. Barry would talk the guard into lending him keys for the night. They were well matched as a pair, and well suited for handling the appeal of Marion Coakley.

The conviction of Coakley had thrown a panic into the people at Legal Aid Society. Everyone involved in Coakley's defense believed he was innocent—and Legal Aid recognized that Coakley had strong grounds to claim that he was the victim of an ineffective defense provided by one of its lawyers. Naturally, Legal Aid couldn't very well handle an appeal that focused on bad work by Legal Aid. So two of the society's alumni, Barry and Peter, were recruited.

Unlike most private lawyers, Barry had access, in the criminal law clinic at the Cardozo School of Law, a branch of Yeshiva University, to a large cadre of investigators who were not only bright but eager to help. Students in the clinic had worked on other Scheck cases, including a gunrunning plot by the Irish Republican Army, and the defense of protesters at the Shoreham nuclear plant on Long Island. Scheck also had been part of a team that, not long before, had freed Bobby McLaughlin, a young Brooklyn man wrongly convicted of murder.

Peter, however, was not an immediately obvious choice for the Coakley appeal. He had withdrawn from the practice of law that year to work in the film business. Besides writing a screenplay, he had spent six months as the unit production manager on a film shot in Philadelphia, *My Little Girl*, that starred James Earl Jones and Geraldine Paige. He kept an office in a ramshackle loft on Thomas Street in Manhattan, where the floors were tilted and pitched and the windows were so grimy that it was impossible to tell if it was night or day, raining or shining, in the outside world.

Still, Peter had developed an expertise on scientific evidence that was matched by few of his colleagues. The year before, Peter had handled another Bronx criminal case in which blood tests were a key part of the prosecutor's evidence. Peter had pushed his finger through so many holes and weak spots in the laboratory work that a judge had ruled that the test results were meaningless and could not be presented to a jury. Peter's coup represented the first time in the history of the New York courts that a prosecutor's novel blood evidence had been thrown out.

Moreover, Peter and Barry collaborated so closely on cases that at times they seemed to function as a single brain locked within two querulous bodies.

———

As Barry pushed open the glass doors to the Helprin Institute, they drew a deep breath, like snorkelers gulping the last sips of air before plunging into an underwater world.

It wasn't all that bad. Bad enough, though. In one corner of the building, the city of New York kept a small and shockingly ill-equipped lab for the study of blood evidence in criminal cases. It was headed by a first-rate chemist named Dr. Robert Shaler, who had all the know-how and none of the resources for the job. Even lay visitors could see the shortcomings of a facility where the blood was splashed on counters, where technicians handled pathology specimens with their bare hands.

So when the two lawyers arrived at Shaler's laboratory, the forensic chemist greeted them cordially, if warily. He knew all about Peter's work, having been the prosecution witness whom Peter had dismantled. And he knew exactly why they were coming to see him about the Coakley case.

Shaler had done some lab tests before Coakley was tried, and initially decided that they proved Coakley had not been the rapist. But he later waffled about their meaning, so the judge did not allow him to testify.

The two lawyers were not long seated in Shaler's cramped office before the scientist told them what they had been hoping to hear.

"I think it's unlikely that Coakley is the rapist," said Shaler.

"That's how everyone at Legal Aid feels," said Barry. "They are very concerned that a terrible mistake has been made."

Crowding the room now was a small, unspoken piece of history in the case—the role Shaler himself had played by changing his mind about the test results.

"If the judge had let me complete more tests, we could have ruled out Coakley as the rapist," said Shaler, a shade defensively.

"What would be involved?" asked Peter. "Can they still be done?"

"Absolutely. They can still be done, and there are even better things that have been developed since then," said Shaler.

These better things might change the criminal law and science. For years, molecular biologists had been pickaxing their way into the nucleus of the human cell, to the genetic material. Every pharmaceutical company in the world was spending money for research on cloning and mapping genes.

"In essence, we can take a picture, with chemical probes, of certain genetic characteristics," said Shaler. "These would be unique to each person."

In England, a Dr. Alec Jeffries had recognized that these DNA probes could be powerful investigative tools for crime solving, much sooner than they would have pharmaceutical applications. If a criminal left biological evidence at a crime scene—semen, blood, flesh—a genetic profile could be developed. Later, a suspect's blood could be tested to see if it matched with that profile.

DNA fingerprinting was the name given to the process by Jeffries. People at the FBI and in Scotland Yard believed that these tests would become a standard part of the criminal investigation process. Soon, police agencies all over the country would have access to DNA testing. Some would even have their own laboratories.

The notion that the Milton Helprin Institute might be performing high-tech DNA tests seemed as likely as NYU's cardiovascular surgeons performing bypass surgery on the IRT subway. Shaler agreed that the place was a mess.

"I've given up trying to argue that we need more money and space," said Shaler.

They were performing hundreds of primitive serology tests every year for sex crimes but were getting results only about half the time. And even those results often didn't tell very much that was useful in court cases. He confided that he would be leaving in a few months to work at a start-up company outside the city, called Lifecodes.

Lifecodes would be the first in the country to use these revolutionary new procedures in criminal investigations.

"If you want to do the DNA fingerprint test, then that's your only choice in this country," said Shaler.

After they left Shaler, the two lawyers walked south along First Avenue, lining up the work on the case. The laboratories might help prove

Coakley's innocence, but they could not count on them alone. Barry would deploy his students to reinvestigate the case, from top to bottom.

If Coakley truly were an innocent man, then they had to scrutinize every one of the proofs that convinced the jury he was guilty. They continued walking south, until Barry reached Cardozo, on lower Fifth Avenue.

He called two students into his office. Both were starting second careers in the law. Ed King, a former Marine and nurse, and Candace Reid, who had raised her kids, sold shoes, designed textiles, and acted off-Broadway, would climb into the Coakley case. They began by putting together a picture of the client, the crime, and his trial. Somewhere, things had gone badly wrong.

Marion Coakley was a simple, homely fellow born March 4, 1955, in Beaufort, South Carolina. That he could inspire a travesty among police, lawyers, biochemists, and judges hardly seemed possible. He had moved to New York in 1979, and fell in, naturally enough, with family and friends from down South who had made homes in the city. For all its high-voltage buzz, New York often has pockets of village and small-town spirit, as if cells of life had been picked up from distant places and carried to the five boroughs. Beekman Avenue in the Bronx could have been any block of apartment houses, just another neighborhood of working-class blacks. But behind the doors on that one block lived a half-dozen people from Beaufort. Marion Coakley's sister and brothers lived on Beekman. So did their friends from the South, the Bryan brothers. Here was a neighborhood where Marion could settle among familiar faces. He did, after all, need some looking after. He had a second-grade reading level. His tested IQ was in the seventies. But he was an easygoing soul, strong of back and willing to work hard when he had a day's work. And often enough, friends from Beaufort made sure that Marion had that day.

He worked for the National Elevator Co.; he unloaded crates of fruit and vegetables at the Hunts Point Terminal Market, the city's wholesale food depot; and he did heavy lifting around a stone-cutting shop. On his sister's block, a man named James Kinard was the superintendent, and Marion would earn $10 or $20 helping clean up the buildings. He drew no welfare.

In the evening, on the way home from work, the men from Beekman Street would gather in one of the basements where Kinard had the keys. He had set up a punching bag, someone else had put in a set of weights, and the fellows would work out or sit around and have a few beers before going upstairs to their apartments. They called themselves the Country Boys, and Marion was happy to be one of their number.

On a bright Saturday afternoon, October 15, 1983, Marion was helping a guy down the block lay pinstripes on his car. Two detectives drove onto the street. "Marion Coakley," called one, Det. Edward O'Toole. Coakley looked up, then found himself thrown up against the wall.

"Hey, what's this, what're you grabbing me for?" asked Coakley.

"Where's the gun you used when you raped the woman?" asked one of the detectives.

"I don't have any gun," said Coakley. "Raped who?"

"We got you for raping the woman in the motel," said the detective.

They put him in the backseat of the car. Coakley insisted that he knew nothing about any rape or motel. It would all be cleared up at the station house.

———

Two nights earlier, on the evening of Thursday, October 13, 1985, Gabriel Vargas left his job as a department store security guard and picked up his lady friend, Irma Lopez, and they drove to the Bronx Park Motel. Lopez, thirty-eight, the mother of five, was divorced from the children's father, a police officer. She lived a couple of miles south of the motel, in a crowded Bronx apartment. Besides her own five children, her sister and brother-in-law were staying with her on an extended visit from Puerto Rico.

For a quiet evening alone, Irma and Gabriel didn't have much choice: the Bronx Park was the only motel for miles. Set three hundred yards from the gates of the borough's famous zoo and botanical gardens, the Bronx Park puts on few airs. The clerk sat behind two inches of bulletproof glass. The room phones were dead appendages. The phone in the office could not be used unless the desk clerk threw a switch. Few people stayed more than an hour or two.

Irma and Gabriel checked in just before seven, undressed, turned out the lights, and climbed into bed for the great American pastime: they watched television. Around 7:20 P.M., Irma heard a noise from the door, the tentative flicks of a key seeking its grooves in a lock. "Gabriel," she said, "did you hear something?"

He half turned in the bed. Gabriel had set the door chain in place before getting into bed. That would protect them from someone accidentally pushing into the wrong room. An instant later, the chain tore away from the wood molding, the door heaved open, and a man burst into the room.

He stood a dozen feet or so from the bed and screamed at them to get up, he wanted the fucking money now, they were not to move, a clatter of orders that could not all be obeyed. Irma and Gabriel had started to their feet an instant after the door had opened. The man stood in the wobbling light thrown by the TV. The shades were drawn. The lamps were off. The events that followed would be lit only by the glow of the TV screen, a nineteen-inch color set.

"Give me the fucking money, or I'll blow your fucking brains out," advised the man. Gabriel grabbed for his pants and plowed into his pockets. He turned to hand a wad of bills to the man. "Throw it on the bed, and go in the bathroom," ordered the gunman. The robbery had taken place in near darkness. Now, with Gabriel out of sight, he ordered Irma to put a towel over her head. "Facedown on the bed," he ordered, and then he raped her. She would remember glancing at a mirror on the wall and catching the rapist's face, alone in the dark room. "Don't peek," he ordered. When he was finished, he wanted a gold necklace she was wearing. She could not undo the clasp and was sent into the bathroom to Gabriel for help. When she came out, the man wanted more money. Irma said she had some at home. No one was there, except her sister, she lied, knowing well that her brother-in-law would be there.

The man ordered her to get dressed. She was to tie up Gabriel with strips of bed sheet and tell him that there was another man watching outside to kill him if he left the room. After she was dressed, he raped her again.

Then Irma and the man got into her car. He took the driver's seat, adjusting it to fit his size, which she guessed was about five feet, eight inches tall. He also adjusted the rearview mirror, ordering her, once again, not to look at him. In stolen glimpses, she saw a man with a short beard, an Afro haircut, and a wide, flat nose. She heard either a Jamaican or southern accent. When they reached her street, he parked and walked alongside Irma into the building.

"Is there any man in the house?" he asked.

"No," she lied. At least, she hoped she was lying, and that her brother-in-law, Jose Rios, would be home. "Just my kids, don't hurt my kids, please," she said.

"I just want the money," said the man. "Nobody's gonna get hurt. But don't look at me, don't talk to no one. Just walk."

They rode the elevator to the nineteenth floor. Irma unlocked her door, pushed it open, and walked inside, passing Jose. She said nothing to Jose but tried to scream with her eyes. The door started to swing shut at her back, but it was grabbed by the rapist. That was when Jose first saw the man, who smiled and fled, almost immediately, although Jose would later say that they looked at each other for two or three minutes. That seemed to be an overstatement. Irma would remember that she went to her room to fetch money, and when she came back, the man already had departed. She rushed to the window. The attacker, nineteen stories below, was getting into her car.

At 8:36, she called the police and said that her boyfriend was tied up in Room 120 at the Bronx Park Motel, and that another man was going there to kill him. She begged the police to hurry to the motel and save Gabriel.

In fact, Vargas already had freed himself from the sheets at the motel. While Irma was driving home with the rapist, he was hunting for a working telephone. He tried the one in the room, but the line was dead. He walked in his socks to the motel office and found the clerk eating peanuts.

"Hello, hello," Vargas called. The clerk continued shelling the nuts. Vargas smacked on a window thick enough to protect the clerk from anything lighter than a howitzer shell.

"What's going on?" asked the clerk.

"I got a problem, where is the phone, I need to call the police, or can you call the police?"

"Call them yourself," said the clerk. Vargas hunted around the office but saw no phone. The clerk disappeared inside and returned with a phone set. "Plug it in over there," advised the clerk, indicating a wall where a soda machine was standing. Vargas frantically searched for a jack, then spotted it behind the machine, which he pushed aside. The line was still dead. Vargas hollered, desperately, that he needed a phone that worked. Finally, the clerk threw a switch, a red light came on, and Vargas was able to dial 911.

When the detectives arrived at the motel, they decided to take Gabriel to Irma's apartment. They had only turned the corner from the motel when Vargas saw Irma's car parked on Southern Boulevard. The rapist apparently had returned from Irma's apartment to the motel neighborhood, then ditched the car.

Later that night, while Irma was being examined in an emergency room, Gabriel Vargas and Jose Rios went to the police station. They were shown into a room with drawers of photographs. Rios, the brother-in-law witness who had the least opportunity to see the attacker—during the fleeting encounter at the front door of Irma's apartment—was the first to pick out a photo. "This is the man," he told Vargas, who looked it over and agreed. They brought the picture to the detectives. A few hours later, when Irma was released from the hospital, she was shown twelve photographs. She, too, picked out the same picture.

A year earlier, the man in the picture had been accused of another rape. He had gone home from a bar with a woman from his neighborhood and had spent the evening. The woman had a career as a prostitute. In the morning, when the woman demanded payment, the man refused to pay. The woman threatened to call the police, and when he declined again, she left and filed a rape complaint. The man waited in the apartment for the police to arrive. The matter had a very short life as a felony charge, since it gave every sign of being a breach of contract dispute. The "victim" did not make a single appearance to swear out a complaint. The case was dismissed, but the man's photograph stayed in the police files of sex offenders. After Irma Lopez chose his picture, he was brought to the precinct for a lineup. Irma, Gabriel, and Jose all picked him as the fiend. His name was Marion Coakley.

From his first contact with the police, Marion Coakley insisted he had nothing to do with the rape or robbery of Irma Lopez. He took and passed a lie-detector test, denying his involvement. A study of the rapist's semen at Helprin Institute seemed to rule out Coakley as the source. And finally, Coakley had an alibi of staggering proportions: On the night of the crime, he had been at a Bible-study meeting in his sister's home on Beekman Avenue.

The reverend had seen him there. Seven or eight other people had been present. They all could vouch for him.

––––––––

Those were the core facts of the crime and Marion Coakley. But they were just the first cut into the guts of the case. For Barry, Peter, and the two law students, it was easy, reading the trial transcripts, to see where things had gone wrong. It was so easy, it hurt. The day before the trial started, the Legal Aid defense lawyer, Donald duBoulay, had begged the judge for more time. He had just finished trying a case and was spent, physically and mentally. Moreover, the judge had ruled that his best witness, the biochemist Robert Shaler, could not testify that the physical evidence showed that Coakley probably wasn't the rapist. DuBoulay was one of Legal Aid's most successful trial lawyers: smart, charismatic, and fast on his feet. But he needed time to regroup, to find other experts, to catch up.

Forget it, the judge said. If the defense could come up with witnesses while the trial was under way, that would be okay.

If not, said Judge David Levy, "then the defendant is going to have to suffer." With that opening fanfare, the parade of prosecution witnesses began.

The first was the victim, Irma Lopez, age thirty-eight, mother of five, a tiny woman herself at four feet, eleven inches tall. Without blinking or breaking, she told of the attack. The door at the motel crashing open. Her boyfriend being confined to the bathroom. The towel over her head as he raped her. The rapist then leading her at gun point out of the motel and into her car, so they could drive to her home for more cash.

"Look around the room," Assistant District Attorney Debra Reiser urged Lopez.

"Tell me if you can see the man who came into the motel room and raped you and robbed you and Mr. Vargas and took you back to your apartment. Do you see that man here?"

"Yes," said Lopez.

"Would you please point him out?" asked Reiser.

Lopez lifted her right hand and pointed across the room to a man with a broad, flat nose, slouched in his chair. When he stood, the jury could see that Marion Coakley was just about five feet, eight inches tall—the description given to the police. They could not hear his voice though, which had no traces of a Jamaican accent—another feature of Lopez's description.

Then Gabriel Vargas, the other victim, came to court. He had been locked in the motel bathroom for most of the episode but betrayed no doubts about who had done it. "Right there," said Vargas, nodding at Marion Coakley. Finally, the jury heard from Jose Rios, the brother-in-law who had been home when Irma was forced back to her apartment by the rapist. "When he had the door opened, we looked at each other about two to three minutes," said Rios. There was no conversation. Just two men staring at each other silently for two full minutes. To take full measure of the extravagance of his claim, one must recall how Irma described events at the apartment. She said the rapist had waited at the door while she went into a bedroom to get some money. By the time Irma got back to the door, the guy had run away. She went to the window and, looking down nineteen stories, could see him already getting back into her car.

This sequence of events, Rios swore, gave him two or three minutes to stare at the face of the rapist—a man who was right there in the courtroom.

"Who are you indicating?" asked the judge.

"The one that is in the center," said Rios, pointing to Marion Coakley.

DuBoulay did his best with these witnesses, delicately trying to suggest that they didn't have a chance for a good view of the attacker. After all, he had directed Irma and Gabriel not to look at him. He was pointing a gun at the time he issued that instruction. Then he shoved Gabriel in the bathroom and covered Irma's head with a towel. He had broken into a room that was lit only by the television screen. When he walked Irma into her home, he again told her not to look at him.

"You didn't want to make him angry?" asked duBoulay.

"I still stared at him," Irma insisted. "I mean, I peeked at him."

Where the trial really went wrong was on the physical evidence. A man breaks down the door of a motel, rapes a woman repeatedly, forces her into a car, adjusts her mirror, and drives to her home—somewhere along that hellish journey some trace of the criminal should have been left. But neither the prosecution nor the defense presented any serological evidence from the rape.

As for the fingerprints and palm prints, the police had not dusted the motel scene—in true Bronx Park Motel fashion, the room was rented out again only minutes after the rape and robbery—but the cops did examine Irma's car, and specifically, the rearview mirror. They had come up with palm prints at the exact spot where the rapist, by Irma's account, had put his hand to adjust the view.

At the trial, the double-talk on this point by the investigating detective would have made Casey Stengel's head spin. Yes, it was true that the Fingerprint Unit had prepared a report saying that there was no match between Marion Coakley and the palm print—but they had compared his fingerprints to the palm prints, and you really can't compare fingerprints to palm prints. Then why, wondered duBoulay, did the report say that a check of Marion Coakley's fingerprints came up negative? I'm not a fingerprint expert, said the detective.

It sounded baffling, but Assistant D.A. Reiser didn't want the jury to be confused. Those lifts from the car mirror "could be a smudge," she told the jury, and the fingerprint experts "are not sure exactly what it is. . . . There is absolutely no evidence in this case that any palm comparison can be done or would be done."

Whatever that meant.

The worst thing Marion Coakley had going for him was his actual innocence. No one thought the case was really going to be tried. As a result, the preparation by both the prosecution and the defense was sloppy, as shown in the meaningless babble about the fingerprint matches. The truth was that the Fingerprint Unit wanted "elimination prints" from Irma and Gabriel, so that they could be sure that the prints they were checking did not belong to people who had legitimate access to the car. In a report written more than eighteen months before the trial, the Fingerprint Unit detective had written, in black and white, what was required: "Elimination prints . . . MUST be submitted for comparison purposes."

That was not done. Possibly, no one had bothered to read the file until the eve of trial. The case had dragged on for nearly two years. Soon after he was indicted, Coakley passed a lie-detector test denying his involvement, which impressed the prosecutors—although the test was not admissible in court. Several times, due to the reports written by the forensic chemist Shaler exculpating Coakley, the prosecution appeared on the verge of dismissing the charges. But victims Lopez and Vargas insisted Coakley was the man. And later, Shaler developed doubts and wanted to conduct additional tests—a shift in position that, he insisted, had not resulted from pressure by prosecutors. The case staggered into court, almost in spite of itself. Basic stuff, like the palm print on the mirror, just hadn't been worked up by the prosecution.

Similarly, the defense's alibi evidence was much stronger than the jury ever learned. Coakley always said he was at a Bible-study meeting in his sister's apartment on the night of the rape. He had nine witnesses ready to say he was there, including the minister. Before the Bible meeting started, he said, he had spent a few hours hanging around with the building superintendent and the other Country Boys from Beaufort, South Carolina, enjoying a drink in honor of someone's birthday. The drinking ended when the preacher arrived in the basement to start the meeting.

Through pinpoint cross-examination, Assistant D.A. Reiser was able to spin the preacher like a child's top. She seemed to ask the Reverend Samuel Manigault everything about an evening twenty months earlier except whether he had used quarters or dimes to pay the toll on the bridge to the Bronx.

Q: When you got down there [to the basement], you saw four or five men right, and you don't recall if one of them was the defendant?

A: That took us down, I don't recall. He was down there when I went down there. I don't know if he took us down there, but he was in the basement.

Q: And what was he doing in the basement?

A: I guess he was helping me to gather up the men to come up to the Bible study.

Q: So he was in the apartment when you first got there?

A: I don't recall whether he was at the apartment when I got there.

. . .

Q: Well, when is the first time that you saw him?

A: When is the first time? I don't recall the first time—how do you mean the first time?

Q: Well, that evening, on October 13th, when is the first time you saw him?

A: I don't know, but I can say he was at the Bible study. That's for sure.

Q: He was at the Bible study at some point?

A: He was at the Bible study during this day.

. . .

Q: How many people were there?

The preacher wasn't sure.

Q: Did everyone read?

Couldn't say.

Q: And on October 6th (the week before), did the class start at 7:30?

Didn't remember.

Q: And where was everybody seated?

A: In the living room.

Q: Did the defendant ask any questions at the meeting?

A: I don't recall.

Q: And do you recall what the weather was like that night?

A: No, I don't recall.

Q: And about what time did you get home that night.

A: I don't remember the time.

Q: Do you recall if the men in the basement were drinking.

A: I don't recall if they were drinking.

Q: Did you notice if there was a television down there?

A: I don't remember.

Q: Do you recall where you parked your car when you arrived?

A: I think it was right in front of the building—not in front, but not far from the entrance of the building.

. . .

Q: So you don't really know what time it was?

A: No I really don't.

Q: And you don't really know what time you saw the defendant that night, do you?

A: Pardon me.

Q: You don't really know what time you started the Bible meeting, do you?

A: No.

After that, the witness had to be mopped off the floor. But even the prosecutors acknowledged that Coakley had been at the Bible meeting at some point during the night of October 13, 1983. The critical issue was the time. Despite the prosecutor's examination, all involved seemed to think the prayer meeting had ended shortly after 9:00 P.M.

To allow Coakley enough time to rape Irma Lopez, rob Gabriel Vargas, kidnap Irma back to her apartment, then return to the motel, and still make it back in time for the Bible meeting, the crime surely had to have been completed by 8:00 P.M.

Yet sitting in duBoulay's file was proof positive that Marion Coakley couldn't have done all that. The defense had subpoenaed the 911 call records and tapes. These showed that Irma Lopez called the police at 8:36—just after she saw the rapist from her apartment window, getting back into her car and driving away. At that point, the rapist was driving her car back to the Bronx Park Motel, where it would be found.

At the moment the 911 call was being made, the Bible meeting in Apartment 3C at 380 Beekman Avenue already was in full gear, and all present swore on the Good Book that Marion Coakley was in there the entire time.

There was one problem with the 911 records. Defense lawyer duBoulay never introduced them. Not only had he just finished trying a case before the Coakley trial opened but he had picked up Coakley as a client because the first lawyer who had been handling it, Elizabeth Schroeder, had left the Legal Aid Society. It was Schroeder who had subpoenaed the 911 tapes, requested the serology workup on the semen, and arranged for the lie-detector exam. But the case lingered so long that she had left for another job before it came to trial. In fact, so had the original assistant district attorney.

The jury was out long enough to get lunch. When they returned the guilty verdict, Coakley still did not believe it. He was led away in handcuffs. A few weeks later, on sentencing day, the prosecutor portrayed Marion Coakley not as a simple, Bible-reading day laborer, but as a terrible danger to the community. The evidence from three eyewitnesses was "overwhelming," said Assistant D.A. Reiser. Coakley "is uncaring and unconcerned about the rights of others. That is certainly obvious from the facts that were adduced in this case. I feel there are no mitigating circumstances in this case, none at all. And for that reason, the People would ask that the defendant be sentenced to a maximum term of incarceration on his conviction of rape in the first degree and robbery in the first degree, that being a term of eight and a third to twenty-five years."

With that, Marion Coakley stood to give his part. He was not a glib man possessed of polished language. But he spoke with a conviction not often heard in courtrooms or, for that matter, most anywhere else.

"I never seen these people before in my life," he began bluntly. "And during the time when this crime happened, I wasn't there when this crime happened. And when the preacher arrived, Judge, that day, seven-thirty, through my sister, we went to her house. And after the prayer meeting I went home with the preacher. And this preacher said he couldn't remember, it was so long ago. And I went home with the preacher and I came back on a Saturday, and that Saturday, I picked up a check for my sister. I was in the Bronx, and that's the day I got arrested. And I never seen these people in my whole life, Judge. I'm an innocent man and I didn't feel—they railroad me. And I never seen these people in my whole life, and it's wrong an innocent man to go to jail for something he didn't do.

"And I worked all my life since I've been in New York City, and all my life, I've always had jobs. I never done anybody no harm, and I never done anybody anything. And I had a good job and I lost that. I lost everything. I lost everything. And I don't never seen these people in my whole life, you know. And the Bronx Hotel, I don't even know where the Bronx Hotel is. I don't even know where it's at. I never drive in New York City.

"I never carried a gun in my whole life. It's a shame for these people to come in court and look in my eyes and say this is the man. And God knows it ain't me, it ain't me. And God knows it ain't me. And it's wrong for you to send an innocent man to jail. I never seen these people before, never seen these people in my whole life. You can't send an innocent man to jail, it's not right, it's not right. I feel to myself someone done this to me.

"In the Bronx, I wasn't expecting this, I wasn't expecting this. But I talked with a couple of friends of mine and I got arrested just like that. I didn't know nothing about the gun I had and I told them I didn't have no gun. And they start asking me—the detective start asking me questions. They start asking me like if I know anybody with guns and people that have it. And I tell him, let him know. And I said, No, I don't do things like that. I never seen these people in my whole life, I never did, you know. And all my life I live in New York City and the first day I got to New York, three weeks I had a job. I was working all my life and I'm an innocent man. You can't send an innocent man to jail, God knows it. I was going to a church all day long. I was with the preacher. The preacher go to work, and I stayed in the church. I clean around the church. All these years I've been working. I don't know these people. I don't understand.

"They got—they probably got someone confused and said they can't find the right person, so they said Marion Coakley. But God knows I didn't do this and I pray every night that God know I didn't do this. It's wrong for you to send an innocent man in jail. I know I didn't do this. It's a shame. I can't come to court and say that's the man. I can't do that. I don't have the heart to do nothing like that. And I don't have the heart to see person do time for something he didn't do. I'm not the one. I never seen these people, Judge. . . .

"These people who got me here, I never seen none of these people in my whole life, I never did. I don't—I never carried a gun in my whole life. I can't drive no car in New York City. I never drove a car in New York City. I can't drive a car. I can't drive a car. That's all, Judge, I have to say."

The judge gave him a fifteen-year sentence, with a minimum of five years before he could be considered for parole. Marion Coakley was dragged screaming from the courtroom by a wedge of court officers. He received his first dose of antipsychotic medication that day. Not only had he been found guilty. Now he was plainly crazy.

———

On the evening of April 9, 1987, the Marion Coakley case was in its fourth unsettled year, with yet another set of defense lawyers—the third—

another new group of prosecutors—also the third—and a new forum to argue the matter of the penniless, borderline retarded man. For Ed King and Candace Reid, the Coakley case could have been the trial of the century. The two law students were riding with Barry to an apartment building on West Farms Road in the South Bronx. They were going to visit, unannounced, the home of Irma Lopez. They needed her fingerprints.

But how would they get past the front door?

"Of course, we have to tell them that we are representing Coakley," said Barry, "and that it is important to clarify whether or not he is the real criminal."

"If they let us in after that, I think I should talk to Gabriel," said Candace. "You guys work with Irma. She will respond to you. He will be interested in proving to me that he was macho and did all he could to protect Irma at the motel."

To have the woman interviewed by the male lawyers was counterintuitive, or at least counterstereotypical, but the whole trip was a shot in the dark. From the backseat, King gave directions to the building. He had grown up in the Bronx and once had dated a girl who lived on the street.

In the law clinic, Barry had assigned King to work on the Coakley case on the grounds that his nursing background might be of some use with the scientific issues. But the biggest of those issues was proving a bust. Just a few days before their trip to the apartment, Barry had received a notice from Lifecodes, the vaunted laboratory. Their attempts to establish a "DNA fingerprint" for the rapist had been unsuccessful. Not only that, but the Lifecodes lab technicians had, in the process, consumed the entire rape kit—all the vaginal swabs taken in the hospital and the semen stains from the underwear preserved after the crime. All the physical evidence of the crime was destroyed.

Now King would be called on to do a much lower-tech kind of fingerprinting. In his briefcase, he carried an ink pad and special bonded paper. If all went well, if they were very lucky, the student would collect the "elimination" prints that the detectives never got around to. These would be compared to the palm print on the rearview mirror handled by the rapist. That was the central purpose of their trip to Irma's apartment.

They decided not to buzz her on the intercom, preferring not to be stopped so early in the game. When someone with a key opened the lobby door, they trailed behind and took the elevator to the nineteenth floor, as Irma had done on that night with the rapist. The two students dropped to the rear of Barry. Let him do the talking at the doorstep. He rang the bell. They could hear the click of the squinting peephole.

"Mrs. Lopez?" said Barry.

She opened the door, evidently satisfied with the eyeball inspection. Barry explained who they all were. She immediately brought him inside and called for Gabriel to join them in the living room. The crime had been the signal event in their lives, and the two victims were welcoming and gracious to these new people who wanted to discuss it yet again. The apartment looked neat as a pin. Irma had worked as a receptionist in the parish house of the local Catholic church for five years, and she surrounded herself with the iconography of her church.

Barry and King situated themselves nearest Irma. Candace moved next to Gabriel. Barry's preamble was honest, without using a bullhorn to announce that their purpose was to overturn the conviction of Marion Coakley and set him free. Instead, he explained that they wanted to make sure the right man was in jail. Barry said he understood, of course, that Irma would like to put the whole case behind her.

"Well, we still have the civil case going against the Bronx Park," said Lopez.

"Of course, that's right," said Barry. This was the first he had heard of it. He told himself to sit still and not leap off the couch. He was thrilled. If the prosecution knew about the civil lawsuit, they had not told Coakley's defense lawyers. And that would mean the guilty verdict would dissolve as soon as they could file papers, because New York courts had held that defendants should be informed if their accusers had a financial interest in the outcome of a criminal case.

"The civil case," said Barry casually. "When did you file that?"

"Right away after the incident, I think," said Irma. She called to Gabriel, using his nickname. "Quirrito, when did we file the lawsuit against the motel?"

Gabriel recalled that the rape had taken place on a Thursday.

"I talked to the detective on the weekend, the fatty one," said Gabriel. "I told him I was going to take pictures of the door where the guy broke in.

He said if I had any problem, I should let him know. I went there on the Monday."

"This was the Monday after the rape?" asked Barry.

"Yeah, I went there, and the handyman showed me the boss's car, and told me to wait until the boss left before I took pictures," said Vargas.

"It sounds like a good lawsuit against the motel," Barry agreed. "If this rapist let himself in with a key, that's really their neglect. And the detective knew about it and was willing to help?"

"He was very nice," said Irma. "I am so frightened that it will happen again. I have dreams that the rapist is running after me in the subway. I am afraid of black men that I see in the streets, they all look like the rapist. I am afraid he will come after me—he took a picture of me from my wallet, and he took my driver's license."

She had been seeing a psychiatrist about these torments, she confided.

"Did the district attorney know about all this?" asked Barry.

"Oh yes," she said.

Perfect, thought Barry, nodding. More reversible error.

"We told them about the lawsuit," said Irma. "The insurance company for the motel is trying to say the whole thing was a setup, that there was no rape. The lady assistant D.A., she knew I was seeing the psychiatrist on Fordham Road."

On the other side of the room, Gabriel chatted easily with Candace Reid. He had been a police officer in Puerto Rico. He had been told by the cops that Marion Coakley was a bad guy—that he was wanted for sex crimes in South Carolina, and that he had raped another woman in New York but she declined to press charges.

"That's right," said Irma. "They told me that he had done this before."

"Who told you?" asked Barry.

"The assistant district attorney, in her office one day before the trial," said Irma.

"That's not really correct," said Barry gently.

They had not even gotten to the fingerprints. They had not been in the room five minutes and already four or five big legal issues had been spilled. Barry was making notes furiously. So were King and Reid. The defense should have been told that Irma was seeing a psychiatrist and felt that every black face she saw reminded her of the rapist. After all, the whole case was based on the strength of her identification of Marion Coakley. And the prosecutor was subtly, and wrongly, endorsing and reinforcing Irma's identification of Coakley by telling her that Marion had raped someone else and gotten away with it, or was wanted in South Carolina.

Not only that, but with their civil lawsuit, Irma and Gabriel had a strong incentive to make sure that *someone* was convicted of the rape—especially since the motel was claiming no such crime had taken place. The defense surely had a right to know about that, and to let the jury know. But these two crime victims were not the appellate court. They did not have to entertain arguments about the fairness of Marion Coakley's trial, and Barry did not make any.

As Candace Reid sat with Gabriel, she talked about his work as a police officer in Puerto Rico and mentioned how the files were incomplete without his fingerprints. Would it be okay if they took his fingerprints?

"Right here?" asked Gabriel.

"No time like the present," said Ed King, reaching into his briefcase. He pulled out the ink pad and paper.

He and Gabriel sat at the kitchen table, and King slowly rolled his hand evenly into the ink pad, beginning at the ball and continuing up to the fingerprints. He noticed a crooked finger on one of Vargas's hand. Then he rolled Vargas's inked hand onto the white paper. A moment later, Irma was sitting in Gabriel's chair, repeating the procedure.

Barry and the students left the apartment, hardly able to believe all they had found out—not to mention obtaining the fingerprints. A few days later, King walked into the lobby of One Police Plaza with his briefcase.

"I'm looking for the fingerprint lab," said King.

"Sixth floor," said a bored cop, not glancing up from his newspaper.

King, with his Bronx Irish face, appeared at the fingerprint office and explained that he needed prints checked for a case he was working on. He gave them Irma and Gabriel's prints, plus a fresh set of Marion Coakley's, which had been taken in prison.

"Do you want to wait?" asked the detective at the counter.

"Can you do it that fast?" replied King.

"We can give it a quick read for you right now, but it will take a couple of days to write up a report," said the detective.

"I'll wait," said King.

A few minutes later, the detective came back. "Sorry," he said.

"The prints are no good?" asked King.

"The prints are fine," said the detective, "but this Coakley's no good on this."

"What do you mean, he's no good?" asked King.

"The print that we lifted off the car mirror is not his. And it's not one of the other elimination prints. Sorry," said the detective.

"Nothing to be sorry about," said King. "That's great news. I'm a law student, working on his appeal."

"A law student?" said the detective, laughing. "I thought you were on the squad, working the case."

"Me?" said King, genuinely astonished. "A detective?"

Barry, in the meantime, had drawn up two affidavits, based on notes of their conversations with Irma Lopez and Gabriel Vargas. The affidavits covered the lawsuit, her psychiatric visits, and the encouragement that the D.A. gave them in their identification of Coakley.

King was dispatched to the Bronx, this time to get the signatures of Irma and Gabriel. Barry worried that the lawyer for the civil case might have shut them down, so he instructed King to get some evidence that the material in the affidavits had come from the couple. Back in the Bronx, King felt quite comfortable about ringing the intercom. No one was home. He lingered on the sidewalk, calling from memory the face of the girl he once dated who had lived on this street. Then Vargas arrived.

"Hey, Gabriel, how are you?" said King.

"Oh yes, hello," said Vargas, who seemed to be in a rush.

"I drew up this statement for you to sign, based on the things you told us the other night," said King.

"Remember I told you we would write up everything so you could check it out?"

"Yes, I remember. But after you left, I called my lawyer," said Vargas.

"He told me I shouldn't sign anything. I'm sorry to make you come back for nothing. I have to follow his advice."

"Not a problem," said King. "Listen, I'm going to turn it in anyway. You don't have to sign it. But would you check it over for factual errors?"

Gabriel did not mind doing that. They leaned over the hood of a car and went through the three typed sheets. "This here isn't right," said Vargas. He pointed to a sentence that mentioned someone else helping him to drive the car home after the rape.

"Could you just scratch that out and make the correction?" said King. Vargas complied. "Just put your initials there, to show that it's your correction," said King. Again, Vargas complied.

"And just to be sure that there are only three pages, that I'm not slipping anything extra into this, would you just write down at the bottom of each page, 1 of 3, 2 of 3, 3 of 3?" asked King. Vargas immediately wrote the page numbers. "That's great, just put your initials next to them," said King. No signed affidavits. But initials everywhere.

A few nights later, King called on Irma. She, too, refused to sign. But she also made corrections and initialed them, just as Vargas had.

Now the Coakley team had plenty of evidence for a new trial that showed major problems with the eyewitness identifications. Anyone could see that if he were given a new trial, these additional details were powerful ammunition for attacking the identifications. Had this fresh information been available during the trial, Marion Coakley very well might be found not guilty. And that, in a nutshell, met the legal standard for overturning a conviction: newly discovered evidence that had a good chance of bringing a different result.

But none of the details proved that Marion Coakley was innocent. For that, his team would have to find evidence that someone other than Coakley had committed the rape of Irma Lopez.

They knew that the rapist was a black man, of roughly Coakley's size and age. But they also knew one other key fact: the rapist either had one of two blood types, type B or type O, or he was a person whose blood types were chemically invisible in semen. That much Dr. Shaler at the medical examiner's office had been able to deduce from the semen stain in Irma

Lopez's underwear before it was destroyed by the DNA test. She had not had sexual relations in the hours prior to the rape, so the only source of the semen was the rapist.

Before his trial, Marion Coakley took a day from work to present himself at the medical examiner's office on First Avenue, two years before his lawyers would find themselves in the same office. His blood was drawn and tested. He had blood type A, which was not one of the types found in the semen left by the rapist. He should have been cleared, then and there, but for one additional issue.

The forensic investigation was based on a simple, but little-known fact: For most people—about 80 percent of the population—their blood group markers can be found not only in the blood but in other bodily fluids such as semen, vaginal discharge, perspiration, and saliva. These people are identified as "secretors." Those individuals whose blood groups don't appear in their bodily fluids are categorized as "nonsecretors."

But what if Coakley were a "nonsecretor"? What if he turned out to be one of the 20 percent of the population whose blood groups do not migrate into his bodily fluids? It was possible that the reason markers for his blood type A were missing from the panties was not due to his innocence in the rape, but because his semen simply didn't reveal any blood types. To answer this question, Coakley also provided a semen sample to the medical examiner's office. Tests showed that he was, indeed, a secretor. So if Marion Coakley were the rapist, his blood type would have been identified in the semen found in the underwear of Irma Lopez. It was not.

"Therefore," wrote Shaler in a report dated May 3, 1984, "Marion Coakley could not be the donor of the semen on the panties analyzed under case 56/84."

At that point, the prosecution had considered dropping the case. But they consulted with Irma Lopez and Gabriel Vargas. They were very eager for the criminal case to go forward. They were quite certain that Coakley was the rapist. The district attorney would not be dismissing the charges.

Moreover, the D.A. was not confident that Dr. Shaler's science was sound. He was testing a four-month-old semen stain. With time, proteins break down, and a blood marker was just a protein. The prosecutor then handling the case, Judy Lang, promised that she would find other experts to challenge Dr. Shaler. That turned out to be unnecessary.

Shaler was the quarterback of technical issues for another case Lang was handling. Asked later if he was pressured to change his findings on Coakley, Shaler said no. "Most attorneys," Shaler would also say, "like to let you know what their opinions of the facts of the case are—irrespective of the scientific conclusions."

A few months later, Shaler testified that his original report might have been overstated. He still thought it was "unlikely" that Coakley was involved. But it was possible, he said, that Coakley was a "low-level secretor"—a person whose blood groups sometimes would appear in his bodily fluids, and sometimes might not. No longer was he certain that Marion Coakley was *not* the rapist.

It was at that point that the judge ruled that Shaler couldn't testify, period. And so Coakley was deprived of his best witness, lost the case, and went to jail.

The first wave of press about the new DNA fingerprint technique was reaching the United States from England, where it had been employed by Dr. Alec Jeffries. But Lifecodes had, in effect, burned the sample through its tests and gotten no results.

For Barry and Peter, that left only one avenue on the serology front: Coakley had to produce new semen samples. These would be tested to find out if his blood type A always could be seen in his semen.

Peter met with Shaler, and they devised an elaborate plan. It would not be enough to have Coakley simply provide one or two semen samples, because each ejaculation would produce different quantities of fluid—and, in the key question, perhaps different levels of his blood type.

Coakley would have to produce samples morning, noon, and night. Sometimes he would have to produce them consecutively. Sometimes he would have to wait several days. And he would have to produce on command.

The lawyers met with him and explained that it could help get him out of jail. He understood but wasn't happy about it. Now people were telling him what times and days he should play with himself. Wasn't right. A phone call would come into the prison from Peter, and while the lawyer held on, the guards would have to fetch Coakley and bring him to the hospital wing. While not under the direct supervision of a nurse, he would have to produce semen into condoms supplied by Shaler's office. The condoms were then frozen. A few days later, Coakley would have to do it again. "I feel like a monkey," he said after the third trip to the cubicle with a *Playboy*. One time, he picked up the phone with the open line to Cardozo to object.

"This is a sin against God," he said.

They calmed him down. He produced thirteen semen samples.

Nearly two years to the day after the jury found Coakley guilty, the tests that should have been done before the trial were finally completed. Each and every time Coakley had ejaculated, his semen had contained blood type A. The semen left by the rapist in the Bronx Park Motel had not been blood type A.

"I can now state to a reasonable degree of scientific certainty that Marion Coakley is not the donor of the semen found in the panties of Irma Lopez," Shaler wrote in an affidavit dated July 9, 1987.

All that was left was to finish the papers. After a conviction, most states set strict time limits on reopening a case on the grounds that "new evidence" has been discovered. However, New York State has none. Prisoners can file a motion under Article 440 of the Penal Code, arguing that if the new evidence had been available to the jury, it would likely have produced a different result. Not only did Barry and Peter have the new evidence—Shaler's affidavit, stating unequivocally that Coakley wasn't the man—but they had assembled a dossier of bad lawyering, bad judging, bad prosecuting, and bad police work. The papers were filed on August 27, 1987.

The trial prosecutor, Reiser, had gone into private practice. She told Barry that she did know about the civil suit the victims had filed, but wasn't sure whether she learned about it before or after the criminal case. Moreover, she said she did not know about Irma's psychiatric sessions and fears of black men in the street. Meanwhile, Reiser's former bosses at the Bronx district attorney's office acknowledged many problems with the Coakley trial, and it was clear they would soon be on board.

Peter called Coakley in prison to explain that there was good news. But this simple, angry man had lost all patience and interest. He wanted to go home right away. On September 3, just a week after the papers were filed for his new trial, he tore apart his cell. He lost more of his good-time credit.

———

By the end of September, the Bronx district attorney's office had agreed that he should be released. Justice had not been served. With the consent of the prosecutor, an appellate judge agreed to parole Marion from prison while the case was resolved. His sister, Janette Coakley Smalls, drove to the state prison in Greenhaven to pick him up.

Marion carried a small bag of belongings, got in Janette's car, and said barely a word.

A few months later, in December, Judge Burton Roberts held a hearing to perform the last rites on the indictment against Coakley. The famously earthy Roberts, the chief administrative judge in the county, had taken over the case when he got word through the grapevine that a miscarriage of justice was likely. Roberts had been immortalized in Tom Wolfe's *Bonfire of the Vanities*. A Bronx original with strong opinions, Roberts brought a child's excitement and curiosity to the assembly-line work of managing criminal cases. Intrigued by the possibility that Coakley had been wrongly convicted, he was thrilled to have a brand-new technology to think about. He had given permission for the defense to arrange for the "DNA fingerprint test" that ended up as a flop.

On the day that he formally buried the Coakley case, Roberts praised everyone, defense and prosecution. It should be their finest hour, he said, much like his own proudest moment. Back when he was the Bronx County district attorney, Roberts himself asked a judge to release a convicted murderer from prison. The man's brother, who had a strong resemblance to him, actually was the killer.

As the judge continued his paeans for all the good work done by lawyers, Marion sat impassively in the courtroom, where he had come on his lunch hour. Since his release, he had gone back to work at the stone-cutting firm, and the dust rose from his pants when he took a seat.

"I was not involved in the original trial," said Judge Roberts. "I came into it when an application was made for a hearing, but insofar as I am capable of representing the judiciary of the state of New York, I am sorry. And those words are so weak. I am so sorry that you have suffered this miscarriage of justice."

"Thank you, Your Honor," said Marion Coakley. He stood and headed back to work. His lunch hour was over.

An Invention

In the early decades of the twentieth century, a patient who lived through surgery stood a decent chance of being killed in the recovery room by blood transfusions. There was a very good reason for this. In 1930, a researcher discovered that people had one of four blood groups—A, B, AB, and O—and that giving patients the wrong blood type was far worse than giving them no blood at all. A test was developed to "type" the blood. Not long afterward, police and prosecutors realized that blood typing could be useful for investigating certain crimes.

For the next fifty years, blood types were as sophisticated as most courtroom science would get. And for all his bad luck, Marion Coakley could have had worse: He might have had the same blood type as the rapist. Within an hour's drive of the Bronx Park Motel, three million males could have been linked to the assault by their blood types. It is not a test that makes fine distinctions. Moreover, the blood had to be protected from heat, light, and humidity—or bacteria would consume the blood molecules.

That was why so many forensic laboratories were excited about the development of the so-called "DNA fingerprint test," and why it was such a disappointment when it failed in the Coakley case. Because DNA is a much smaller molecule than the blood antigens that define a person as type A or O, bacteria do not eat it until after they have gobbled up, Pac-Man-like, the larger blood particles. And each person's DNA is different. The problem with the DNA fingerprint test—known as restriction fragment length polymorphism, or RFLP—was that it could work only when there was a lot of DNA available. That was fine in the laboratory. But in the messy reality of crime scenes, DNA is a scarce commodity. There just wasn't enough DNA left by the Bronx Park Motel rapist to test with the RFLP process.

It just so happened that the very year Marion Coakley was arrested, someone was building a better DNA test.

On a spring night in 1983, Kary Mullis, a bored genius, was driving to his ranch in the Alexander Valley, three hours north of San Francisco. He had a job at the Cetus Corp., one of the first Bay Area biotech companies, although it demanded little attention. He synthesized chemicals for other biochemists. Mullis had figured out how to automate much of the work with homemade computer programs, so he was able to spend a fair amount of time on the Cetus roof, sunning himself. His other main interest was chasing and marrying women. "He loves weddings," explained one of his four ex-wives. "Getting dressed up and all the ceremony."

As he drove across the mountains toward the Pacific Ocean, his current love interest, a woman from the laboratory, was dozing in the front seat. Mullis was thinking about technical problems in a diagnostic test Cetus was developing for sickle-cell anemia, a disease based on a genetic mutation passed from parents to children. The aim of the test was to diagnose the disease before the child was born. The problem was a lack of sensitivity; the test often failed to detect the broken gene.

So as Mullis steered the car along the curling mountain road, his mind was wrapped around the curves of a molecule, the famous serpentine helix known as deoxyribonucleic acid—DNA. Everything that lives has DNA. Mullis would remember the fragrance of the flowering roadside buckeye that washed in the car windows, their white stalks bobbing in the headlights.

How could you find a single spot on the long, fragile DNA molecule? In a series of acrobatic mental leaps from one chemical principle to another, he realized that a section of DNA containing a gene or fragment of a gene could be marked off and then forced into copying itself, employing the same replicating techniques that DNA uses when a cell divides. And then he realized something that was so startling he pulled the car to the shoulder and scrounged for a pencil. He would remember the spot as mile marker 46.7 of Route 128.

When he had been messing with computer programs that would automatically answer his office E-mail, he had been mightily impressed by the power of a reiterative computer loop, in which the same process is repeated over and over. Respond to two messages, and there are four. Respond to four, and there are eight total messages. By the fourth response, there are thirty-two copies of the messages. By the fifth, sixty-four copies. He also played with fractal photography, which involved exponential numbers. He enjoyed, for instance, running a picture of a naked woman through one of his fractal programs and having sixty-four images on the screen. The process showed him how fast numbers can climb when they increase exponentially.

As he worked out the cycles, he realized that his process for replicating DNA would work just about the same way: By adding the right chemicals, the little section of DNA could keep reproducing itself automatically and exponentially—so that the first fragment would double. Then each of those two pieces would double, creating four. Then those four would double to eight. In miniature, it was a replica of cell reproduction.

Next to him in the front seat, Mullis's companion woke up.

"I'm on to something big," he told her.

She muttered something crankily and went back to sleep. He worked by the map light.

In practical terms, after ten trips through the process, he wouldn't have ten copies of the gene—he'd have 256. And as it doubled, by the twenty-second cycle, he'd have 1,048,576. By the thirty-second, he'd be up to 1,073,741,824—a billion copies of a single gene, inside three hours. Bottomless vats of DNA.

"Can we get going?" asked the woman in the front seat.

Mullis pulled back onto the highway, still in the grip of the idea. It kept moving forward. Not only would this process give endless copies of a single gene or fragment, but it could be any single gene or fragment. He stopped the car again. They could find any gene they wanted to find, even if it was chemically invisible, and just keep reproducing it until the "signal" from all those copies of the original gene could be read.

"Dear Thor!" Mullis would later claim he said, explaining: "I had solved the two most annoying problems in DNA chemistry in a single lightning bolt: abundance and distinction."

Those very problems faced biotechnologists and forensic scientists investigating criminal cases.

By the time they reached his cabin, Mullis could not sleep. He opened a bottle of Mendocino County cabernet and poured a mug full. Working under kerosene lanterns in the electricity-free cabin, he scrawled notes and mathematical squares on every table, wall, and flat surface.

It would be months before he was able to make the process work in the laboratory, or even stir up much interest among his colleagues. By Christmas 1983, he had proved it could work. Ten years after his trip across the mountain, Mullis was called to Stockholm to receive the 1993 Nobel Prize in chemistry for his invention, called the polymerase chain reaction, or PCR. "I can't keep up with the things people are doing with PCR," said Mullis, who has retired to a life of surfing along the coast off La Jolla. "What will happen to it? It's like asking what stories people will write with a new software program. PCR is the word processor of biochemistry."

———

Almost immediately, corporate war broke out for the rights to PCR because its applications for pharmaceutical and biomedical purposes approached infinity. Hardly anyone realized, though, the revolutions that would be made in the courthouse.

In the late 1980s, two young biochemists working in the Bay Area, Henry Ehrlich and Edward Blake, recognized that the Mullis invention could be used in criminal investigations. With it, any fragment of tissue could become evidence, because the same genetic material is found in every cell from the brain to the big toe. When dealing with drops of blood or shafts of hair, a major concern is the ability to show that the evidence has not been tampered with or contaminated.

That would not be an issue in sexual assault cases, Blake realized, because the evidence itself could reveal contamination. Anyone who has ever used a mild soap and couldn't wash out a stubborn stain will be able to follow his logic.

To remove genetic material, cell walls must be broken open, allowing the DNA to escape. A simple, mild detergent does the trick for most cells. But the walls of sperm cells are different—tougher and thicker. Put sperm cells and skin cells in the same mild detergent solution, and the DNA from the skin cells will drain quickly, while the sperm cells remain intact. If a harsher detergent is used, then the walls of the sperm cells will break open, releasing the genetic material.

This mundane fact would alter the history of criminal justice. After a sexual assault, a mixture of two types of cells are collected with swabs—sperm cells from the rapist and skin or epithelial cells from the victim. In the laboratory, the first, mild detergent breaks open the epithelial cells. The victim's DNA is extracted and set aside. That leaves behind the sperm cells from the rapist and his DNA. A second, stronger detergent is then used to break open the tough outer shell of the sperm, freeing the rapist's DNA.

In effect, the ability to isolate and remove the male and female DNA—known as differential extraction—creates a biochemical videotape of the assault, yielding evidence from both victim and attacker. Whether that swab is tested the following week, or the following decade, the presence of the woman's cells in the mix tells the investigators that they are looking in the right place for the rapist.

The critical point is that a sperm cell won't open up with other types of cells. Even if a male police officer or technician somehow tainted the evidence with his own blood or saliva, the DNA from those cells would come out in the first rinse, with the female portion. Only the sperm from the rapist remains intact. That process, refined by Blake, has become the standard practice in laboratories around the United States and the world. In 1987, Blake was the first scientist called by prosecutors to testify about PCR results in a rape case.

A year later, Blake also provided the evidence in the first DNA exoneration of a wrongly convicted man. Gary Dotson of Chicago had been jailed for more than a decade for rape. He never stopped protesting his innocence. When Dotson heard about the DNA work of Dr. Alec Jeffries in England, he asked that the evidence be sent there for analysis. By then, it was far too degraded for Jeffries's RFLP, so it was returned to the United States and sent to Blake, who was able to use the new PCR invention. It showed that Dotson was not the source of the semen, and he was freed from prison.

Since then, the tests have become much more sensitive and discriminating. This means they can work with older, more deteriorated bits of evidence, and have greater power to tell one person from another. The tests are accepted in every court in the country, both as proof of guilt and innocence.

The acronym *PCR* may be unfamiliar, but the technique has become central to molecular biology, to rapid diagnosis of infections, to the matching of organ tissues for transplantation, even to the investigation of the past and the future. Scientists have used PCR to find the sparse remnants of DNA in ancient fossils. Researchers have read the genetic material inside an eighteen-million-year-old leaf, in a woolly mammoth that has been frozen dead for forty thousand years, and in a human brain that has marinated in a bog for seven thousand years. It is the technology that made *Jurassic Park* plausible. Now scientists can know what these creatures were like, how they lived, how they changed. In effect, the technique can roll back the stone from the tomb of extinction and catch the light from dead stars.

Moreover, the Mullis invention truly is a looking glass into tomorrow, capable of revealing the aging self to the youthful self. With it, the DNA can be read in a human embryo, only two hours old and four cells large. Almost from the instant of creation, a certain kind of destiny can be predicted. Will the child have cystic fibrosis or sickle-cell anemia? Young men and women can gaze into their futures, too, and find out if they are doomed to a fatal, wasting disease such as Huntington's Chorea.

When Kary Mullis pulled off the road that night and scribbled his arithmetic, no one could have dreamed the places to which his breakthrough would go. That it would travel through the history of the American judicial system hardly seemed possible. PCR can look anew at long-forgotten evidence and find long-standing injustices. For all its power, though, the invention cannot explain why.

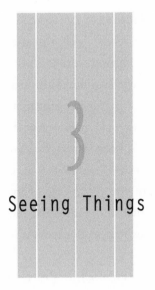

3

Seeing Things

One day in 1902, a large seminar class at a university in Berlin, Germany, was being taught by a Professor von Liszt, then a criminologist of some renown. Unknown to his students—an audience that was quiet, respectful, and male—the classroom was perched on a melodrama that would make history.

Professor von Liszt's topic that day was a chapter in a long-forgotten book. As he spoke, a shouted objection suddenly rose from a student in the audience. He insisted that the discussion was too secular. "I want to throw light on the matter from the standpoint of Christian morality!" hollered the student, a senior.

The outburst, like a fish leaping from a quiet pond, startled the class. Across the aisle, a younger student scoffed at the mention of religion.

"I cannot stand that," announced the underclassman.

The senior jumped to his feet.

"You have insulted me," said the senior.

"If you say another word—" said the underclassman, abruptly swallowing his threat when the senior man drew a revolver from the folds in his robes. Seeing this mortal peril, the younger student lunged forward, struggling to wrest the gun from the senior. Professor von Liszt also stepped in to grab for the weapon. At that instant, a blast was heard, the report of gunfire, a shot, devouring all other sounds. After a moment, it was clear that no one had been hit, and the two combatants backed off.

In a few moments, Professor von Liszt was able to recapture a semblance of order. He informed the shaken students that it was their obligation to provide detailed information about the events they had just witnessed.

The entire episode had been staged. Professor von Liszt had just conducted the first scientific test of eyewitness accuracy in the spanking new field of human inquiry known as psychology. The events in that Berlin classroom would become a minor landmark when the eyewitness accounts were reported by Hugo Munsterberg, a German American scholar at Harvard. Wrote Munsterberg:

"Words were put into the mouths of men who had been silent spectators during the whole short episode; actions were attributed to the chief participants of which not the slightest trace existed; and essential parts of the tragi-comedy were completely eliminated from the memory of a number of witnesses."

These hardly seem like revolutionary findings today, after a century of psychological research, but the discipline was only in its infancy when the von Liszt experiment was carried out. With the rising profile of the machine during the nineteenth century, a high premium was placed by society on precision and measurement. People were viewed as "perceivers" who absorbed information, recorded it, and could be counted on to produce reliable versions of what they saw happen.

By 1908, though, Munsterberg had written a book, *On the Witness Stand,* arguing that scientific evidence showed eyewitnesses were just as likely to be wrong as right. As a disciple of William James in the Harvard philosophy department, Munsterberg's writings were taken seriously.

After all, his argument was backed by concrete research: In the von Liszt experiment, the student with the best recollection of the event made errors on about 26 percent of the significant details. Others were wrong in their account of 80 percent of what they had seen. These healthy young German university students not only made history; they also made it up.

Were they simply inattentive, sloppy, or just inferior at recording what happened in front of their eyes? Were there special conditions in the Berlin seminar room that needed to be taken into account? The obvious questions quickly moved beyond the interests of Munsterberg, who drifted into psychic research. He left the field wide open. The von Liszt experiment became a favorite trick of academic and research psychologists. For most of the twentieth century, variations on that scene have been reenacted in classrooms all over the world.

Thousands of eyewitness tests later, with all the ritual rigors that modern social sciences can bring to bear, it can be said, with great confidence, that the German students were extremely average.

Just as physicists in the twentieth century have provided humanity with quantum mechanics, and biochemists have decoded the structure of DNA, psychologists have proved one concrete insight: What happens in front of the eyes is transformed inside the head, and is refined, revisited, restored, and embellished in a process as perpetual as life itself. Over the decades, elegant experiments have shown again and again the fungibility of memory. Starting in the early 1970s, and spurred by interest from the U.S. Supreme Court, the demonstrations became increasingly dramatic.

On the evening of December 19, 1974, a short documentary film was shown on the local NBC newscast in New York. In it, a young woman walks in a hallway. A man lurks in a doorway, wearing a hat, leather jacket, and sneakers. The man bursts from the doorway, grabs the woman's handbag, and runs straight toward the camera, full-faced. The entire incident lasts twelve seconds.

After the film was shown, the show presented a lineup of suspects. The viewers were provided with a phone number and asked to choose the culprit from among those six, or to say that he wasn't in the lineup. "We were swamped with calls," Robert Buckhout, a professor at Brooklyn College who organized the experiment, would later write. They unplugged the phone after receiving 2,145 calls.

The "thief" was seated in lineup position Number 2. He received a grand total of 302 votes from the callers, or 14.1 percent of the 2,145. "The results were the same as if the witnesses were merely guessing, since on the basis of chance (1 out of 7, including the 'not in lineup' choice), we would expect only 14.3 percent identifications of any lineup participants, including No. 2," Buckhout wrote in an article with the charming headline NEARLY 2,000 WITNESSES CAN BE WRONG.

Not surprisingly, those involved in such demonstrations often find themselves feeling deflated, and slightly put out, upon learning that they might as well have picked the culprit by throwing darts, blindfolded. When Buckhout used the same purse-snatching documentary with panels of lawyers and judges, he reported similar inaccuracy. But the members of the bar were peeved. They complained that the suspects in the lineup were not wearing the same clothes as the thief in the film!

By far the most significant implication of all the studies was the danger that innocent people would be put at risk of wrongful conviction. One of the leading researchers in the field, Elizabeth Loftus, illustrated the phenomenon of "unconscious transference," in which the mind drafts a vaguely familiar face to play a role that could not otherwise be cast.

Loftus described a case from real life in which a railroad ticket agent was held up at gunpoint. The agent was brought to the police station, where he viewed a lineup of suspects. He picked a sailor from a local naval base as the robber.

But when the police investigated the sailor, he turned out to have a solid alibi and was freed. How did the mistake happen? The ticket agent said the sailor's face looked familiar—and he was right. Because the sailor was based near the railroad station, he had bought train tickets from that very same agent three times before the robbery. But on the day of the robbery, the sailor was at sea. To the psychologists, the sailor was an obvious victim of the unconscious transference phenomenon.

The same process was neatly demonstrated in laboratory settings. Professor Buckhout staged an assault on the campus of California State University at Hayward. In view of 141 witnesses, a student attacked a professor. Another man, about the same age as the student-perpetrator, was a bystander at the crime. Buckhout videotaped the scene. A few weeks later, the witnesses—who did not realize that this was a study and thought they were participating in a criminal investigation—were asked to view a photo lineup.

This time, the eyewitnesses performed far better than those who had watched Buckhout's film on TV. Some 40 percent of the students chose the bad guy. But one witness in four picked the photograph of the bystander, a person who had no involvement in the attack. The remainder picked the "fillers," persons who were not present during the crime. This was another example of the unconscious transference phenomenon, and yet another warning about the risks to innocent people of eyewitness testimony.

Psychologists have measured the accuracy of people under stress, of groups collaborating on a description of a suspect, of the young and old, male and female, black and white. People under stress don't do well. As people try to identify across racial groups, they become even less reliable. And the people who are most certain of their identification often are the least likely to be correct.

All the published papers, and all the experiments in college classrooms, faced a gap: They were in the laboratory. They were simulations. Not real. No one could argue that the psychological studies of eyewitnesses were not consistent in results. But critics could argue that the bar should be higher before they were used to change rules in the courts. In the language of the social scientists, they required "external validity."

"Quite literally, in the legal domain, people's futures and lives depend on inferences from research results," wrote Vladimir Konecni and Ebbe B. Ebbesen of the University of California at San Diego. "A close examination of the run-of-the-mill studies in legal psychology shows that most offer only lip service, if any, to external validity."

What, after all, could these studies tell the real world?

———

Faye Treatser raised the shades on the window, opening a bright November afternoon into her living room. Then she settled herself on the living room couch to watch the world go by. A slim, brown-haired woman of thirty-five, Faye worked as an accounting manager in the suburbs of Washington, D.C. She lived with a big cat, Aggie, in a one-bedroom apartment on the ground floor of a town house in Alexandria, Virginia. It was, in its way, a lonely place.

From her couch, Faye looked out on Ashby Street, a lane of small, tidy homes, each with a little comma of a lawn that punctuated the street. Her side of the street, with the town houses, was anonymous, nearly invisible, easily ignored. She came and went by a back door, directly to a parking spot. She had moved in a year earlier, in July 1984. Of her neighbors on the other side of Ashby, mostly middle-class black families, she knew little. It was a Sunday. The churchgoers had come home. A few kids were playing on the street. Others were planted in front of the TV to watch the Redskins.

From the house directly across the street, Faye saw a muscular young black man emerge, carrying a bucket of water and sponges. A red Volkswagen was parked in the driveway, and he set to washing it. As he bent to dip a sponge in the bucket, Faye recognized something. He leaned over to soap a fender, and she saw it again.

That's him, Faye said to herself.

She sat on the couch, watching.

Him.

Two weeks earlier, Faye and another woman had gone to dinner at a Mexican restaurant on Glebe Road, just a mile from the town house. After dinner, the friend had walked Faye home, and then left in a cab. Around 9:30, Faye put on a big sweatshirt and climbed into bed. It was a chilly night, good sleeping weather, and she had left the window ajar.

Just before 2:00 in the morning, she awoke. She could hear the shade rattling. The darned cat was playing with it. She waited in bed a minute, thinking that if he kept making noise, she'd have to get up and move him. Suddenly, the light went on. She blinked her eyes open and saw a young black man standing a few feet away. He looked at her for a few seconds, then shut off the light and crept up to her bed. He said nothing. Faye dropped her head onto the pillow, afraid that she might actually be awake. The man draped a soft cloth over her face.

For the next twenty minutes, he raped and sodomized her. When her face was not covered with the cloth—a diaper, she thought—it was pressed down onto a pillow. He said nothing. She could see nothing. In the dark, she collected scents and touches: a musty body odor, cigarettes and alcohol; soft, smooth hands. When he turned her over to begin yet another attack, she could take no more. She groaned, feigning a heart attack. It was the first sound she had made. He paused, startled. "My heart," she groaned again, and at that point, the rapist quickly slipped into red shorts and tennis sneakers, then bent down to climb out her window. Faye, pitched on her side, watched him leave.

The moon was full, and as the man leaned over to climb out the window, he stepped into its light. In profile, Faye saw a muscular man with a short haircut. When the police arrived five minutes later, she met them at the door, carving knife in hand. They took her to the hospital. She was examined by a doctor. A nurse collected an evidence kit. Her private parts were swabbed with cotton to collect any seminal fluid that might have been left by the rapist. Her pubic hair was combed for traces of his hair or skin. Her body was a crime scene.

The next morning, the case was turned over to Investigator Barry Shiftic, one of the two detectives in the Alexandria police sex crimes unit. Shiftic canvassed the neighborhood. Had anyone seen a young black male wearing shorts? He left his card with neighbors, and not long afterward, a woman from Ashby Street called. She had seen a man wearing shorts and drinking a beer around nine or ten o'clock on the night of crime. He was standing in the street outside his house. The name was Walter Tyrone Snyder, and he lived directly across the street from Faye Treatser.

Snyder once had been charged with trespassing, the police files showed. He and some friends had gone into a school playground after hours to play basketball. It wasn't much of a criminal history—not even a photograph was on file—but Shiftic had to start somewhere. On November 8, 1985, he called on Snyder at his job, as a boiler mechanic for the T. J. Fannon & Sons oil company.

Snyder agreed to come to the precinct, have his photo taken, and give fingerprints. Yes, said Snyder, he owned red shorts—he boxed at 150 pounds for the Alexandria Boxing Club—and he also had a few pairs of sneakers that he wore for training or fighting. Snyder was directed to a fingerprinting office on another floor.

As he rose to leave, he felt his work gloves in his back pocket. He pulled them out and placed them on the table. As he did, a $20 bill was tugged from his pocket and fell to the floor. Snyder did not notice.

In the fingerprint office, Snyder rolled his fingers in ink and spread them one by one into the little boxes on the card. He washed up and returned to Shiftic's office to collect his belongings.

"Here," said Shiftic, holding the $20. "You dropped this."

Snyder was shocked, pleasantly.

"Thanks, man, I didn't even know it fell out," said Snyder.

"No problem," said Shiftic. "You can go now."

Their interview over, Shiftic dropped Snyder back at his job. Then he called in Faye Treatser to look at photographs of men who fit the description of the rapist. He gave her a pile of seven pictures. On top was the photo of Walter Snyder snapped that morning. She looked at his face and dropped it in the discard file. Didn't do anything for her.

Eventually, she separated four that looked familiar, then decided none of them was close enough to the rapist. She and the detective chatted for a few minutes. Then she idly picked up the first photo, the one she had rejected. "There is something about those eyebrows, something about those eyebrows," she told Shiftic. But no, she was not prepared to say he was the man.

That day, November 8, would be a busy one in the investigation of the rape on Ashby Street. Having taken Snyder's picture and shown it to Faye Treatser, Detective Shiftic then drove to the Snyder home with a search warrant. He was admitted by Snyder's mother, Edith, a postal clerk who worked nights. She directed him to the basement apartment that was the domain of her son, who was still at work. The detective picked up two pairs of red boxing shorts and two pairs of white sneakers and brought them back to his office, capping a full Thursday for Investigator Shiftic.

It was three days later, on the Sunday after this flurry of activity, that

Faye Treatser sat in her living room, looked across the street, and saw a man washing his red Volkswagen. She knew that face and shape. He was the first picture she had seen. She phoned Detective Shiftic to say that she had seen the guy, across the street. It was him.

For most of the next three months, little happened on the investigation. Faye Treatser went back to work at a home-improvement company, trying to recapture the life that had been tattered by the rapist. Walter Snyder was busy cleaning oil burners by day and boxing by night. But he also had a stubborn streak, and he was annoyed by the whole engagement with the police over the attack in his neighborhood. Shiftic had come to him at work, Snyder had cooperated fully, and the cop had even returned his $20. Then he had gone to the house and taken Snyder's stuff, an unnecessarily sneaky and underhanded move, in his estimation.

The national amateur boxing championships would be held at the end of February in Texas, and Shiftic had been sitting on his gear since the first week in November. Every time Snyder went to train, he was reminded of the episode. He stewed. On the morning of January 28, he stopped at the police station on his way to work. He asked for the detective at the reception desk and was steered to Shiftic's office.

"I came down to pick up the materials that you came and got from my house," said Snyder.

"You can't have them," said Shiftic. "They are out at the lab. They are part of this investigation."

They argued for a few minutes.

"I am sorry," said Shiftic, cutting off the debate. "You are going to have to leave."

"I am not leaving until you get me someone with authority to tell me why I can't have my belongings," said Snyder.

"If you don't leave, I am going to lock you up for trespassing," said Shiftic.

Furious, Snyder left the station. Later that morning, the problem of his purloined shorts seemed minor. The space shuttle *Challenger* had exploded seconds after launching, killing the seven crew members. The sight of the rocket streaking into the sky played over and over on television, the announcers explaining that signs of the disaster could be seen in the bend of the flame, the sudden peeling away from vertical.

Snow fell the next morning in Alexandria. Walter Snyder did not care to drive on slippery roads, so he loaded his backpack to jog three miles to work. As he ran, the matter of his shorts came to mind again. His mother had told him to stay away from the police station. But he was nineteen years old, and he could make up his own mind; they were his shorts, and he wanted them back. Shiftic had no right. Snyder appeared, once again, at the police reception desk.

"I want to talk to you about getting my stuff," said Snyder.

"Walter, I don't want to talk about your stuff anymore," said Shiftic. "I want to talk about things on my mind. Come on down."

They sat in a small interview room. Walter allowed that he was in pretty good shape from boxing, so an early-morning run was no problem. They talked about the *Challenger* disaster. Then the topic shifted.

"Would you do a crime like this?" asked Shiftic.

Of the conversation that followed, there is no agreed version. By Shiftic's account, Snyder spoke about being physically present at the rape but his mind not being there. Snyder recalls speaking about a person having to be out of his mind to commit such an act, so that his body could do such evil only if his mind and better instincts were absent.

"I want you to go sit upstairs and wait for me," said Shiftic.

Snyder agreed. He sat in the reception area. It was still early in the morning, not yet eight o'clock. From his office, Shiftic dialed Faye Treatser's number.

"Good morning," he said. "What are you doing?"

"I'm just starting my day," said Treatser.

"Are you busy?" asked the detective.

"Do you need me to look at someone?" asked Treatser.

"Can you come down to the station?" replied Shiftic.

"I am on my way," she said.

Three months after she had been raped in her home, Faye Treatser arrived in the Alexandria Police Station, fully expecting that the police were ready for her to identify the attacker. She asked for Barry Shiftic, and the police receptionist pointed to a door behind Treatser, and directed her to go that way.

She turned. She froze. Sitting in the front row of chairs, the only other person in the room, was Him. The man in that first picture. The man who had been washing his car. The man, she was sure, who had raped her.

"I can't go that way," she urgently whispered to the receptionist. "That's my assailant there."

––––––––

Faye Treatser's glance lasted no longer than an instant, a spark really, but it was enough to incinerate the only life Walter Snyder had known. Not that he had the faintest idea at the time. He was focused on his boxing togs. Slumped on a bench, he didn't notice Treatser arriving, looking at him, or panicking. He certainly did not realize that he had just undergone the equivalent of a flash trial and conviction. Few laypeople would have guessed the gravity of such a moment, but for the next seven years, Snyder would bend under its weight.

Treatser turned her back on him and faced the police reception desk. The receptionist did not seem to understand what she was whispering.

"To see the investigator, you just go down those stairs," said the receptionist.

"I don't think I can go that way," said Treatser, speaking in hushed, urgent tones. "That's him. That's the one."

She looked over her shoulder at Snyder. With that, the receptionist caught the drift. A violent criminal was sitting just a few feet away. She led Treatser down the back stairs to see Shiftic.

"The man who raped me is upstairs in the lobby," Treatser declared by way of greeting.

"Let's go over to the office," said Shiftic, with some satisfaction. Things had worked out just as he had planned. Faye had come down to the police station. In a "chance" encounter with the suspect, she had identified him as the rapist.

He poured a cup of coffee for her and called a rape companion, a woman in the office who helped victims of sexual assault.

"Now, Faye," Shiftic told her solemnly, "I don't want you to make a mistake. We are dealing with a serious crime, so I want you to be positively sure."

"I am one hundred percent sure," declared Treatser.

"Would you bet your paycheck on that?" he asked, teasing.

"Yes," said Treatser, "I would."

When the rape companion arrived, Shiftic left to prepare an arrest warrant. He dispatched another officer, George Burnham, to bring Snyder back downstairs. He found Snyder waiting in the lobby, just as Shiftic had said.

"Hey, Tony, how d'you feel?" asked Burnham, calling him by his family nickname.

"George," said Snyder, surprised. Burnham had coached various members of the Snyder family on baseball teams when they were younger.

"Come on downstairs," said Burnham. "We can wait down in one of the rooms for Investigator Shiftic."

They sat talking for a while about old times, people who had played on the teams and gone on to make something of themselves. They talked, too, about Snyder's desire to join the Marines, and how Burnham had agreed to not push the prosecution of a trespassing charge against Snyder when he caught him playing ball after hours in the schoolyard. Much later, each man would have distinctly different interpretations of other parts of the conversation.

For Snyder, at least, when Shiftic strode into the interview room, he had one thought only: At last, he would be getting his shorts and sneakers returned.

"Walter, I've got good news about your clothes," said Shiftic. "They're back from the lab."

"Fine, let me get them, get myself going," said Snyder.

"The bad news, Walter," said Shiftic, "is that you're under arrest."

"Arrest? Get out," said Snyder. "What is this? A minute ago, you had nothing. Now you're arresting me?"

He rose to leave, but Shiftic insisted he sit down.

"I want to leave," said Snyder.

"Just so it's clear where things stand," said Shiftic, suddenly snapping a handcuff around Snyder's wrist and the chair.

As Snyder sat there, dazed, the detective plucked some hairs from his head to use for lab tests and set them on a sheet of paper. For sure, Snyder thought, those hairs would be planted somewhere as evidence. He leaned over and blew them away with a gust of breath. He was slapped in the face by Investigator Shiftic, who would later say that he acted only because Snyder had stood, chair dangling by the cuff, and bulled his way to the door. He had fifteen years on the detective, and the brawl rolled into the hallway. Five police officers jumped in. Snyder's nose was broken. The officers hauled him back into the interview room. To complete the investigation, Shiftic needed pubic hairs. The other officers combined to pin Snyder, arms and legs, while Shiftic plucked hairs for the evidence kit.

As things turned out, the fracas over the hair produced no evidence linking Snyder to the crime. No matter.

With the single glance from Faye Treatser in the lobby, the case had been closed. Naturally, there were other rites to perform—blood tests, the formalities of indictment, trial, and conviction—but for the Alexandria Police and the commonwealth of Virginia, a case of first-degree rape, sodomy, and burglary had been solved.

The wet concrete of Faye Treatser's memory had cured in phases around the form of Walter Tyrone Snyder: On her very first visit to the police station, she had passed over his picture but somehow was drawn back to the pile of pictures and happened to pull one at random. Both Barry Shiftic and Faye Treatser would say it was mere chance that brought her back to the picture of Walter Snyder, that she had not been steered to look more closely at the very picture Shiftic had taken that morning. And on that second look, she thought she saw something familiar. Maybe his eyebrows.

Three days later, the police picture came to life in her living room window. Snyder was washing a car on Ashby Street, across from her home, in his driveway.

At last, summoned by the detective on that snowy January morning to look at a suspect, after three months waiting for an arrest, she had only to take a few steps in the police station when she encountered one man, and only one man. Now she was certain. It was twelve weeks after the rape. The concrete had set. Her memory had hardened. No amount of jackhammering by a defense lawyer ever would make it budge. "It all came back," she would explain. "Everything just came back on the thirtieth. I don't know why. Just what I saw was not a picture, or somebody washing his car. What I saw was my attacker."

———

The trial of the *Commonwealth* v. *Walter Tyrone Snyder* opened in the circuit court for the city of Alexandria on June 23, 1986. The first witness, Faye Treatser, was explaining that when she rushed to the police precinct on the morning of January 30, she presumed the detective at last had arrested the man who had been haunting her memories for three months. She was ready to identify him.

"Whenever Investigator Shiftic called me, he represented authority and I assumed—I assumed they wanted me to come down for something like that," Treatser testified. "I did not give him an opportunity to tell me. When he called, I jumped. I wanted to go and do whatever I needed to do."

Her assumption was logical. Never before had she been summoned on short notice to the police station, at breakfast time or any other time. As she told her story to the jury, the details rang with the certainty that could come only from one who was telling the truth as she knew it. Faye Treatser was not a prominent person, but it is the gift of the judicial system that the violation of a thirty-five-year-old single woman, an accountant for a home-improvement company, was taken as injury to the people of the commonwealth of Virginia. And she brought her own dignity to the proceedings.

Under questioning from a soft-spoken prosecutor, Joseph McCarthy, Treatser sketched the night of the attack in quick, sure strokes. The Mexican dinner with a friend, the walk home, turning in early for the night. The window shade rattling her from sleep. A light clicks on, a man standing in the bedroom. Her face being covered with a soft cloth. The attack.

The events were distant in time and place, months and miles away from the courtroom, but suddenly, they were happening again, fresh in the telling from the witness box. Watching Faye Treatser, the jurors could picture the moment and its terrors. Yet a trial is more than remembered narratives of victims, the emotionally detached reports of fingerprint experts, or the flourishing grandiloquence of lawyers.

The crime must be connected to the accused person, on the spot, in the courtroom. For at least an instant, the action must move into the present tense.

Faye Treatser was led gently out of recollection by Prosecutor McCarthy.

Q: How long had you lived there on that date?
A: A little over a year.
Q: Did you have a chance to see the defendant that day in your apartment?
A: Yes, I did.
Q: Do you see him here today, Faye?
A: Yes.
Q: Would you identify him for the jury? Who is he?
A: He is the defendant.
Q: What color is his shirt?
A: Pink.
Q: Is he seated there with Mr. Stafford [the defense lawyer]?
A: Yes.
Q: Are you positive about that?
A: Yes, I am.

It was a short trial. In rapid order, an emergency room nurse and doctor testified to Faye Treatser's injuries and the collection of physical evidence from her body. A laboratory technician said that Walter Snyder shared the blood type of the rapist—as did 32 percent of the population. A policeman said that he and his tracking dog tried to follow a trail from the Treatser back window, but they lost it not far from her condo. A fingerprint technician said that the only prints he found in the bedroom were Faye Treatser's. Most of the witnesses were neither illuminating nor, in the lawyers' terms, probative.

Faye Treatser was the first, and lengthiest witness. For emotional weight, nothing came close to her presence. She had described the attack for the record at least three times—once, immediately afterward, when she called the police and gave a description to the patrolman who came to her door. The second time was a day later, in a detailed interview with the detective assigned to the case, Barry Shiftic.

And now, once more, in the courtroom.

Each telling of her attack had been precise. In court, she said again that her face had been covered or pressed into a pillow for the worst of it, and that she had glimpsed the rapist when he first turned on her light, and when he bent over to climb out her window. But she did have a chance to pick up his scent. And only in this detail did her memory make a subtle, important shift.

When the first policeman came to her door, Faye Treatser told him that the assailant had "a strong body odor and the odor of alcohol on his breath." The next day, she gave Detective Shiftic an extensive statement that was transcribed. "He definitely had an odor," she said of the rapist. "I mean, we are not just talking about a bad odor, but just a very unique odor. . . . He had kind of a musky odor, a combination of sweat and alcohol and possibly cigarette smoke."

Seven months later, Prosecutor McCarthy asked:

Q: Now, when he was lying on top of you, did you have a chance to detect any odors?

A: Yes.

Q: What odors did you detect, Faye?

A: His face was right next to mine. I was able to—I smelled tobacco smoke or smoke. I smelled alcohol and I smelled a musky-type odor.

Q: Could you describe that odor in any more detail?

A: The musky, it was kind of—it was kind of a combination of *oil* and a *basement*—a musty smell.

Never before had she used the words *oil* or *basement* to describe the odor of her attacker. Perhaps those were the words she meant to use on the night of the crime, or the next day, when she was interviewed. Far more likely, though, is that someone told her where Snyder lived and what he did for a living. And those two facts about Snyder—his quarters in a basement apartment, and his work as a fuel-oil boiler repairman—became part of Faye Treaser's memory of the odors she recalled.

Later on, the prosecutor brought in Snyder's boss from the fuel-oil company to testify about his work. "The Commonwealth, through this witness, wants to establish contact with oil through his work," said McCarthy. "That was the odor that the victim detected on the person that raped her."

The criminal had been all but invisible to Faye Treaser, but suddenly, the very air around Walter Snyder would incriminate him. Only when Snyder emerged as the defendant did Faye Treaser remember an odor of "basement" and "fuel oil."

On another detail, Treaser had consistently described her attacker as wearing red shorts, and indeed, two pairs had been found in the Snyder basement during Shiftic's search. Both belonged to Walter. In court, Prosecutor McCarthy produced a paper bag, Exhibit 6. Inside were the shorts. He held them aloft so Faye Treaser and the jurors could see them.

Q: Have you had a chance to look at those before?
A: Uh-hum.
Q: Do you recognize these at all?
A: Uh-hum.
Q: Are these similar to the boxing shorts you saw the defendant wearing on October 28th?
A: Yes.

In a moment of small drama, Snyder's defense attorney, Bobby Stafford, also questioned her about the shorts. He pulled them from the bag.

Q: I show you Exhibit 6. Do those appear to be the shorts you saw that evening?
A: Both of them do. I remember the red.
Q: Okay. Now, if you remember the red, do you remember anything about any writing or white on them?

A: No.

Q: Do you know any reason why you would be prevented from seeing red and white?

A: No.

With that, Stafford turned both pairs of shorts inside out. What the jury and Faye Treatser had been shown by the prosecutor were the insides of the shorts. When turned right side out, they no longer were solid red. They had an inch of white piping at the hem and the waist, and the letters ABC emblazoned in white, for the Alexandria Boxing Club. The word EVERLAST also was blasted across the front in white. To have displayed them as solid red—which is how they appeared when turned inside out—was a sleight of hand.

Q: Seeing those now, do you believe that if you had seen those that night, you would remember whether these were the same?

A: I don't know.

She was sure she had seen red, and she was sure they were about that length. But Stafford pressed again and won a small concession:

Q: Can you identify these as being the shorts?

A: I do not remember the writing.

In court, Walter Snyder's red and white shorts were made to appear red. In court, the boozy, smoky-smelling rapist became a rapist with an odor of "basement" and "fuel oil." They were only small, telling details. Whether they were tricks of the mind, or tricks of the prosecutor, mattered little. They had become part of the story of Walter Snyder's rape of Faye Treatser.

One other question. Did Treatser know that Snyder lived across the street from her home? After all, she could be identifying a familiar face, rather than a criminal one. It was an obvious issue, and Prosecutor McCarthy dealt with it early in her testimony. In the year and a half that she lived on Ashby Street, Treatser said, she rarely encountered any of the neighbors. Her car was parked behind the apartment complex, and she came and went by a back door.

Q: Do you know where the defendant lived that day, on October 28th? Do you know where he lived?
A: No. I didn't know where he lived at that time.
Q: Do you know where he lives?
A: Yes . . . He lives directly across the street from my apartment.
. . .
Q: Had you ever seen him before?
A: I don't recall seeing him, no.

How then did she come to know that Snyder lived across the street? Defense attorney Stafford pressed on the question. The slow-motion identification of Snyder was pregnant with areas of potential abuse. Treatser conceded that she had been told by Investigator Shiftic that the suspect lived in her neighborhood.

Q: When did he tell you that the defendant lived across the street?
A: I don't recall. It might have been after I talked to him about seeing [Snyder] wash his car.

The defense lawyer tried to draw out Investigator Shiftic on the same matter. Had he told Faye Treatser that Snyder lived across the street? "I don't think I mentioned his name," said Shiftic. "I don't recall saying that he lived across the street. I think I said 'the neighborhood.' I honestly don't recall."

In fact, on the day after the crime, it was Treatser herself who suggested that the style of the rapist's haircut was similar to that worn by a neighbor. "I know exactly what kind of hairdo that you are talking about," she had said. "In fact, there is a fellow that lives right across the street that is very much like what I am talking about, and he has a hairdo like that."

This discussion was contained in a twenty-eight-page statement on the rape that the Snyder family says it first saw seven years after the trial.

The crime had a beginning and an end, a rape and an arrest. But the middle of the story sagged. How did she happen to return to his picture in the precinct, after having rejected it? When did she learn that he might live in her neighborhood? Why wasn't a lineup conducted? On these and many other questions, neither the victim nor the investigator could provide much detail. Snyder had been seen wearing shorts on the night of the crime, and by default, he became the only suspect ever examined. Investigator Shiftic had done little investigation and even less pursuit of Walter Snyder. Not until Snyder pestered him on two consecutive mornings for the return of his shorts did he summon Treatser down to view him and bring the case to a head.

Besides Faye Treatser, the state had one other piece of evidence implicating Walter Snyder. The prosecution said Snyder confessed to the crime—not once, but twice, on separate days.

On the morning of January 29, Shiftic testified, Snyder made his first visit to the precinct to retrieve his boxing shorts. He confessed to the rape, but Shiftic said he wasn't ready to arrest him, so the detective sent him home. His account is bizarre.

"He wanted to box or to use those shorts for some reason. I explained to Mr. Snyder he couldn't have them," Shiftic said. "They were still part of the investigation, and I couldn't release them.

"We talked about a lot of things. We talked about boxing, sports, and he made some statements. He said the woman raped him, he didn't rape her. We kept going in and out of a lot of conversation.

"I still wasn't sure what his point was for coming to see me. He repeated several times, 'No, she raped me. I didn't rape her. I was there mentally but not physically,' and then, 'I was there physically, but not mentally.' The conversation continued."

After two hours of this, Shiftic claimed, "I was trying to get Walter to talk a little more since he wouldn't stay on the line of thought. Finally, I had more appointments and Walter was still my number one suspect. I wasn't positive and asked Walter to leave my office."

"Why didn't you arrest him?" asked Prosecutor McCarthy.

"We are talking rape, next to murder in severity," replied Shiftic. "I don't make arrests unless I am sure the individual I arrest has done the crime."

This was an astonishing leap. Because the crime was so serious, Shiftic decided to let a man walk away who, by his account, had confessed to the attack. Not until the following morning, when Snyder again appeared at the police station in search of his boxing shorts, did Shiftic decide to present him to Faye Treatser.

After she spotted him in the lobby, Shiftic told his colleague, George Burnham, that Snyder had been fingered in the rape. Burnham sat with Snyder in an interview room. They chatted about baseball. Then Burnham, who knew next to nothing about the case, put it to Snyder: You have been named as the rapist.

"I told him I knew he had committed the rape. I told him a lady had identified him as one committing the rape. At that time, he started crying and stated he did not rape her, that she had raped him."

Burnham conceded that Snyder had, during most of their time together, denied any involvement. At points, the officer said, Snyder had said, "I am not Walter. I am Jesus Christ."

There was no record of this conversation—no tape recordings, no memos, not even written notes. Even in Burnham's telling, it was not a persuasive, forthright, assertion of guilt by Snyder.

Still, taken with the identification by Treatser, it was clear that Walter Snyder had to answer a case. His alibi was not a knockout. On the night of the rape, he had been home in bed, asleep. His parents were asleep, too. One brother, Christopher, came to court and said he had been awake at the time the police came to the Treatser apartment. He had noticed the cars while he was out smoking a cigarette. He had passed Walter's bedroom and remembered that he was asleep. The brother's account was scoffed at as a well-meaning, hard-to-credit story by the prosecutor. At 2:00 in the morning, though, most people are in bed.

Then the defendant himself took the witness stand. Walter Snyder wanted, in the first place, to discuss his encounters with the police. He had cooperated at all times with Investigator Shiftic, leaving his job to meet him in the police station for an interview. There, he voluntarily gave his fingerprints and permitted Shiftic to take his photograph. Later, although the jury did not learn this, he also had taken a polygraph.

All he could say about the night of the crime was that he had been home asleep. And all he could say about his arrest was that he had been prod-ded by the police to admit the crime, and in the course of the interrogation, even heard suggestions that Treatser had seduced him.

"I said, 'It never even happened. Nothing happened. I was never there.' They were trying to get me to admit to the crime myself." Then, he said, the officers suggested again that Treatser somehow had initiated the encounter. They said, according to Snyder, "'She asked you. She started fondling with your body.' I said, 'No, it didn't happen like that. I was never with this lady.' 'Say she came on to you.' 'What, she raped?' And that was my reaction, 'She raped me.' 'No there wasn't nothing even like that.' . . . I had nothing to do with that woman at all."

In his closing statement, Prosecutor McCarthy dwelled on Faye Treatser's identification of Snyder.

"She was there twenty to twenty-five minutes," said McCarthy. "She had a chance to see his face. She saw him for three to five seconds before he turned the light off at the beginning of the attack. She told you she had opportunities to see the man. The man seated here, Mr. Snyder, took the stand. He's the man that attacked her. She's one hundred percent sure. She's in a better position to know. She saw, she experienced it."

He also reminded them of the odors.

In about two hours, the jurors came back with the guilty verdict on all counts.

At sentencing, defense attorney Stafford could do little more than point out that Walter did not have a criminal record, and that the victim had said her attacker was gentle. The lawyer also raised the possibility that an-other man in the neighborhood was a better suspect than Snyder, resembled him, had a criminal record, and had been seen wearing red shorts near the rear entrance to Faye Treatser's home. That effort went nowhere.

When Snyder spoke to the judge, he was curt, angry, and expressed no contrition.

"I tried every way I could to prove my innocence in this whole thing," said Snyder. "It is very ridiculous. I don't see—humans aren't infallible. They cannot pass judgment, and, I have been convicted on, I believe—and I know very strongly that I did not do this, and I don't believe that I received a fair trial in this entire matter. That is all I have to say."

In Virginia, jurors recommend sentences on high felonies, and the judge can revise their suggestion. Prosecutor McCarthy characterized the jury's recommendation as a "very, very light sentence," but Judge Albert Swersky thought the recommendation was just about right and followed it to the minute.

He sentenced Walter Tyrone Snyder, who had not yet reached the age of twenty-one to forty-five years in prison. Snyder looked around the courtroom. His parents were stricken, particularly his father, Walter. The number of years his son would serve, forty-five, clanged inside the elder Snyder's mind. It was not a time beyond reckoning. On that very day, the father had turned forty-five.

———

Seven years later.

The prosecutor had retired to private practice. The judge had retired, period. The detective had moved to other cases. The city of Alexandria was booming, and Walter Snyder was busted.

By the first week of 1993, he was awaiting his twenty-seventh birthday in the Nottoway prison, deep in rural Virginia, and looking at thirty-nine more years of incarceration. His dog-eared case had settled into obscurity, after getting the once-over lightly by the appellate courts, and vanishing into the hands of attorneys indifferent, timid, or both.

Then Edith Snyder delivered the legal carcass into the office of Peter in New York.

"We have legal proof that our son is innocent," she told Peter. "You and Mr. Barry Scheck would be the sixth lawyer."

"Sixth?" said Peter.

With that, she began a recitation that went on for some minutes, a wander through the looking glass.

From the moment Walter went to jail, his family had fought in his corner, chasing tips, digging up money, hiring lawyers. The most promising lead came from Walter himself, right after the guilty verdict. It had taken only six and a half years to pan out. While he was still in Alexandria, awaiting the formal sentencing, Walter had picked up a copy of *Newsweek*. An article told of Alec Jeffries, a brilliant scientist in England who had invented the technique and coined the term *DNA fingerprinting*, and had used it to solve a crime. Not only had his work nailed a serial killer in the English countryside, but he also had exonerated an innocent man, wrongly accused.

On his mother's next visit to the jail, Walter had an instruction.

"Get this article," he told her. "This DNA test will clear me and get me out of here."

Edith Snyder went home and began making phone calls to international directory assistance. She tracked Jeffries down to his laboratory in Leicester. No, said the scientist, no one in the United States was doing that sort of work yet with DNA. A company he was associated with, Cellmark, however, was building a facility in Germantown, Maryland, not far from the Snyder home in metropolitan Washington, D.C. The Snyders called a contact person at Cellmark. The roof was not yet on the building, but they could stay in touch.

Walter moved into the state prison system. For the first year and a half, he let it be known that he was in for murder. Killed a man. Rape? Not him. He did not want a reputation as a "tree jumper," someone who hid in the bushes and attacked women. A course for sexual offenders was required even to be considered for parole ahead of the forty-five years. Snyder refused to sign up for it. He would not hang out with those people. He would not take the sex-offenders' therapy program because he was not a sex offender. Looking good for the parole board was not on his agenda. He would never get to parole. He would be out of prison long before. Of that, he was certain.

At home, the legal fees for the Snyders had not ended with the criminal trial, which had cost them more than $10,000, paid for with a second mortgage on their home. They tapped benefits accounts, cashed in insurance policies, took on additional work shifts. Walter Sr., besides working as a postal engineer, set up a locksmith business in the backyard and hung a notary public shingle on the front door.

Now they were on to the appellate lawyer. He was paid nearly $4,000 to attack the trial court's decision permitting the police officers to testify that

Walter had given them a sort of confession. Other appeal issues concerned the exclusion of young black males from the jury and the eyewitness identification process.

All these were secondary, in Walter's mind, to proving his innocence. He wrote to his attorney on May 12, 1987, not long after he arrived in prison, begging him to explore DNA tests.

"I have spent almost one whole year in prison, waiting for something to happen relating to my case," wrote Walter. "I didn't know anything about a test such as this. I know for a fact that my sperm will in no way match the semen found at the scene of the crime." The tests should go forward along with "any other procedures of business you may be conducting at this present time. I feel this test will refute all statements and allegations made by the Commonwealth's Attorney and others.

"The analyzing of spermatozoa will undoubtedly prove my innocence. . . . My life is passing before me, everyone I love and care for are far from reach. I am more than curious as to what's happening in my case. It would be most appreciated if I was informed of the progress and all anticipated factors concerning my situation. . . .

"I am not trying to tell you how to do your job, but I'm very concerned as to how long it may be until I'm reunited with the outside world. There are many questions I would like to ask, but do not have the means of doing so.

"A response to this letter will be highly regarded and helpful. Thank you, Walter T. Snyder, Jr."

He got no answer. He never heard from the lawyer about DNA tests. The case had been tried in two days. It would be nearly three years before the appeal was filed, and the legal arguments were dismissed by a panel of three appellate judges on December 15, 1989, three and a half years after the conviction. That left the DNA tests as his final shot.

For the DNA work, the family decided to move on to another lawyer, to whom they paid $5,000. She turned out to be much friendlier and seemed to take a great interest in the case. By then, in 1989, Cellmark's laboratory was up and running in Maryland. The new lawyer prepared the papers, but things dragged on.

After nine months with no word, Walter called the lawyer from jail. "Unfortunately, the lab wasn't able to get results," she told him. "There was not enough molecular DNA."

When did she get these results? Why had she not told him sooner? Why was it left to him to call her? Angry questions formed in his mouth, but he swallowed them. It did not matter. He had been sure that this test would prove his innocence. Despair rose like floodwater. He was four years into a prison term, he had spent his appeals, and now the magic DNA card was a dud. Justice was a mirage that vanished when you reached for it. He began to think about chiseling into his forty-five-year sentence. The next morning, he signed up for the sex-offenders' class so he would one day be eligible for the parole he was not supposed to need, ever.

At home, the Snyders discovered a few other blind alleys to chase. One memorable afternoon found Edith Snyder sitting in a lounge at National Airport. Just the other day, she had seen a lawyer on Sally Jessy Raphael's show. He presented himself as a specialist at correcting injustices, particularly in rape convictions. Even when cases seemed hopeless, he had wrenched fairness from the constipated guts of the criminal justice system. Edith Snyder had called him on the spot. He agreed to meet her at the Washington airport if she would pay $500 in transportation costs. In advance. She did.

"From what you told me about the case on the phone, I believe that we can help your son, Mrs. Snyder," said the lawyer. Edith leaned over. She knew he was edging in for the kill. She did not care. "The thing is," he was saying, "is that there will be a considerable amount of investigation involved. We will be working with the top people in the field, very cutting-edge stuff."

Around them, all the world and its brother were scurrying from taxi-cabs to flights, down long corridors to the boarding gates. Indifferent to the clamor, Edith Snyder, postal worker, listened to the man make a smooth pitch to be her son's lawyer. On that day, Walter Snyder had been in prison for more than five years. She and her husband had spent thousands of dollars defending their son during his trial, and more again on his appeal.

He listened to her recite the details of the case. He nodded sympathetically, shook his head at the hint of a foul-up by an earlier defense counsel, clenched his teeth so that his jawline rippled with anger at the indifference to the truth of the police and prosecutor.

"We would need a retainer of twenty thousand dollars before we begin our work," said the lawyer. "A significant amount of research will be involved."

"Up front?" she asked, already knowing the answer.

"That's the policy," said the lawyer.

"Let me see what I can do about another mortgage," she said. But her bank had done two mortgages and was not ready for a third. She all but searched between the cushions of the couch for lost change. Then she called the lawyer in New York and told him the places she had been for money.

"I have been able to put together eighteen thousand now, and we will work on getting the rest," she said.

"Let me know when you have the twenty thousand," he had said, and that was the last of him.

───────

On that winter afternoon in New York, Peter listened to Edith Snyder's voice on the phone as she recounted her pilgrimages from one grotto of false hope to another. She was matter-of-fact, giving him the lay of the land as she saw it. Now she would explain what had brought her to the Innocence Project.

Edith worked the night shift at the Alexandria post office so that she would be home during the day to care for her young grandson while his father was in prison. Over the years, she became friendly with another woman in the post office, Tommie Kuramoto. By 1992, in chats over a million pieces of mail, Tommie had lived the Walter Snyder case, backward and forward. She, too, had felt the hammer blow of the failed DNA test. One day, she was talking with her own daughter, Susan Moffit, a reporter for the *Los Angeles Times*, who was working on a story about the identification of military men and women who had been killed in the Gulf War during Operation Desert Storm.

From her daughter, Tommie learned about an amazing new DNA test that would work on mere fragments.

"Edith, they have this new technique that can work with tiny pieces of DNA," Tommie told her one night. "It's called PCR. Maybe it's something for Walter."

The next day, Edith Snyder was back on the phone to Cellmark. The earlier test might not have worked because there was insufficient DNA. But how about this PCR, which could take tiny pieces of DNA and analyze them?

Sorry, said the man at Cellmark, but the company wasn't set up to do it yet. She could try a laboratory in Boston. A Dr. David Bing was using the PCR technique.

"Get a lawyer to send the evidence to us, and we will do the test for you," said Janice Williamson, who worked with Bing.

Edith Snyder thought for a moment about the woman lawyer to whom they already had paid $5,000, and the papers she had produced for the first round of DNA tests. No reason not to recycle them. Having paid boutique prices for lawyers too many times, she now hunted down a general-purpose, will-writing, house-closing attorney and asked him about writing a letter. Actually, the term *writing* overstated the task. He merely had to retype a letter written by the previous lawyer, changing the address where the evidence should be sent. Instead of Cellmark in Maryland, it would go to CBR in Boston. For $50, the lawyer would be willing to do just that. On May 23, 1992, a certified-mail package arrived in Boston from the Alexandria court clerk's office. Inside was all the physical evidence from the trial: the blood samples taken from Faye Treatser and Walter Snyder, the underpants that she put on after the rape, the swabs taken of her vagina and anus at the hospital.

These were critical records of the crime, immune to suggestive questions, unimpressed by sudden confrontations in the lobby of a police precinct, incapable of remembering an "oily" smell that did not exist. The laboratory staff opened the package and photographed each of the fifty separate items as they were unwrapped. In the earlier Cellmark tests, most of the rapist's sperm had been consumed. But enough was left for Dr. Bing to tease out the rapist's DNA. While Faye Treatser had a steady boyfriend, she had testified in court that they had not had sexual relations for more than ten days. The underwear she put on after the rape had been freshly laundered. It was impossible that the semen of anyone but the rapist was in the evidence.

On the morning of October 27, 1992—seven years, minus one day, to the date of the rape—David Bing and his associate, Janice Williamson, tested the underwear.

The Snyders waited, but watchfully. In December, when results were expected, they began phoning their $50 lawyer to see if he had heard from Bing's lab. He did not return their calls. Then he left for vacation. On Christmas Eve, Edith Snyder called Boston herself.

"We're just trying to find out the results," she said.

The woman at the lab, Ms. Williamson, was surprised. They had sent the results three weeks earlier to the lawyer in Virginia. She thought the Snyders knew.

"We're really only supposed to be dealing with the lawyer, but I thought you would have heard by now," said Williamson. "The news is good. Your son is excluded."

Edith Snyder did not need any translation. She called the Nottoway prison in rural Virginia and left word for Walter to contact her. He was playing cards when a guard walked up to him.

"Your mom wants you to call," he said. Snyder folded his cards, left the table, and waited his turn at the pay phone. He dialed collect to the house on Ashby Street in Alexandria.

"Son," said Edith Snyder, "you're coming home."

———

And that, as she told Peter, was the story up to the present. Walter was still in prison. How could they get him out and how much would it cost?

"The first thing we have to do is contact the prosecutor, to see what position they are going to take," said Peter. And the legal work would be done for free.

Edith had her doubts about getting any cooperation from the county prosecutor. The small-town politics of Alexandria had come to resemble a vise. The disregard for the truth about her son by so many officials, the lassitude of even their own defense lawyers, all seemed to be a product of good-old-boyism taken to a toxic level. The case was now in the hands of a new prosecutor, S. Randolph Sengel.

"You think Sengel will buck the rest of them?" asked Edith.

"If he doesn't agree that this test definitively excludes Walter as the rapist, then we will fight them," said Peter. "But if he is willing to help, it would be good to have him as an ally.

That day, Peter researched Virginia law on "newly discovered evidence" that would allow a court to reopen the Snyder trial. The results were grim. The law specifically said that a motion based on new evidence had to be made within three weeks of the conviction.

By that law, the DNA evidence was approximately six years and seven months too late for it to matter. That left one recourse: executive clemency.

The next morning, Peter called the commonwealth attorney's office in Alexandria and introduced himself to Randy Sengel. The prosecutor knew the technology and its value.

"It's a clean exclusion of Snyder," Peter told him.

"I want my lab to take a look at the work," said Sengel, not unreasonably. "If you're right, you won't get a fight from me."

Dr. Bing had a solid reputation, and the Virginia crime laboratory was not long in agreeing that the Boston tests were reliable. The FBI laboratory also concurred. Still, the prosecutor's office wanted to be make doubly certain. They asked Bing to repeat the tests. On February 18, 1993, a second set of tests came back with identical results. Walter T. Snyder was not the rapist.

A few weeks later, the prosecutor called Peter.

"I'm on board," said Sengel. "Let's go to the governor."

Peter and Barry drafted a four-page letter, explaining why Snyder was innocent, and sent it to Sengel for use as a template in the request to the governor for clemency. In the prosecutor's letter, composed a few days later, Sengel dwelled on the explanation of why Snyder *seemed* guilty—even including the noisome evidence of the "oily" odor that Faye Treatser suddenly had remembered at trial, coinciding with Snyder's work in the fuel-oil company. This was institutional self-protection. But, Sengel wrote on behalf of his boss, the scientific evidence was regarded as reliable by all responsible authorities. That left one conclusion: "In view of all the facts and circumstances now known, reason and justice require that action be taken on Mr. Snyder's behalf." The letter was signed by Sengel's boss, John E. Kloch, the commonwealth's attorney.

In prison, Snyder was, for the first time, receiving regular correspondence from a lawyer about the progress of his case. Peter always took his collect calls. And now, for the first time, Snyder and his family had two lawyers on their side—not only a defense lawyer, but a prosecutor who was far more useful than many of their prior attorneys.

Yet, even with the combined weight of the prosecutor and the defense lawyer, they had one slight problem: There was no way to get Walter out of jail.

Even with the prosecutor agreeing that Snyder was completely cleared of the crime for which he was serving forty-five years, no courthouse in Virginia could entertain a motion for his release. Innocence had nothing to do with it. The commonwealth of Virginia in 1983 gave Walter Snyder just twenty-one days after his conviction to prove his innocence. The best minds in science needed 150 years to come up with DNA tests after the science of genetics had been invented by the Bavarian monk Gregor Mendel.

In theory, Snyder could have gone to federal court and asked for a writ of habeas corpus—a powerful tool that allowed the national court system to reach into the state system and correct injustice. But even that avenue was becoming cloudy. Just as Bing's laboratory was clearing Snyder, the chief justice of the Supreme Court, William Rehnquist, said that the federal courts did not have to entertain claims of innocence. A person convicted in state court could bring a claim to federal court that a trial had been unfair in its procedures but not its results. Nothing in the Constitution said that the federal courts were required to examine proofs of innocence. "A claim of actual innocence is not itself a constitutional claim," wrote Justice Rehnquist. He said prisoners who maintained their innocence should ask the governors of their states for pardons or clemency.

So the Snyder case now rested uneasily in the hands of Gov. L. Douglas Wilder, a Democrat in a conservative state. Snyder's freedom had become a political, not legal, issue. And Wilder's staff was concerned that he not be tarred as a soft-on-crime liberal. By releasing Snyder, the governor would be acting against the adamancy of Faye Treatser, who continued to insist that Snyder had been her attacker.

All this was conveyed to Peter by the governor's public-relations aide. The case was a problem, and it was analyzed in political terms. Peter understood. Politics was the reason Walter Snyder sat in jail as February turned to March, and as the spring flowers cut the winter out of the hills of the Blue Ridge Parkway, and as the yellow ribbons on his parents' front gate faded and tattered. Peter understood that Snyder's innocence was a political liability to the governor, just as he realized that his innocence was a legal corpse that the courts had no interest in reviving.

Peter rang the leading newspaper in Richmond, the capital of Virginia. A few months earlier, a reporter had called to ask about the petition for clemency, and Peter had ducked. Now the lawyer called back. Not only was this hot news—a pardon petition from both the defense *and* the prosecutor— but it was a terrific human-interest story. For seven years, Edith Snyder, a hardworking postal clerk, had doggedly fought to prove her son's innocence. She and her husband had taken second mortgages and second jobs. Now Edith's journey was all but complete. She had concrete, irrefutable evidence of his innocence. Even the prosecutor agreed. How about that! Any day now, Governor Wilder would be signing an order of executive clemency. The Snyder family was tying yellow ribbons around the fence on their lawn. The story got great play. The governor's public-relations man called Peter in a rage.

"What are you doing?" he screamed.

"We think it's a great story," said Peter. "Don't you?"

"The governor could get hurt here," said the aide.

More stories ran in Richmond about the valiant Snyders. On April 23, Governor Wilder signed an executive order freeing Walter Snyder, grumbling that he had been dragged into the fray. The law had to be changed. "It's too much power (for a governor) to say that an innocent person should not go free," Wilder said. But, he acknowledged: "I'm convinced he's not guilty. . . . If (DNA) can be used to convict, it must also be used to protect the innocent."

For Walter's release, Peter flew to Richmond, where he was to be met by Edith Snyder. They had never seen each other, although Peter and the Snyders were in touch daily, sometimes hourly. The airport in Richmond is not a busy one, and they had made no complicated arrangements for the rendezvous. Edith Snyder is a big woman, and Peter is a tall man. She spotted him first, sprinted across the tarmac to him, and lifted him in a bear hug clear off the ground. Then they drove to Nottoway prison to bring Walter home.

On Ashby Street, TV cameras filmed the fresh yellow ribbons, the smiles and hugs on the lawn. Peter gave interviews, and so did Walter and his mother and father. DNA was a great marvel, everyone agreed. The *Washington Post* described the tests as a "get out of jail card."

The other local paper, the *Washington Times,* reported: "Laughing, he said the first thing he wanted was a 'cheese deluxe pizza.' He said he will probably go to work in the family's locksmith business. 'I received a new life. Thank God for DNA,' he said."

To the end, everyone in power insisted that there was good reason Walter Snyder spent seven of the prime years of his life locked in a cell. "In the absence of that DNA, the evidence would have been pretty damning," Gov. L. Douglas Wilder was quoted saying.

Damning evidence? Yes. But not of Walter Snyder.

The case against him was built on evidence that was, by any reasonable standards, compromised, corrupted, and unsafe. Yet his trial was judged fair by the highest court in Virginia. Even after the result was catastrophic failure, the governor, prosecutor, and police all defended the process by which the unjust conviction was obtained. "I can find no fault with the findings that were made by the jury based upon the evidence that was available to it at that time," said Governor Wilder. His comments were echoed by the chief prosecutor, Kloch, and the chief police investigator, Shiftic.

It was as if a building had fallen down and the architect, the engineer, and the contractor held a press conference to proclaim the soundness of their techniques.

In a study of DNA exonerations by the Innocence Project, 84 percent of the wrongful convictions rested, at least in part, on mistaken identification by an eyewitness or victim. Dramatic as these results are, they only confirm a century of social science research and judicial fact-finding. Professor Borchard's 1932 text, *Convicting the Innocent,* studied sixty-five cases of wrongful conviction. Wrote Borchard: "Perhaps the major source of these tragic errors is an identification of the accused by the victim of a crime of violence. This mistake was practically alone responsible for twenty-nine of these [sixty-five] convictions. . . ."

Is the law totally helpless when eyewitnesses make mistakes?

Hardly. Walter Snyder was a toddler in 1967, when the U.S. Supreme Court attacked the problem in three separate rulings known as *Wade, Gilbert,* and *Stovall.* "The vagaries of eyewitness identification are well-known; the annals of criminal law are rife with instances of mistaken identification," wrote Justice William Brennan in *U.S. v. Wade.*

Once a sympathetic witness identifies a suspect, the court noted, investigation ends for nearly all intents and purposes. "The trial which might determine the accused's fate may well not be in the courtroom," Brennan wrote, "but that at the [initial] pretrial confrontation."

Therefore, the Court said, a person arrested and placed in a lineup should have an attorney present. A cartoon once showed a lineup that included a refrigerator, a hen, and a black man with a big Afro haircut. In the foreground, a woman points at the man, saying, "He's the one!"

Finally, in a ruling that might have changed the course of Walter Snyder's life, the Court warned that "show-ups" were dangerously suggestive. A show-up differs vastly from the lineup. In a show-up, a victim or witness is shown one suspect, typically in the back of a patrol car or some other custodial setting, clearly because the police consider him or her to be a likely perpetrator. Walter Snyder had been told to wait, by himself, in the lobby of a police station so that Faye Treatser could look at him. That was a show-up.

Except in rare circumstances, the show-up should not be used, the Court said in *Stovall v. Denno,* because it was, "so unnecessarily suggestive and conducive to irreparable mistaken identification that [it denies the defendant] due process of law." An exception could be made when a witness was gravely ill, the Court said, and the police brought a suspect to the hospital room for identification.

With those decisions, the Court was tapping at the crust of the human mind. It had tried to fashion a drill bit that could reach buried truths about knowledge and how people acquire it, but one that would work delicately, without disturbing or transforming that knowledge.

By the time Walter Snyder went on trial, nearly twenty years later, all those protections had been eroded by a new Supreme Court and through police practice. Instead of staging lineups after an arrest, police use photo arrays 60 to 70 percent of the time, or hold lineups before formally filing charges, so no lawyer is required. Worse for Snyder, the Supreme Court ruled in *Neil v. Biggers* and *Manson v. Brathwaite* that a show-up could be used as evidence if the witness had a good chance to see the criminal and was really certain in the identification.

When the Court dismantled the *Wade, Gilbert,* and *Stovall* rulings, Justice Thurgood Marshall issued an important but unheard warning. As well as anyone, he knew of simmering anger at legal decisions that seemed to make truth subordinate to process. The most obvious target was the exclusionary rule, which often prevented juries from hearing important evidence of guilt due to some error in how the police collected it.

For instance, if the police seized a murder weapon from under a suspect's bed and the victim's pearls from his pillowcase, it was possible the evidence could not be presented at his trial if the officer had not obtained a warrant to search the home. The purpose of the rule may have been to shape police behavior and protect people from government invasions of their privacy, but the obnoxious side benefits to criminals were most prominent and galling.

Yes, said Marshall, the exclusionary rule sometimes wasted reliable and relevant evidence, in the name of punishing disobedient police officers. Not so in eyewitness cases. The sole purpose of the rulings in the *Wade, Gilbert,* and *Stovall* cases was to safeguard evidence, and to protect it from being recast or reshaped to fit the form of a suspect. "Suggestively obtained eyewitness testimony is excluded, in contrast, precisely because of its unreliability and concomitant irrelevance," Marshall wrote dissenting from the majority in *Manson v. Brathwaite.* Locking up the wrong man would mean "the real outlaw must still remain at large."

When the Virginia judges dismissed Walter Snyder's appeal, the court said Snyder was right to complain about the show-up—but not right enough to overturn the case. Quoting Virginia precedents, they said: "We agree that, when the circumstances permit, a lineup is preferable to a show-up. However, our task is to decide if the identification procedure that was utilized violated due process; not whether that procedure was the best that the authorities could have employed."

The testimony of eyewitnesses will, of course, remain a central element of human inquiry, including the investigation of crime. For all the shadows cast on witness reliability by social scientists, the studies also found ways to improve it. The leading researchers, Gary Wells, Elizabeth Loftus, and Stephen Penrod, made these suggestions:

• All lineups, photo spreads, and other identification processes should be videotaped. These are by far the most critical moments in the whole process, and the only people present are the investigator and the witness. Months later, there is no way to reconstruct bias, suggestiveness, or hints.

Faye Treatser and Investigator Shiftic gave divergent accounts of how she came to pick Snyder's photo from the pile, and her reaction. A video recording would settle such questions.

• An independent examiner should run the lineups and photo spreads. The examiner should not know who the suspect is, to avoid dropping hints. Investigator Shiftic personally showed the picture of his one suspect to Faye Treatser.

• The witness should be asked to rate his or her certainty at the time of the identification. Months after Faye Treatser first tentatively thought something was familiar in Walter Snyder's eyebrows, a loop of suspicion and half-truth had solidified into certainty.

• Police and prosecutors should be trained about the risks of providing corroborating details. Faye Treatser obviously learned that Snyder worked at boiler cleaning, and amended her description to say that he reeked of fuel oil.

These reforms do not require new legislation or new dogma from the Supreme Court. They could be undertaken as policy changes by local authorities as a means of improving both crime fighting *and* justice. Many of these are outlined in "Eyewitness Evidence: A Guide for Law Enforcement," a 1999 U.S. Department of Justice study prompted by the explosion of DNA exonerations. To do less, the experts say, would effectively leave the most important work of the justice system out of sight.

"We do not assume that these risks are the result of police procedures intentionally designed to prejudice an accused," wrote Justice Brennan in the Wade case. "Rather we assume they derive from the dangers inherent in eyewitness identification and the suggestibility inherent in the context of the pretrial identification."

On the day he was released, Walter Snyder had little time to justify the tactics of Investigator Shiftic. "Man is so unjust to man," said Snyder. Few heard him. That first bite of pizza led the evening news reports.

———————

The next day, a Saturday, there was a knock at the door of the Snyder home. It was T. J. Fannon, the owner of the oil-burner company.

"You have anything lined up?" he asked Walter.

"Not yet, no," said Walter.

"Come on down Monday morning."

A few weeks later, Walter was cleaning a furnace in Alexandria. He was not much for socializing with the customers, and on his way out the door, he passed the ticket to the homeowner for his signature. Walter checked the name on the slip of paper. He stopped.

"Are you *the* Randolph Sengel?" asked Walter. "The deputy state's attorney?"

"That's me," said Sengel.

"I don't know what to say," Walter said. "My name is Walter Snyder, and I just gotta shake your hand."

4

False Confessions

Even in April, Denver was blustery and cold. Barry had been sent to the Mile-High City by NBC News to provide legal commentary on the trial of Timothy McVeigh, accused of bombing the Alfred P. Murrah Federal Building in Oklahoma City. By 6:00 every morning, a line formed for seats in the courthouse, victims' families and journalists and officials moving slowly through the security checkpoints.

One morning, the man ahead of Barry turned and offered his hand. "Ray Elliott," he said. He was in Denver from Oklahoma to visit his wife, who was working on the case for the feds. The name was well known to Barry: Elliot headed all criminal prosecutions in the office of the Oklahoma City district attorney.

"You're the same Ray Elliott who still wants to try our client Robert Miller for murder?" asked Barry.

"The same one," said Elliott.

On that morning, Robert Miller had been on death row in Oklahoma for nine years. For six of those years, the state had DNA tests proving that he wasn't the killer. Yet he had languished. The whole plot of Miller's life stood between the two men in their pinstripe suits, shuffling toward the metal detectors.

"I just don't understand what's taking so long," said Barry. "The DNA shows who the real murderer is. And it's not Robert Miller."

"All the DNA proves is that there were two killers, not just Robert Miller," said Elliot. "All we know from the DNA is that he was not the donor of the semen. We know from Robert's own statement that he was there. He knew things only the killer would have known."

"You know he made one hundred and thirty-three wrong guesses in that videotape," said Barry.

Elliot smiled.

"His own words put him at the scene of the murder. Don't you worry about it, Barry, we're gonna needle your client."

Needle our client? Barry was bewildered.

"I am sorry," Barry said. "I don't know what you mean."

"You know, lethal injection, the needle," explained Elliott. "We're going to needle Robert."

Just then, the queue for the courthouse forked into two different metal detectors, and Barry lost sight of Elliott.

———

By the time the grandson of Zelma Cutler discovered her body, the Military Park section of Oklahoma City already was reeling with fear for its elderly neighbors. Zelma was ninety-two years old. She was dead in her bed. Apparently, she had been suffocated by the weight of a man who raped her. Four months earlier, in the house catty-corner to Cutler's, the same thing happened to Anna Laura Fowler, age eighty-three. In between the two murders, a man had been seen on the back porch of a third elderly woman, unscrewing a lightbulb and trying to force his way inside. He was chased off before he could do any violence.

Now, Zelma Cutler had been killed. Both dead women were widows who lived alone in corner houses. No property was taken, and there was no sign of ransacking. Knotted rags were found in both bedrooms. Telephone lines were wrenched from the ground in both yards. The circuit boxes at both houses were switched off. In the semen left by the rapist in both victims, blood type A+ was detected. Three "Negroid" hairs were found on the gurney sheets that were wrapped around Mrs. Cutler's body. "My grandmother lived out there," recalled one young woman, Lee Ann Peters. "I was among many citizens wanting the police to get this case solved."

The city put twelve detectives on a task force. They swept the streets of the Military Park neighborhood. "There was mass hysteria," Ray Elliott would recall. "Especially in that neighborhood. A lot of old-timers there. One victim had lived in her house for sixty years. The city police stopped everything that breathed or moved." Some 173 black men were questioned and listed as suspects. Of these, twenty-three gave blood. Among those whose finger pricks showed A+ blood was Robert Miller, a twenty-seven-year-old unemployed heating and air-conditioning repairman. He lived three blocks from the scenes of the murders. On February 23, 1987, detectives visited Miller and asked if he could help. Miller felt unwell. He was a regular user of drugs, and he believed that someone had slipped PCP into something he had ingested. But, he said, he, too, sensed the unease heaving along the streets following the murders. Anything he could do to help, he would. He rode to the police station with the detectives, and they sat him in an interview room, where Det. Jerry Flowers asked him what he had to offer.

"I've got these powers," said Miller. "I can see things through the killer's eyes."

With that, Flowers made a signal. Watching through a mirror, his partner, David Shupe, switched on a hidden video camera.

"I was dreaming about it one night and you know, probably almost the same night it happened," Miller said. "You know I have dreams like that, you know, come to me all the time."

The next twelve hours were a numbing drone of hallucination, interrogation, exorcism, revival, and nonsense. The detectives held a Bible. They prayed. They cast out demons. They coaxed Miller, accused him, walked out on him, begged him to peer deeper into his visions. Miller spoke of enemies who stole his hair from garbage cans, pilfered his clothes, poisoned his days. An ancestor had predicted that he would be a great federal lawman, perhaps another Marshal Dillon, perhaps the Lone Ranger, he told the police. At times, he invoked the memory of his hero, Bruce Lee. He concentrated ferociously when asked to envision the killings, and what the murderer was doing. Like a TV set with a weak antenna, Miller's details were fuzzy, and sometimes he changed channels without warning. The detectives played with his mind-set and even prayed with him to get him back in tune.

At the end, the detectives decided they had their man. With a flourish, the District Attorney of Oklahoma City, Robert Macy, announced that he was moving quickly to file capital murder charges against Miller.

He had committed "incomprehensible crimes," said the district attorney.

"I want to let the public know this man is in custody, and the danger has been removed," said Macy.

Robert Miller never actually admitted the crime, but he didn't have to. In the prosecutor's telling, he had coughed up inside details, fine points that would be known only to the investigating detectives—and the killer. A few months later, District Attorney Macy would tell a jury that Miller put himself into deep trouble with his own words, even if the videotapes were a lengthy display of "mind games" between the detectives and their quarry.

"You may not approve of their techniques, but you've got to remember what was going on," said Macy. "You have two cops sitting in there who knew very early on, before they got too far in there, they knew that they had the killer, these two men sitting across the table from him. And they knew it was their job, if they could, to get incriminating statements out of him that would identify him as that killer. And they did. He may have got tired. They got tired, too. They worked real hard at it, and they got damning—they got evidence that only the killer knew."

What was that evidence?

"He knew what rooms they were in. He knew how the rooms were decorated. He knew precisely how the killer got into the houses. He knew how the killer and why the killer disconnected the telephone lines so they wouldn't, couldn't call out. And he told you exactly what the killer was feeling and thinking. And there's only one person on the face of this earth that knows that, and that's him right there."

Indeed, at trial, the jury heard those very tapes. They ran nearly twelve hours, often indistinct, or when audible, often incoherent. In those days, Robert Miller had been a drug user, and he would later say that he thought someone in his household had doped his food or drink on the day the detectives came for him. The tapes sounded bad, even if Miller denied having anything to do with the crimes, over and over, and insisted he was merely channeling a vision, a power sent him by his deceased Choctaw grandmother.

Then there were a few hairs, described by the state's so-called hair expert as "Negroid" and supposedly consistent with Robert's hair. Then there was the ample residue of semen found at both crime scenes. "He put Mrs. Cutler through a sexual nightmare," Macy declared. "He climaxed more than once." And the blood type showed that his A+ was the same as that found in the rapist's semen.

Still, for drama by the ton weight, nothing beat the twelve hours of tapes. One of the detectives even claimed to have counted up the number of times that Miller slipped and used the term *I*—gutting the defense claim that the killer was a "he," a character who dwelled within Robert's mind only in the third person.

When the defense had its turn, Miller denied having anything to do with the killings, just as he had on the tapes. All the details he discussed with the detectives were simple rumors he had picked up in the neighborhood— he lived only a few blocks from the murdered women—and from news accounts, including a TV broadcast of *Crimestoppers*. His discussions with the detectives were not based on any firsthand knowledge of the crime but on a mystical experience.

"I had visions from the Lord. An angel came to me—I assume it was my grandmother—warning me someone was trying to frame me," Miller swore.

Another defense witness, a neighbor, described Miller as a "peaceful" man who often helped with chores. The murders had been the talk of the neighborhood, she said, and many people knew that the killer had gone in the back door—one of the details that the prosecutor had claimed only the killer would have known.

None of that could match the closing arguments of District Attorney Macy, who silenced the courtroom with supreme stage craft. He paraded along the jury box, holding an elastic band from a pair of men's underpants. As he walked, Macy remembered aloud something Miller told the detectives. They had wanted to know if he could see that the killer had left something behind.

"It might have been underwear or something, he left something in the house," Miller had said on the videotape.

And there was Macy, holding an underwear band in his hand. It was Fruit of the Loom, same brand worn by Miller, and it had been found near the body of Anna Laura Fowler. "As I recall, well, he [said he] may have left a shoe, he may have left a glove, and then he said, no, he may have left his underwear," thundered Macy.

And there was the foul little piece of cloth, the band of the underwear. He approached the jury and displayed it.

After the fierce power of this relic had settled on the jury, Macy continued with other incriminating evidence. It was Miller's blood type in the semen. His type of hair on the bed. His knowledge of secret details about the murder.

"And he sat there and he laid it out without one tear, without one sign of remorse. Did you ever see one sign of remorse? Instead, he was able to tell you the killer felt good, that he didn't like white women. How does he know that he didn't like white women? How does he know—if he's not the killer—that the killer doesn't like white women but he likes to have sex with them?"

As he said this, Robert Miller, a dark-skinned man of African American and Native American lineage, sat at the defense table in front of an all-white jury. What Macy said was not even remotely related to proof that Robert Miller knew about the crime. In fact, no one knew what the killer liked sexually, or disliked socially, so there was no way of knowing whether Miller's statement was true. The prosecutor, however, had managed to end up with a jury of twelve whites, and it was more than likely that among those twelve would be at least one person stirred by some primal fear of black men as sexual predators.

High-octane prosecution was Macy's specialty. He wore string ties and Stetson hats, in the manner of the old western lawman, and it was his frequent boast that he personally had brought more death penalty cases to verdict than any other prosecutor in the country. As of early 1999, that figure was fifty-three. Now and then, he would lose a case on appeal or be slapped on the wrist for some extraordinary excess—withholding exculpatory information, playing fast and loose with the facts, or using rhetoric that perverted justice—but Macy said he never strayed from honest prosecution of people he believed were guilty. In the Miller case, he held back nothing. He told the jurors that they would be shirking their duty if they did not convict Robert Miller.

"We're not burning witches at the stake," said Macy. "We're not seeking out Communists. We're trying to seek justice. We're trying to bring a killer before the bar of justice. And that's why the twelve of you are sitting there, because a man who committed these crimes has got to be brought to justice. He sits right there. Only the twelve of you can do it. You can do it by going up in that jury room and finding him guilty as charged on all seven counts.

"Because if you do anything less than that, it's an assault to the memory of these two little ladies and everybody that cares about them."

In the days running up to the trial, an Oklahoma television station had done a poll on the case, Miller would recall. Before a single word of evidence had been heard, 68 percent of the viewers voted that he was guilty. The jury, having heard his twelve-hour videotape and the forensic evidence, convicted him of two murders, two rapes, two burglaries, and one attempted burglary. After that, a minitrial was held on the suitable penalty. A man came to court who lived in the Military Park section of town and reported that he had surprised a black man who was wearing a bandanna and trying to break in. Months later, when he saw Robert Miller's face in the news, he felt that this was the same man.

The judge sentenced Miller to two death penalties, plus 725 years. "I couldn't do none of it. I needed me a little red wagon to pull all that time out of that courtroom, it was so heavy," said Miller.

On his first night on death row, he listened to the howling and chaos and wondered if he had been born to suffer this hell.

———

Lee Ann Peters scanned the transcript of the Miller trial. Once the young lawyer had fretted for the safety of her grandmother while the Military Park murderer was at large. Now, as an appellate lawyer for the Oklahoma City public defenders office, she was trying to save the life of the very man convicted of being the fiend. Her tools were a sharpened pencil and an even sharper mind. In the trial record, she discovered a peculiar fact.

The state's serologist had provided the names of twenty-three black men whose blood had been tested as part of the investigation. Then the serologist gave the names of all the men whose hair had been microscopically examined. Peters made a list of all the names, checking them off. Suddenly, she stopped.

There had been twenty-three blood tests, and twenty-four hair checks. That meant there was one extra name on the hair list. Someone's hair had been examined but not his blood. Why?

The one extra man was named Ronald Lott, a name unknown to Robert Miller. In a few days, Peters and a retired homicide detective, Bob Thompson, would learn some astonishing details about the crime spree in the Military Park neighborhood. It had not stopped with the arrest of Robert Miller.

After Miller was taken into custody, after he had made the twelve-hour videotape, after District Attorney Macy announced that "the danger has been removed" from the community, identical crimes were continuing.

Two other elderly women who lived in corner houses were attacked by a man who broke in their back doors. Knotted rags were left at the scenes in these cases, too. The electricity and phone lines were disabled—just as they had been in the two murders. Once again, it seemed that the point of the crimes was not robbery but rape, as little property had been taken. These two women, in their seventies and at least a decade younger than the earlier victims, had survived the rapes, not suffering the crushed chests of the two older women. One woman actually pulled a handgun on the attacker and bopped him on the head. He then wrested the gun away from her.

A few days after the second of these rapes, Ronald Lott was stopped on the street and found with that very gun, registered to the victim. His fingerprints were found at the other victim's home.

In August 1987, six months after District Attorney Macy had announced that Robert Miller was the Military Park rapist and killer, secret tests were done on Ronald Lott's blood to see if he could be linked to the crimes. Police reports found by Peters and Thompson showed that the detectives considered Lott a strong suspect not only for the rapes but also in the two murders charged to Miller.

As the lawyer and the investigator dug into the details about Ronald Lott, they learned even more remarkable facts. The same prosecutor assigned to the Miller trial also was handling the Lott case. One Friday afternoon, the prosecutor, Barry Albert, had asked for a recess during a hearing on the Miller case because he had to go across the hall to another courtroom. There, Ronald Lott was pleading guilty to the two rapes that bore such similarity to the Miller case.

And that very day, Prosecutor Albert would say later, he realized that Lott could be a suspect in the crimes that Miller had been charged with.

"This is déjà vu," Albert said he told the judge and bailiff in the Lott case. "This is exculpatory information [for Miller]."

Did he walk across the hall and share this information with the lawyer defending Robert Miller? Albert claims he did. Never happened, insisted Miller's lawyer, Ron Evans.

In any event, Prosecutor Albert withdrew from the Miller case, turning it over to Ray Elliott and Robert Macy. And no mention was made by the defense during the Miller trial of Ronald Lott or his involvement in these amazingly similar crimes. The jurors never heard that Lott had admitted to doing identical crimes in the same neighborhood. They never learned that Ronald Lott had a record of felonies in Kansas, unlike Miller, whose biggest crime was not paying parking tickets. The jurors never knew that he had the same blood type as the rapist and Miller.

Instead, they had heard Ray Elliott argue passionately: "We have a semen donor of an 'A' blood type secretor status. [Miller is] 'A' blood type secretor status."

Many years later, Elliott would say that he knew the admitted rapist Lott also had the blood type of the man involved in killing the old ladies, but believed that more sophisticated tests had ruled out Lott. The prosecution and Miller's appellate lawyers argued for years about whether the defense also knew of Lott and had been deprived of a chance to name him as a better suspect during the trial. Certainly, the prosecution gave no hint at trial that anyone other than Robert Miller could be responsible.

Robert Macy told that the jurors they would have little to ponder if they merely reviewed all the physical evidence suggesting that the killer was black, wore a baseball cap, stood about the same height, had A+ blood, etc.

"There can be only one man, only one person that fits all of this criteria, and he's sitting right there," said Macy, pointing at Miller. "He fits every one of them, and he's the only man in the state of Oklahoma, or maybe in more, that would fit all those criteria."

In short order, Lee Ann Peters would prove otherwise. She sought DNA testing of the evidence. Not surprisingly, the first results, based on the RFLP technique, were inconclusive. So much time had passed that the semen samples had started to degrade. Then PCR tests were done, and they clearly excluded Robert Miller. He had not been the rapist of either dead woman.

"We'd be waiting outside a judge's chambers, and Ray Elliott would say: 'It's a damn shame they didn't kill him before this DNA testing.' I would get sick to my stomach," Peters recalled. "I had past experience with Ray Elliott that made me think he was a person of integrity."

She was not the only person to report a conversation of that nature with Prosecutor Elliott about Robert Miller; Barry and Garvin Isaacs, another attorney who took up Miller's cause, also said Elliot wished for his execution on separate occasions in their hearing. Elliott would say in 1999 that he did not recall ever making such remarks.

Before one hearing, Lee Ann Peters learned that the murders still bothered other courthouse employees.

"A bailiff mentioned that because one of the victim's grandsons was in prison, he always thought someone down in prison would kill him," Peters recalled. "By that time, though, every one on death row knew Robert was innocent."

Not only had the DNA cleared Miller, but it pointed directly at Ronald Lott. The first argument made by Peters—that Robert Miller had been denied a fair trial because his attorney didn't bring up Ronald Lott as an alternative suspect—now took on even greater weight. But the district attorney had a strong-sounding rebuttal. So Lott raped and killed the women. All that meant was that there had been two rapists at the scene. After all, Robert Miller himself had confessed. It was there on the videotape.

Actual innocence

In 1660, an Englishman named William Harrison suddenly disappeared. Given that it was the seventeenth century, nobody could phone around to his haunts. So a servant, John Perry, was sent to find him. The constables became suspicious when Perry did not return to his own home that evening. Perry was questioned for days, then finally confessed. He had done away with the boss. His mother and brother had helped. All three were hanged, even before the body of William Harrison was found.

The master's body was never found, and for very good reason. Perry had not killed Harrison, and Harrison was not dead. He turned up two years later, claiming to have been kidnapped and sold into slavery in Turkey. This was a little bit late for the Perry clan, all of whom had swung based on John Perry's confession.

The vanishing corpse is a recurring theme in Edwin Borchard's *Convicting the Innocent*. All through the eighteenth and nineteenth centuries in America, Professor Borchard reported, people would go missing. Others would be blamed, often forced to confess, and then brought to some terrible end—only to have the corpse reappear, "hale and hearty."

In 1883, a tough, charming, and brutal man named Thomas F. Byrnes persuaded the legislature of the state of New York to give him command of all detectives in New York City. Until then, the city detectives had operated independently from precincts, where their primary function had been the collection of payoffs from the underworld. Byrnes's chief credential for the job was his investigative successes, most notably, solving a spectacular, $3-million robbery from the Manhattan Bank. Byrnes excelled where others failed in the extraction of confessions. His techniques involved beatings, questionings, then more beatings until the suspect gave the desired admissions. The process of coercive interrogation became known as the "third degree," a play on Byrnes's name. When a reformer named Theodore Roosevelt took control of the board overseeing the police department, Byrnes retired—not because of his brutality but because of the exposure of a $350,000 portfolio Byrnes had accumulated somewhat mysteriously.

The third degree survived Byrnes until the 1930s, when a combination of factors led to its end. Borchard's book was published in 1932, documenting the conviction of the innocent, often based on confessions that were extracted through threats, torture, and beatings, using blackjacks, billy clubs, rubber hoses, phone books, and fists. Other reformers also were shining lights on the practice. "The so-called roughneck," Emanuel Lavine wrote in a 1930 exposé, "is hit with everything but the foundation of the building." The Wickersham Commission, headed by a former U.S. attorney general, reported that use of the third degree was rampant throughout the United States. "Suspects were hung out windows, drugged, deprived of food and sleep and questioned for days. Or stuck in the 'sweatbox'—a tiny dark room transformed into a little hell by a scorching stove stoked with a noxious combination of coal, old bones, rubber and garbage," wrote Peter Carlson in the *Washington Post*. "Or given the 'water cure,' which consisted of dunking the suspect's head in a toilet until he nearly drowned."

Upon hearing that three black men were tied to a tree in Mississippi and whipped until they confessed, the U.S. Supreme Court in the 1936 decision *Brown v. Mississippi*, outlawed the use of physical force during interrogations. Into the vacuum stepped a new wave of interrogation theorists, most prominently, Fred Inbau, a professor of law at Northwestern University, and John Reid, a former Chicago police officer. Coauthors of the seminal police training text, *Criminal Interrogation and Confession*, they were among the most influential proponents of psychological interrogation techniques used across the country, and seen every week on such American police dramas as *NYPD Blue*, *Law and Order*, and *Homicide: Life on the Street*. On nearly every episode, the detectives win confidence, play good cop–bad cop, tell lies, and use a high-risk technique called "maximization-minimization."

A suspect is told that he is being fitted for a first-degree murder charge, but the detective thinks there might be a better explanation for his actions. Perhaps the killing was an accident or was done in self-defense. This often leads guilty suspects to confess. And under circumstances of high pressure, with vulnerable people, the "maximization-minimization" technique also provides a strong incentive for innocent people to make false admissions.

The psychological pressures of the Inbau-Reid techniques were cited by the Supreme Court in the 1966 case, *Miranda v. Arizona*. The court created the famous formula of rights, to be read to suspects at the start of questioning: "You have the right to remain silent. Anything you say can and will be used against you in a court of law. You have the right to an attorney. If you cannot afford an attorney, one will be appointed for you without charge."

Contrary to the loud worries that this provision would cripple law enforcement, most people do talk to the police. Upward of 80 percent of suspects waive their Miranda rights, studies have found. And of those who do talk, about three in four make some sort of incriminating statement. Such statements will have tremendous weight with jurors, social scientists have found. But how reliable are confessions?

• In Phoenix, Arizona, a mental patient called police and admitted to a mass murder at a remote desert temple. He implicated Leo Bruce and two other acquaintances from a barrio in Tucson. Bruce, a factory worker, was arrested at his mailbox in Tucson. His only previous involvement with the law was a speeding ticket, and he thought that was why the police had come to see him. He denied the crime, but after thirteen hours of interrogation, he broke down and admitted shooting six of the victims in the back of the head with his own .22 rifle. Ballistics proved this to be untrue. All three suspects broke down under interrogation. All were later shown to be innocent when two teenagers were arrested with the actual murder weapon.

• Gary Gauger was an ex-hippie and recovering alcoholic who lived on an Illinois organic farm with his mother and father. In April 1993, his parents were murdered, their throats cut. During twenty-one hours of questioning, Gauger was told that he had failed a polygraph test about the murders and was shown photographs of his parents' bloody corpses. Then he described a scenario for the murders which investigators viewed as incriminating. The confession was not recorded, nor was any statement signed by Gauger. The police searched the farm for eighteen days and found no physical evidence linking Gauger to the crime. He had not failed the polygraph test; the examiner said the results were inconclusive. At the trial, Gauger said he had not confessed to the slayings but merely had suggested a hypothetical scenario in which he blacked out during the murders as an explanation for failing the polygraph. Convicted in three hours, he ended up on death row in

Cell No. 1 of the maximum security unit in the Stateville prison. The previous occupant had been John Wayne Gacy, the pedophilic serial killer. An innocent man was the next person to close his eyes on that fiend's old bunk.

Gauger's case was taken up by Larry Marshall, who argued that the "confession" had been illegally obtained. The appellate court agreed, and Gauger was freed. Later on, an FBI wiretap picked up conversations among motorcycle gang members who said that they had killed the couple as part of a bungled burglary. A federal racketeering indictment charged two members of the gang with killing the Gaugers.

• In New York City, Glenville Smith of Queens volunteered to police in January 1998 that he had murdered his landlady's teenage daughter. He led detectives to thirteen places where he expected the body to be. Then the girl showed up—alive.

• In Goshen, Indiana, the sixteen-year-old daughter of Edgar Garrett was slain one Sunday morning in 1995. Accused by detectives of murdering the girl, Garrett denied any involvement—only to be told that eyewitnesses, blood evidence, and a polygraph all marked him as the murderer. That was a ruse. After hours of denial, Garrett was persuaded by the police that he had killed her and was suffering from blackouts, possibly due to alcohol. Garrett confessed—but using terms and descriptions so untrue to the original case that a jury acquitted him.

• In Chicago, after eleven-year-old Ryan Harris was raped and killed, a police dragnet snared two young boys, seven and eight years old. They were questioned about Harris's death without their parents nearby. After some hours, both admitted to killing her. When they left the police, they immediately denied it. Later, forensic tests found semen in the girl's body, showing that the dead girl had been raped. Since it is highly unlikely that boys of ages seven and eight would be capable of ejaculation, all charges were dropped. Later, DNA tests proved that they could not have been the source of the semen even if they had been able to produce it.

• Johnny Lee Wilson, a timid twenty-year-old janitor with mild mental retardation, was accused of robbing and killing a seventy-nine-year-old woman in Aurora, Missouri. He was fingered by a special-education classmate who claimed to have heard Wilson make incriminating remarks. (Years later, the classmate said he had made up the story in hopes of getting a cash reward but was afraid he would get in trouble if he admitted that.) For hours, Wilson denied any involvement, insisting he had been shopping with his mother at the time in a mall. After questioning that stretched over two days, most of it accusatory, Wilson conceded that he must have been involved in some way. Even though many of the details he provided to the detectives were wrong, and he often contradicted himself, some of his account was consistent with the crime scene. In fact, tapes showed that he had learned most of them from the detectives. He was sentenced to a minimum of fifty years in April 1987. A year later, another man, in prison for robbing and beating an elderly woman, voluntarily admitted that he had killed the victim. Wilson was pardoned by the governor of Missouri in 1995, some eight years and five months after his conviction.

How often false confessions are made and result in convictions is a question that social scientists have not been able to answer with much confidence. Nationally, estimates range from a low of 35 up to 840 annually. Among DNA exonerations studied by the Innocence Project, 23 percent of the convictions were based on false confessions or admissions. Most jurors can't swallow the idea that people would admit to crimes they had not committed. Confessions retain a unique power in courtrooms: 73 percent of juries will vote to convict even when admissions have been repudiated by the defendant and contradicted by physical evidence, studies show. Almost none of these defendants come to modern courtrooms with physical scars from interrogation-room beatings. The third degree of Inspector Byrnes and his prodigy has been replaced by psychological techniques too subtle to leave visible marks.

"The difference between the third degree and psychological interrogation is akin to the difference between getting mugged and getting scammed," wrote Peter Carlson in the *Washington Post*.

Faced with DNA tests that showed Robert Miller had not raped Zelma Cutler or Anna Fowler, the Oklahoma City district attorney's office at first disputed their validity. More tests in 1993 came back with the same results: indisputable proof that Miller had not raped the two dead women. "I thought he would be home by Christmas," said Lee Ann Peters, who had left the Legal Aid agency that represented Miller but continued to follow the case. Not a chance.

The Oklahoma County district attorney's office clung to the Miller conviction. "The bulk of the evidence presented against Mr. Miller was Mr. Miller's own videotaped statement to police detectives," Assistant D.A. Ray Elliott wrote to a member of the public who protested the continuing incarceration of Miller. "The DNA tests have proven only one thing, that is, that Robert Lee Miller Jr. was not the donor of the semen left at the crime scene. The DNA tests do not prove that Mr. Miller was not present during the commission of these crimes. The DNA tests do not prove that Mr. Miller did not commit murder.

"Furthermore, the DNA tests do not erase the statements given by Mr. Miller himself concerning these crimes."

Indeed, the DNA did not erase the videotapes. And for the first time, people took a very close look at what Miller had said.

Elliott argued in public and in the press that Miller told the detectives things about each of the murders that were so knowing, he had to have been part of the murders. During the questioning, Miller was brought to the scenes of the crimes, which included the two murders and a third case, an attempted break-in on Thanksgiving Day, 1986, that was thwarted when the police arrived and the burglar fled. At the scene of the break-in, Elliott said, Miller showed the detectives the escape path. "He was like a bird dog on point," said Elliott.

Yet on the transcribed tape, Miller seems to know little about the flight of the burglar until he is prompted by the detectives. Asked about the events of that Thanksgiving in 1986, Miller says he ate turkey dinner with his sister. The detective, Jerry Flowers, lays out the basics.

FLOWERS: Think . . . Go into your vision, I wanna see this, I wanna hear it, this is real important, by that church Thanksgiving morning, it's a full moon, something happened up there around one of those churches, or up around that church.

MILLER: That must have been when this stuff happened.

FLOWERS: What happened?

MILLER: Something happened up that way . . .

FLOWERS: Did this demon, did this demon, working through this body, this person, try to do something that day or that night?

MILLER: Maybe.

FLOWERS: What?

MILLER: Did something, I can't, I can't recollect. They did something.

FLOWERS: What?

MILLER: 'Cause that was when I left my sister's house . . . Naw, I was with my parents, my brother came for Thanksgiving from the penitentiary, and we had dinner with him.

FLOWERS: Okay. Now let me ask you this. . . . Is that the day that this demon-possessed person nearly got caught, that morning, early that morning?

MILLER: I think so.

FLOWERS: How did he nearly get caught? Look through your eyes and see. . . .

MILLER: I think the police was chasing him, somebody was chasing him.

In this exchange, Miller says nothing about an escape until Flowers tells him about it. A few minutes later, they return to this attempted break-in.

FLOWERS: You're there, you're there right now, you're there at the back door, looking through the eyes of the person kicking on the back door, trying to get in, you see that? You're there, you see the police, you hear the police coming up here, you're scared, you want to run away.

MILLER: It's not me.

Some 130 times during the tape, when detectives switch from the third person to the second, from "he" to "you," Miller cuts off the conversation and denies that he is present.

Then there was the matter of the underwear. No one could forget the dramatic presentation by District Attorney Macy of the underwear band dropped at one of the murders. Fruit of the Loom, the same as that worn by Miller.

That Robert Miller had a "vision" of underwear left at the scene was not surprising at all: early in the interrogation, he was asked repeatedly what the killer had left at the scene. Miller guessed about articles of clothing, tools, until he at last hit on the underwear. Then the detectives locked in on that detail.

FLOWERS: When the man got through doing what he was doing to the woman, think really hard 'cause this is really important. Did he leave anything with her?

MILLER: He might have.

FLOWERS: What would he have left, look into your dreams and tell me what he would have left. Did he leave any articles?

MILLER: Yeah, something.

FLOWERS: What did he leave.

MILLER: 'Cause he was in a hurry.

Five questions. Miller is on a verbal wander. The help of a Higher Power was summoned.

FLOWERS: Jesus, help this man to recall. . . . What would he have left there with that woman?

WOODS: Help this man remember, Jesus.

MILLER: He left something.

Maybe he ran out and left something behind, not knowing it. Maybe he did it on purpose. Maybe . . .

FLOWERS: Was it some type of article or what kind of article was it, a rock, was it some type of object, was it a clothing item?

MILLER: Maybe.

FLOWERS: Maybe what?

MILLER: 'Cause I have some clothes missing, too, at 29th Street.

What kind of stuff, Flowers wanted to know. Pants, said Miller. Tools. Coats. Slacks. Shirts. Many things. He would have to go through it all.

FLOWERS: What did—look at me, Robert. Let's go back in your dream. Let's go back in your dream. What did this person leave inside that house, that maybe it was stolen from you . . . ? What was left in the house?

MILLER: Might have been something of my hair. I don't know.

Frustrated, the detectives returned to the subject of clothing. Close your eyes. What kinds of clothes would he have left?

MILLER: Maybe a shoe or something. I don't know. I'll have to check my shoes again.

That wasn't the right answer. Look in the dream and see what the killer was holding in his hand. Or did he forget something?

MILLER: He might have left that knife or he left something out of his pocket.

That wasn't it, either. The detectives pressed on. What would he have left to set you up, Robert. Miller suggested hair.

FLOWERS: Look at this person's body, what's this person missing off of his body. Does he have his shirt on, what is he missing?

MILLER: It might have been the shirt.

FLOWERS: What is he missing, look at the person.

MILLER: She tore something off of him. . . . She tore some of the clothes. Probably the knife.

FLOWERS: Does he have shoes on?

MILLER: I don't . . . He might have left one.

FLOWERS: Does he have pants on?

MILLER: Uh-huh.

FLOWERS: Look at this person, he's fixing to leave, but he realizes he's leaving something, what is it he's leaving?

MILLER: It might have been underwear or something, he left something in the house.

FLOWERS: Did he intentionally leave it in the house?

MILLER: Un-huh.

FLOWERS: Accidentally?

MILLER: Uh-huh. Didn't know he left it. He left it, but he didn't know he left it.

WOODS: What is it. Look at your dream. What is it?

MILLER: When he raped her, he took his clothes off, he might have left his underwear or something, but he left something I know, he didn't know he left it, though, but he left it.

FLOWERS: He left what?

MILLER: He, uh, when he took his pants off and raped her, I don't know.

What, what, what, they demanded.

MILLER: He might have left his hat, ski mask, or something he left because . . . He forgot to put something back on because he was in a hurry.

FLOWERS: What would it be?

MILLER: I don't know.

A moment later, he suggests it was gloves. By that point, Miller had suggested virtually every stitch or tools that a rapist might have carried.

Many hours later, they return to the underwear. This time, the police deal with it as an established part of Miller's memory.

FLOWERS: You know, you told me a while ago that uh, this guy that's in this vision that you see, even left some clothing articles, either he brought them or forgot to, forgot to, take them.

MILLER: Maybe.

FLOWERS: And you told me that, ah, you this uh, was his underpants, his shorts, that he left at one of them, which one did he leave that at, the first one or the second one?

MILLER: I was trying to tell you then, did you write it down?

FLOWERS: Yea, we was trying, we was doing it but you never really elaborated on it that much. Did he leave that at the first one or the second one?

MILLER: I don't know for sure right now.

FLOWERS: What kind, what kind of underwear was it?

MILLER: I don't know. I don't know exactly.

FLOWERS: Are you hungry?

MILLER: Yes.

They discuss getting hamburgers.

FLOWERS: What kind of underwear do you have on?

MILLER: I think they're Fruit of the Loom.

FLOWERS: Let's see.

They inspect his underwear, see that it is Fruit of the Loom, and that it is size 30–32.

———

In the last hours of the interrogation, they return again to the topic of the underwear.

FLOWERS: What does he do now?

MILLER: Leaves the room.

FLOWERS: Did he put his clothes on?

MILLER: Some of them.

FLOWERS: What did he not put on?

MILLER: I don't know. . . .

FLOWERS: Did he forget to put something on?

MILLER: I think so. . . .

FLOWERS: What? You're there, you can see him, Rob, now tell me, he wants you to tell me.

MILLER: He left something.

FLOWERS: He's wanting you to tell me, Rob. . . . This is it, he's wanting you to tell me. . . . What does he leave in that room?

MILLER: (shakes head no, trying to clear head)

FLOWERS: Look real close. . . . Where does he leave this item in the room, where is it?

MILLER: He forgot something, either his underwear or a glove. . . .

Another powerful detail cited by the prosecution was Miller's supposed knowledge of the method of entry into the women's homes. "He picks the glass out of the frame and stacks it in a sack next to the trash—in the trash next to the door," Assistant D.A. Ray Elliott told the jury.

"Now who knew that trash—that glass—had been stacked in the trash? The police detectives that were there. Who else? The defendant."

In fact, Robert Miller didn't quite describe the glass going into a sack. But he did describe the killer removing the glass with some care. With the cheerleading Detective Flowers pushing for more and more details from Miller's "vision" of the killing, he describes the burglar's entrance to the Cutler residence.

FLOWERS: What's he doing, what's he doing?

MILLER: Trying to get in the back door . . .

FLOWERS: He's cut the lights off, what's he doing to that back door . . . ?

MILLER: Broke the glass . . .

FLOWERS: He broke the glass, how did he break the glass?

MILLER: Some kind of object.

FLOWERS: What's he using?

MILLER: (no answer)

FLOWERS: What's he using on that back door?

MILLER: Tools.

FLOWERS: Has he broke the glass? Where's the glass, what's he doing with that glass, where is it . . . ? Where is the glass?

MILLER: Takes it out.

FLOWERS: What's he doing with it, he's taking it out what . . . ?

MILLER: Out the frame . . .

FLOWERS: He's taking the glass out of the frame, what's he doing with it . . . ?

MILLER: Put it somewhere . . .

FLOWERS: Where's he putting that glass . . . ? Look at him, Robert, you seen him. . . . What's he doing with that glass?

MILLER: I don't know. (inaudible)

FLOWERS: Look, Robert, he's taking it out of the frame, what's he doing with that glass?

MILLER: Puts it somewhere.

FLOWERS: Where's he putting it, Robert, what's he doing with it . . . ? You see him, don't you?

MILLER: He lays it on a back porch somewhere. . . .

FLOWERS: He's laying that glass on the back porch. . . .

MILLER: Somewhere.

FLOWERS: What's he doing with that glass . . . ?

MILLER: He takes it out. . . .

FLOWERS: Is he just throwing it down, what's he doing with it?

MILLER: He's removing it.

FLOWERS: He's removing it from the frame. . . .

MILLER: Uh-huh.

FLOWERS: Now what's he doing . . . ? You see him, what's he doing?

MILLER: He puts the glass somewhere. . . .

FLOWERS: Puts the glass on somewhere.

MILLER: On that back porch . . .

FLOWERS: How's he put it down, what's he doing to it?

MILLER: He's trying to be quiet. . . .

FLOWERS: He's trying to be quiet, now then the glass is broke, he's removed the glass from the frame, what's he doing . . . ? You see him. . . . Look through his eyes.

MILLER: He sticks his arm through.

FLOWERS: He sticks his arm through the door. . . . What's he doing?

MILLER: Trying to unlock the door.

As Ray Elliott said, the DNA did not erase the videotape. Indeed, the videotape saved his life.

———

The so-called insider revelations of Miller's "confession" are, in fact, buried under piles of mistaken information. For every flimsy statement that could be tied to the crime, there are dozens of details that Miller was just wrong about. He said that the killer stole jewelry, a TV, a radio. Nothing was stolen from any of the homes. He said the murderer stabbed one victim numerous times until she was covered with blood. That did not happen. He described one victim as being middle-aged—a few years older than he was himself. At the time, Miller was twenty-seven. The victim was eighty-three. He said the killer had left his knife on the floor of one house, had left a shoe behind, had torn all the victim's clothes off. All untrue. He said the victims were strangled with lamp cords. There was no sign of ligature.

Experts say an accurate, objective record of interrogations is an indispersable protection that ought to be adopted everywhere.

"He has done so many of these crime scenes, he gets confused," Ray Elliott would say in 1999, by way of explanation. "At a minimum, he was the lookout for Ronald Lott."

———

By the time Lee Ann Peters left the agency that was defending Robert Miller, she had filed a potent appeal arguing that the defense either should have been told about or acted upon the suspicions relating to Ronald Lott. She also had arranged DNA tests that cleared Miller of the rape and implicated Lott. The case then languished as the prosecutors disputed the validity of the results and new tests were arranged. In 1994, his new public defenders encouraged Miller to accept a deal with prosecutors that offered him life without parole. He declined. He remained on death row from 1988 to 1995, when the district attorney agreed that he should have a new trial. Simultaneously, his new appellate lawyers dropped the claim that Miller was denied information about Lott. The shift greatly troubled Peters and Miller, but they had been waiting seven years—from the first test results exonerating Robert—for the prosecutors to give any ground.

Miller was moved from the state penitentiary to the county jail in Oklahoma City. A young nurse, Kim Ogg, had taken a room in an apartment with Robert's brother. One weekend, she accompanied the brother on a visit to Robert in jail.

"I need help," he said.

Kim wrote to the Innocence Project, explaining that exculpatory DNA evidence had been found in 1991, but Miller remained in jail, five years later. With Miller already having both favorable DNA results and local defense attorneys, there seemed to be little need for intervention by lawyers in New York.

By 1997, a judge held a hearing to decide if there was any basis to keep Miller for a trial. The state had thrown out all its forensic testimony, conceding that the DNA showed that Miller was not the source of the sperm. A jailhouse snitch who testified at the trial had recanted, then disappeared. And only Miller's interrogation remained.

"There is nothing in these statements by defendant which would in any way be considered a confession," ruled district court judge Larry Jones. He then talked about a lower standard for an "admission," in which a suspect reveals some guilty knowledge of a crime, as opposed to a full-fledged confession.

"In my view," said Judge Jones, "the statements made by the defendants in the taped interviews taken as a whole, or even divided into parts, do not constitute an 'admission' either. Mr. Miller's statements come to the detectives as visions and dreams—even images he receives from deceased grandparents and so forth.

"Virtually every item of information is hedged with 'maybe' this happened, 'probably' this occurred. Admittedly, after some prompting, he becomes more definite in certain answers. I get the impression, however, taking the statements as a whole, that Mr. Miller was attempting to tell the detectives what he believed they wanted to hear. And it is evident from the video that the detectives are directing many of his responses.

"To the extent defendant's statements are consistent with known facts, the consistencies are not such as to compel even probable cause to believe he committed these crimes."

The district attorney's office immediately appealed to a Judge Karl Gray, higher ranking and far more sympathetic to the prosecution than Larry Jones. Even Judge Gray granted that the confession wasn't worth much—but said some of his accurate statements "might be deemed to be admissions or at least evidence which could be considered in making a probable cause determination."

Miller could be held for a trial.

Kim walked out of the courtroom, weak at the knees. There was no chance. She found a pay phone and dialed Barry's number at the Cardozo School of Law.

"We are just desperate for help," she began. "Robert was exonerated six years ago. He is still in jail. They want to try him again."

She ran through the facts again. Barry had one name for her.

"Garvin Isaacs," said Barry.

Barry had met Isaacs twenty years earlier and regarded him as a heroic figure, willing to take on cases and causes that other attorneys shunned. Barry called and asked him to speak with Kim about Robert Miller.

Isaacs told Kim that he would have nothing to do with the case until he met with Robert himself. He took himself up the street to the county jail and went in to meet with Miller.

"Never been down there on death row myself," said Isaacs. "What's it like?"

Miller told him. There was the cell mate, a notorious murderer and pedophile. Another man, a pure lunatic, who had sat next to Robert watching *The Flintstones*, suddenly got up and bashed Robert on the head. In time, though, people recognized that he didn't belong in the fraternity of the damned. So the other inmates didn't mess with him. The company wasn't even the worst of it.

"You know, I'm a country boy," Miller told Isaacs. "Grew up outdoors, huntin' and fishin'. Played basketball outside with relatives and friends. I played basketball, here, too. It's not the same.

"Never saw the sun go up or down, never walked under the moon at night, the whole time I was in here. Never heard a bird singing, or saw a squirrel running in my path. Never felt the wind on my back or the rain in my face. I never went swimming here, got my feet wet, walked up in the mud and felt the mud between my toes."

Bingo, thought Isaacs. That's my closing argument.

"We'll do it," he said to Miller.

As he walked back to his office, he was astonished to hear Miller's words playing again in his head. Isaacs had grown hard with the work; thought the politics of his courthouses were incestuous and rotten; took a cold, clinical view of his clients; and now, tears were running down his face. The mud between his toes.

Kim was waiting in the office.

"How did it go?" she asked.

"There's the matter of my retainer," said Isaacs.

"Of course," said Kim, bracing for a fierce number that would indebt her for life. "How much?"

"One dollar," said Isaacs.

Solemnly, she handed him the dollar. Then they both laughed as she signed the retainer agreement.

The law firm of Garvin Isaacs all but shut down. Bob Thompson, the former cop and investigator who had dug up so much with Lee Ann Peters, moved over full-time to Isaacs's shop. Another investigator from the public defender's office was on loan part-time to the Miller team. They went to the crime scene, re-created the trial, played the videotapes over and over again until they had a perfected transcript.

Isaacs called experts in the psychology of confessions and communications to analyze the statements. Richard Ofshe, one of the top people in the field, said he couldn't even call Miller's statement a false confession because it contained so little original information about the crime.

Miller took a polygraph test. The questions were:

Did you murder Anna Fowler?

Did you murder Zelma Cutler?

Did you participate in the murder of either of these women?

He answered no to all three and, in the opinion of the polygraph operator, was telling the truth.

Isaacs filed motion after motion. One afternoon in December 1997, sitting in the courtroom for a hearing, he was approached by Ray Elliott. There were a few spectators from the ACLU on Isaacs's side of the room, Bob Thompson, and Joan Bell from his office.

"We're going to give Robert Miller the needle in this deal," said Elliott. "He's just blowfish."

Isaacs lost his temper, volunteered that he would kick Elliott's ass outside the courtroom. Eventually, the two were separated. A few weeks later, the district attorney's office dropped all charges against Miller. The case had been disintegrating in public. But there was another, secret element in the district attorney's decision.

Ray Elliott had been negotiating with the attorney for Ronald Lott, who already was doing forty years for the two rapes of the two old women who did not die. Lott was likely to face the death penalty based on his semen being found at both murders.

Lott was presented with the following offer. If he could implicate Robert Miller in the crimes—as a lookout or participant—Lott would not have to face any additional time. The prosecutors would agree that any sentence for the two murders could run concurrently. It was a tremendous deal, basically, a chance to be given a free pass for two murders that would ordinarily send him off for a lethal injection.

"I offered him a straight life sentence, which meant he would have been out in thirty or forty years, and saved his life—if he would finger Miller," said Elliott. "He sat right there in my office and shook his head. Just shook his head."

Elliott, who insists he never told Isaacs or Barry that he wished he could give Miller "the needle," held to his belief that Miller had guilty

Actual innocence

knowledge of the crime. Lott's refusal to take a plea deal did raise strong questions in the prosecutor's mind.

"It's clearly a good argument that if Miller really were involved, to save his own life (Lott) would take the plea. It's a damn good argument," said Elliott. "I gave him that out. I gave him that option."

With Lott's rejection of the deal, Elliott decided that Miller should not be tried again.

Miller was released on Thursday, January 22, 1998. A few months later, Ray Elliott was elected a judge in Oklahoma County. His boss, Robert Macy, still brags about holding the record for most death penalty cases tried to verdict.

5

White Coat Fraud

The dollar amount scorched front pages across West Virginia and popped, syllable by syllable, from the mouths of TV news anchors. *One million dollars.* Just about every important politician in the Mountain State was lining up to utter the number in tones of outrage, shock, confusion. Some of them even meant it.

The state was set to dole out a million bucks to a gravedigger from Charleston, Glen Dale Woodall, who had spent four or five years in jail for crimes he didn't commit. Mind you, nobody was saying that Woodall didn't have something coming. What galled folks was the size of that something, and even worse, the sneaky way the deal was cut. After all, the man's lawyer hadn't even started the suit, just talked about filing papers, and the state's insurance board hurled its maximum discretionary cash settlement at him, all very hush-hush. Why so much? Why so fast? What was the big secret?

Of course, everyone knew the case was going to be embarrassing, but it was nothing people hadn't seen before. Two women were grabbed at the back of the Huntington Mall, driven away, and sexually assaulted. It turned out that the victims had been hypnotized to enhance their memory, a practice forbidden in many courtrooms. That wasn't such a hot idea. Neither were all those margaritas that the mall security staff poured into one of the victims on the day Woodall was arrested, supposedly a celebration, but one that ended with her signing a form, after she was good and sloshed, that absolved the mall of any responsibility for the attack.

Still, all that was just run-of-the-mill sloppy practice. The man did get out of jail, after all. Someone calculated that the million-dollar payoff to Woodall was 28.5 times more than the highest previous settlement of a wrongful imprisonment claim. Not only that, it was done at the speed of light, at least as measured by litigation standards: just three months had gone by between Woodall's final exoneration and the pact.

"That's about the fastest settlement I've ever seen," said Chuck Chambers, the speaker of the West Virginia House of Representatives.

"I don't disagree that the state has some obligation to him. But to make him a millionaire is unreasonable."

"The legislature must stop this settlement," the *Charleston Daily Mail* declared in an editorial. "Two wrongs don't make a right."

And the *Charleston Gazette* wondered if there was a dark secret hidden behind the fast, big payout: "What necessitated the huge payment? We can't imagine, unless state troopers or prosecutors committed serious misconduct. . . ."

As things developed, no one could even guess how serious matters were behind the false imprisonment of Glen Dale Woodall. Not even Woodall. He had been paid so fast that he could catch only glimpses of the vast scale of corruption that had sent him and dozens of others to prison. Backstage, unknown to Woodall and the public, the state had uncovered a massive fraud in his prosecution. Just how bad was spelled out by a lawyer who had been hired by the state to forecast how things might go if Woodall were to get a full-blown trial.

If a civil jury—and the public—found out what really happened in the Woodall case, the lawyer concluded, things would go very, very badly indeed.

"You have asked me to investigate the allegations to determine the potential exposure of the West Virginia State Police," wrote the lawyer, Steven McGowan, on July 29, 1992.

"Based upon that investigation, I have recommended that the case be settled as quickly and quietly as possible, as the potential exposure is catastrophic."

Rarely do people commit to writing, in such stark terms, the need to cover up wrongdoing. McGowan pulled no punches. At issue was the work of a state trooper, Fred Salem Zain, who was in charge of serology for the state's crime laboratory. Practically the entire case against Woodall was based on "scientific" evidence provided by Zain, since the two victims in the case had seen virtually nothing of their attacker. Zain had come to court and given a folksy lesson in blood and semen, and explained that his tests proved only six in ten thousand people could have attacked the woman, and Glen Dale Woodall was a member of that very narrow group. It was powerful evidence, with one slight problem: Zain's laboratory couldn't perform those tests. Even if he had done the tests, his statistics were off by a mile. He had made up a story to make people happy about a suspect. And it wasn't the first time.

"Our investigation has also revealed," wrote McGowan, "that the trooper who falsely reported the laboratory examination results has done so in other cases on other occasions and may have testified to those false results. . . .

"The publicity which will result from the Woodall action and any public settlement or disclosure of the facts in the case would cause irreparable harm to the State Police and, perhaps more importantly from your perspective, will precipitate a number of claims from persons against whom the testimony of this trooper was used in criminal cases. . . . Some of that exposure cannot be avoided, as the Department is beginning an audit of files which may compel it to advise prosecuting attorneys of the potential problem files.

"Nonetheless, a quiet, pre-suit settlement of the Woodall case would preclude a media circus and allow for some form of damage control," McGowan wrote.

Everything McGowan wrote in that confidential letter was true, with one exception: the desperate efforts to keep the secrets of Fred Zain would not succeed. The unmasking of one corrupt, twisted man would reveal dangers that reached far beyond West Virginia. What passes for "scientific evidence" in courtrooms frequently goes unchallenged, and carries tremendous weight with jurors panning for nuggets of truth in the muddy rivers of con-

Actual innocence

flicting stories and rickety memories. Too often, though, the "scientific evidence" is fool's gold. Not only juries are bamboozled by phony scientific evidence. Reassured by malarkey dressed up as science, many ordinary eyewitnesses, police officers, and prosecutors twisted, tweaked, and simply changed stories to make them fit the ironclad decrees of the superior beings in lab coats. "He was a god," one West Virginia prosecutor said of Zain. The warning from Steven McGowan—that it would be "catastrophic" to poke too deeply into the Woodall case—would prove prophetic.

———

Dusk arrived on January 22, 1987, before the sun ever got out of the starting block. The whole day had been blustery and snowing, and the Huntington Mall was close to empty. Walking to her car at the rear of the mall, a young woman was approached by a man in a ski mask, carrying a knife. He forced her to drive a few miles away, then attacked her. Afterward, he taped her mouth shut. Three weeks later, it happened again, to another woman.

One of the victims said she caught a glance of a man with a reddish-brown beard. The ski mask was described as yellow and brown.

It so happened that a few hundred yards from the rear entrance to the Huntington Mall worked a man with reddish-brown hair and a minor criminal record. Glen Dale Woodall, twenty-nine, was the head groundskeeper at the White Chapel Memorial Gardens cemetery. A search of his home found a brown ski mask, not quite the brown and yellow mask described by the victim, but the police report was hidden, so the discrepancy went unnoticed. The tape used to seal one victim's mouth was similar to that sold in a store at the mall where Woodall's wife worked. After hypnosis, both victims said that Woodall was their attacker, recognized both by his appearance and a singular scent. Most courts don't allow witnesses who have been hypnotized to testify because the process is as apt to warp a memory as it is to enhance it.

Woodall, meanwhile, swore seven ways to Sunday that he had nothing to do with the crime. And he was, at best, a weak suspect. Still, his blood was drawn to be tested against the semen left by the attacker, and samples of his hair were taken for comparison with a single hair found in one of the victim's cars.

Here Fred Zain worked his magic—and showed why he was the most wanted serologist in all of West Virginia, at least by prosecutors trying to prepare a case with no strong witnesses.

At the trial, Zain discussed the blood type disclosed by the semen recovered from the victims. He reported his astounding statistics on the match between Woodall's blood and the blood type discovered in the semen: only "six in ten thousand" would have the same combination of blood traits.

Then there was the single, reddish-brown hair recovered from the car. Could the hair have come from anyone but Glen Dale Woodall's beard?

"Highly unlikely," was Zain's answer.

Well, could he say beyond a doubt that the hair had originated from Woodall?

No, he couldn't say that, said Zain, but he could say this: "All characteristics are the same. . . . I had no reason to believe that the hair could not have originated from Mr. Woodall."

Woodall testified that at the time of the rape, he was at work. His brother backed up the alibi. Woodall said he would take truth serum to prove his innocence. He even had heard of a new procedure, called DNA testing, and asked that it be done. The prosecution opposed that motion, saying DNA tests were unproven. Zain tests, on the other hand, were known commodities.

The jury made short work of the rest of Woodall's life: they found him guilty of all nineteen counts of abduction and sexual assault. Their recommendation was a sentence of life, with no mercy. The judge doubled that, giving him two sentences of life without parole, plus an additional 335 years. Woodall's new wife, Teresa, wept.

"I am," said Cabell County prosecutor John Cummings, "tickled to death."

Woodall staggered off to jail and spent his time with a small typewriter, pecking at motions, writing letters. He wanted a DNA test. It would prove him innocent. The prosecution resisted. Woodall said if they would agree to the test and it showed he was the rapist, he would waive all his rights to appeal the convictions. Finally, the evidence was sent out for testing, but the first round was inconclusive because the sample had degraded. Then a private

Charleston attorney, Lonnie Simmons, hired by Woodall's family, read an article in a Sunday *New York Times* about another kind of DNA test, polymerase chain reaction, or PCR, that could work with minute samples.

The use of the test in court proceedings had been pioneered by Ed Blake, the forensic scientist in California. He explained the procedure to Simmons, then had a thought.

"You'd better call these two lawyers in New York who have been handling DNA cases," said Blake. "They are running an Innocence Project to retest evidence in old cases. The names are Barry Scheck and Peter Neufeld."

The new tests by Blake showed that Woodall was not the source of the semen, and the case began to crumble—although slowly. The prisoner was brought from the state penitentiary back to the county jail as a judge tried to figure out what the DNA results meant. On the day the prison van carrying Woodall arrived in Charleston, one of the victims was waiting in the parking lot, weeping. She ran to the door of the van and banged on it, keeping it shut. She was convinced that Glen Woodall was the attacker she had never seen. Her public opposition to his release stiffened the back of the prosecutors when they were presented with the new DNA results.

Even so, with help from Barry and Peter, Simmons and Woodall prevailed in court. The conviction was overturned. Woodall was released in July 1991 on home confinement, with an electronic bracelet to monitor his whereabouts. The following May, the state agreed that he should not be retried. And the monitoring bracelet barely had been unlocked when, in September, the state agreed to the million-dollar payout for Woodall's wrongful conviction.

What had happened? The testimony of the California scientist, Ed Blake, nudged open a door into Fred Zain's closet of horrors. Not only did Blake show that Woodall could not have been the source of the semen found on the victims, but he strongly questioned the validity of the original blood work that Zain claimed to have done.

The state's secret investigation of its liability in a Woodall lawsuit backed up Blake's findings. "The trooper testified that he performed laboratory tests on seminal fluid that the laboratory was incapable of performing at the time the test was conducted," wrote Attorney McGowan.

"Based upon the tests actually conducted, the trooper should have reported that . . . the violator's blood was shared by approximately 3% of the population.

"Instead, the trooper, utilizing test results which were fabricated, testified that the violator's blood was shared by 1 person in 10,000."

Zain had painted a bull's-eye on Glen Dale Woodall's back, claiming the blood work was three hundred times more discriminating than was actually the case.

And what about the incriminating hair evidence? McGowan did not deal with that in his letter, but Attorney Simmons had discovered that Zain's testimony on it was bogus, too. Just three months before the trial, Zain had written a report stating that it was a pubic hair—not, as he would testify in court, a beard hair from Woodall. The other expert who examined the hair said that it bore no similarities to any of Woodall's hair, from any part of his body.

After the Woodall case was settled, the state police performed an internal audit of the laboratory and found "certain improprieties" but no big problems.

"There is no need to take further action," the superintendent of the Division of Public Safety declared. To call his inquiry and response a whitewash would not do violence to history. A second investigation of Trooper Zain was launched by the West Virginia Supreme Court, spurred by Simmons, George Castelle, the chief public defender in Charleston, and Bill Forbes, the new prosecuting attorney for Kanawha County. This time, everyone vowed, there could be no cover-up.

Zain had given evidence in hundreds of serious felony cases, including murder and rape. With help from the American Association of Crime Lab Directors, a prominent group of forensic scientists, the investigator reviewed Zain's testimony and evidence, where it still existed, in a representative sampling of thirty-six cases. The findings were breathtaking. For a period of ten years, Fred Zain faked data in every case. The pattern was identical to his performance in the Woodall trial: Zain claimed tests had been performed when they had not been done. He stated that samples of biological evidence were "conclusive" proof of someone's guilt when he hadn't tested the evidence, and even if he had, the tests could not have supported his sweeping conclusions. In the Woodall case, his arithmetic in calculating the odds of Woodall being the rapist—based on the semen—would have been laughed at by a high school sophomore.

He had failed organic chemistry in college. He flunked an FBI course on forensic sciences. His assistants said he would make statements about evidence based on slides that had nothing on them.

A magic wand was taped by one of his associates to a machine at his lab bench. "Magic was the only way he could have been coming up with the answers he got," explained Gayle Midkiff, Zain's former assistant. Years before Woodall was convicted, she and another worker had written a letter of complaint to the head of the state labs. Zain's supervisors pooh-poohed it as a personality clash, and the matter went no further.

The state supreme court had heard enough. Taking note of the "shocking and egregious violations" found by its special investigator, the court punted Fred Zain, professional prosecution witness, clear out of the West Virginia judicial system. "As a matter of law, any testimonial or documentary evidence offered by Zain at any time in any criminal prosecution should be deemed invalid, unreliable, and inadmissible," the court ruled unanimously in 1993.

By then, Zain had long since moved out of the state. In fact, he was gone even before the Woodall scandal broke open, working as an all-around forensic expert in Texas. He was treated in the press as an aberrational figure, a lone sociopath, a one-man wrecking crew. Yet others helped, in one way or another, and in time, the breadth of that collaboration would become clear as prisoners went into court seeking to have their convictions overturned. They argued that without Zain's tainted evidence, they would not have been found guilty. Most of these claims were rejected, on the grounds that even discounting Zain's phony lab reports, other, nonscientific evidence had put the prisoners in the soup.

The prosecution of William O'Dell Harris showed that Zain's perjury could contaminate even witnesses who weren't presenting "scientific" evidence. The Harris case is a classic example of how criminal investigations can become echo chambers, where answers are shaped by what people believe ought to be true rather than what they know to be the facts.

William Harris had been sent to a rat-infested Civil War–era dungeon in 1987, convicted of attacking a woman in the rural town of Rand. At the time of the rape in December 1984, Harris was seventeen years old, a star linebacker and state champion wrestler, with colleges lined up for his enrollment. By July 1994, he was among the prisoners given a habeas corpus hearing because Zain had been a witness in his case.

The formula used in the review worked like this: First, the court would discard the serologist's testimony. Then, the remaining, non-Zain evidence would be weighed, to make a determination if the conviction should stand. In the Harris case, the most powerful evidence came not from Zain but from the victim herself, a registered nurse named Jeannie. At the trial, she had been asked about the lineup where she picked Harris as her attacker.

"He was in the middle," she testified.

"How did you recognize him?" asked the prosecutor.

"I just recognized his face, and I just—I don't know, I just started crying. It was more—I guess I don't know, but I just started crying hysterically."

"Why did you do that?"

"I guess it brought back what he had done to me," said Jeannie.

"Was there any question in your mind that that was the man who had done this?"

"No," she said.

The sheriff's deputy who had organized the lineup recalled in court: "She had no doubt in her mind. It was probably the, the most dramatic sort of identification I had ever seen."

Even disregarding Zain's phony blood evidence, the weight of the evidence against Harris was heavy. The only chance for Harris to overturn his conviction was to retest the original rape kit evidence. But the prosecutor's office reported that it was no longer in storage. Just didn't know where it had gotten to. The matter would have ended there except for the dogged work of George Castelle, the public defender, and his investigator, Peggy Longwell, who traced the chain of evidence. The hospital that performed the original sexual assault examination of the victim had kept a single laboratory slide, preserved and labeled. The sperm on that slide was tested, and the results said that it could not have come from Harris.

Yet the story was not done. When Harris brought a lawsuit for his wrongful conviction, he and his attorney, John Curry, found two astonishing documents. The first was a police report of an interview with Jeannie. In it, the investigator stated that Jeannie had been shown a picture of Harris:

"Suspect [William Harris] eliminated with photo lineup on March 6, 1985. Victim stated she knew him and it wasn't him." Indeed, Harris lived just three doors away from the victim, who had reported that her attacker was five feet, seven inches tall—some six inches shorter than Harris.

The second document was a chart the police had prepared of suspects in the attack. Under Harris's name, the police reported that he had been eliminated by the victim.

Of course, the failure to give these critical documents to the defense at trial was patently illegal and helped to pervert justice. That was bad enough. Even more intriguing, however, is the sequence in which the victim Jeannie changed her view of Harris. She had, after all, told the police that she knew him and he hadn't done it. Months later, she saw Harris and wept that he was the attacker.

Her mind changed after a blood test was completed by the state police laboratory, under the supervision of Sgt. Fred Zain. He had come up with one of his classic, patent incriminating reports. The police learned the result. Jeannie went to another lineup. Suddenly, William O'Dell Harris was the rapist.

The string of misconduct was so appalling that the settlement of Harris's civil suit was nearly double that of Woodall's: $1.88 million. This time, there were no cries of outrage.

Sham has passed for science in criminal cases all over the United States, at times to shocking effect. Zain was a prosecution witness in twelve states. He was responsible for false evidence in scores of cases in Texas, where he had taken a position as chief serologist for the county medical examiner in San Antonio. On the word of this dangerous fraud, a jury convicted Jack Davis, a janitor at an apartment complex, of murdering a tenant whose body he discovered. Zain miraculously came up with a DNA test showing blood from Davis on carpet fibers near the body that was otherwise soaked in the victim's blood. As word of Zain's antics in West Virginia reached Texas, a team of lawyers led by Stanley Schneider and Gerry Goldstein exposed

Zain's DNA test as a phony and exonerated Davis. The same thing happened to Gilbert Alejandro. Zain's contribution to his wrongful conviction in 1990 consisted of testimony that DNA tests showed semen on a rape victim's clothing "could have only originated from [Alejandro]." In fact, these tests were inconclusive. Additional tests showed he was innocent. Four years later, a Texas judge found that Zain knew that Alejandro had been cleared by the tests but failed to report them to anyone.

Texas already had another superstar of forensic deception in Ralph Erdmann, who had proclaimed himself the "Quincy of the Panhandle." As the medical examiner for forty-eight counties in west Texas, he claimed to have personally performed four hundred autopsies a year, an astonishing rate. "Call him McErdmann," said one prosecutor. "He's like McDonald's—billions served."

How did Erdmann work so fast? By skipping a few formalities. One family read his death report and was surprised to see that the weight of the dead man's gallbladder and spleen were reported by Erdmann. Years before the man died, both organs had been surgically removed. His body was exhumed and showed that no incisions had been done. In another case, Erdmann claimed to have examined a woman's brain. Once again, the corpse was exhumed—and there was no sign that the head had been touched. He became known as the king of the drive-by autopsy. When a few honest cops and prosecutors started an investigation, they dug up seven bodies and found none of them had incisions. Erdmann often would want to know the police theory of the death before he wrote up his report on the cause of death, the investigators said, to keep his story straight.

In Odessa, Erdmann did an autopsy in a possible murder case and somehow misplaced the head. When the police arrested a man with the victim's credit cards, he blurted out: "It wasn't me that shot the woman in the head." ("In law enforcement," said one deputy sheriff, "we call that a 'clue.'") However, since Erdmann was the last one to see the head, the murder charges against the suspect had to be dropped.

Elsewhere, officials in Plainview said they sent Erdmann the headless body of a woman they found in a ditch. Eight years later, he returned the woman's bones, throwing in the head of a fourteen-year-old boy for good measure, like a dutiful shipping clerk sending out a complete package, even if all the parts didn't match.

Lubbock County had to pay one man $15,000 because he spent four months in jail, charged with killing his infant son, based on Erdmann's autopsy. A second autopsy showed the baby drowned accidentally.

"That I'm human and can do errors, yes," Erdmann said at a court hearing. "But intentionally? Never."

One police officer wrote a letter of official complaint about another unusual practice of the coroner: "The second assistant who Dr. Erdmann has brought to the last three autopsies is Dr. Erdmann's thirteen-year-old son. This child dons gloves and apron and proceeds to finger the wounds on the body, as well as handle evidence."

He certainly brought his work home, as Ed Bradley of the CBS TV show *60 Minutes* discovered when he visited the makeshift laboratory Erdmann had set up. Bradley poked his nose into Erdmann's fridge.

BRADLEY: So what—what are these tubes up here?
DR. ERDMANN: Those are blood samples, urine samples.
BRADLEY: And over here you've got . . .
DR. ERDMANN: Hey, that's mustard. Now, don't do that to me.
BRADLEY: Mustard?
DR. ERDMANN: Are you trying to discredit me?
BRADLEY: Cola . . .
DR. ERDMANN: I'm just—this is—as I've said . . .
BRADLEY: No, I . . .
DR. ERDMANN: . . . it's a fairly simple operation.
BRADLEY: Right, but you—Dr. Erdmann, look, I mean, you've been here for a year.
DR. ERDMANN: Yeah. Well—so?
BRADLEY: But you don't keep . . .
DR. ERDMANN: Exactly, this is—this is something that I didn't expect.
BRADLEY: You keep blood next to jelly?
DR. ERDMANN: No, no. I don't keep blood next to jelly. That is the blood over there and . . .

BRADLEY: The blood's over there and the jelly is over here and the hot sauce is over here.

DR. ERDMANN: This hasn't been used in a long time, sir. Since a year this hasn't been used at all.

BRADLEY: Well, realistically, I'm not trying to embarrass you here, but . . .

DR. ERDMANN: Well, yes you are.

BRADLEY: I opened the refrigerator, and I see picante sauce.

DR. ERDMANN: But you saw it . . .

BRADLEY: Next to the blood.

DR. ERDMANN: I've shown it to you before.

BRADLEY: No, you've never shown that to me. That's the first time I've seen it.

DR. ERDMANN: OK. Then . . .

Erdmann pleaded no contest to lying about his autopsies and was given a ten-year suspended sentence. Later, however, he moved to Redmond, Washington, and was found to have an arsenal of weapons in his home, including illegal machine guns. Texas revoked his parole.

Dr. Erdmann of the missing heads was sent to jail. Fred Zain was indicted several times in West Virginia but as of late 1999 has not been convicted. He is due to stand trial in 2000. In Texas, purportedly due to statute of limitations problems, no indictments were ever brought.

Were Zain and Erdmann, two men who engaged for years in systematic forensic fraud, just two bad apples? During the Zain mop-up in West Virginia, one of the people who had been involved with hiring him was questioned under oath. Zain wasn't the only bad guy in a lab coat, he said. And the West Virginia crime laboratory wasn't alone as a safe harbor for phonies. "This is not the only place in the nation that this has occurred," testified former police lieutenant Kenneth Blake. "I saw it in San Francisco, they had to dispose of about one thousand drug cases because of a bad chemist." He could have also cited the incredible fingerprint framing scandals. In Orange County, California, a police officer photocopied fingerprint cards from suspects and then pressed the wet photocopy of the prints onto blank "lift" cards from armed robberies. Another time he took a fingerprint card from a suspect, placed it under a Baggie that had been filled with drugs, photographed it, and cropped out the outlines of the card.

In upstate New York, state troopers resorted to planting fingerprints on evidence in tough cases. The practice was discovered only when one of the troopers applied for a job with the CIA and bragged about his craftiness. The information was passed on to the FBI, which sat on it for about a year before notifying state authorities. While the FBI dillydallied, more people were framed.

The stink of Zain and his ilk smells worst in the nostrils of honest and conscientious forensic scientists, who make up the great majority of the field. Yet it would be naive to write him off as a freak occurrence. After all, there is no sign that there was any more money in fraud for Zain, Erdmann, and the fingerprint fakers than there would have been in honest science. What drove them?

Zain himself has not responded in any public forum to specific questions about his reign of fraud. During civil suits arising from the scandal, he consistently failed to appear when subpoenaed. No doubt his own vulnerability in ongoing criminal investigations played a part in his silence. He did speak to Susan Spencer for CBS-News's *48 Hours* and insisted he did nothing wrong.

"I personally know that I've never done anything intentionally to harm or hurt anybody in my entire life. They're simply unjustified accusations," said Zain.

He said he never believed that his work carried tremendous weight in court. "I have never thought in any case that I've ever testified on that anything that I said would be the turning point. Never. Never meant it to be, never wanted it to be."

Asked if he had ever invented results that seemed to fit the crime, Zain was categorical. "Never. Why jeopardize a career, family, criminal proceedings, civil proceedings? There was no benefit in any avenue to ever do anything like that."

The résumé of Fred Zain may provide a clue to his behavior. A failure in the classroom, in only one place was he a hero: on the witness stand. Even after Zain moved out of West Virginia, county prosecutors continued to hire him because they suddenly discovered that Zain's successors were not coming up with the consistently useful results that the master had achieved. After Glen Woodall was convicted, thanks to Zain, the West Virginia State Police superintendent W. F. Donohoe wrote a letter of congratulations to the serologist for his work on that case and others.

"It is to your personal and professional credit that the citizens of Cabell County who served on that jury believed the prosecution evidence presented," Donohoe wrote on July 10, 1987.

"You, in both your personal efforts and your professional presentation, along with others in the law enforcement community, presented evidence that was so credible that 19 guilty verdicts were sustained.

"If my 33 years of experience as a law enforcement officer places me in a proper position to make predictions, then I can predict that there will be some bleeding hearts (who were not a part of the investigation, were not a part of the jury process established by our national and state laws) that will question the outcome."

In closing, Donohoe assured Zain that if "bleeding hearts should drip on your apparel in the future, please know that the great number of good people support your very proper and proficient action and that I stand ready to assist you in every possible way as we stand proudly together in the law enforcement community."

Fred Zain reached the title of sergeant before he left West Virginia, and as Superintendent Donohue wrote, a cherished member of the "law enforcement community." Not a scientist but a cop in a lab coat, as Zain himself once said: "We weren't considered really scientists. If there were funeral details, disaster details, we were policemen first."

No self-respecting cop would think the fabrication of evidence a duty of the job. No lay witness, for that matter, would knowingly twist the facts. The mistakes made by eyewitnesses or victims rise from the very core of their humanity: emotional, wounded spirits trying to make themselves or someone else whole. The very opposite quality, a detachment from passion, endows scientific evidence with its power as a truth teller. Lab results should not be as malleable as the human mind and memory. A thousand people can witness a crime and recall a thousand different details. In the laboratory, if a thousand people perform a test, they all should come up with the same results. Among scientists, the result that can't be replicated carries little weight.

That is how DNA testing derives its power as a gold standard for truth telling. The test has been proven accurate—it is now used to match tissues in organ donation, for instance, and to diagnose specific viral diseases—and the results have been validated. Along the trail of fraud and errors revealed by DNA tests, the work of unreliable laboratories has turned out to be among the most dangerous to the innocent. Cloaked in the robes of science, the "facts" churned out by charlatans such as Zain seem most remote from human distortion, and unassailable.

Scientific evidence, properly handled, can be the best evidence in a case. Clearly, forensic science has yet to achieve the status of an independent third force, unbeholden to prosecutors or defense lawyers, consisting of professionals who will not misrepresent or slant data for either side. The abuses of Fred Zain and those like him simply could not exist in a truly independent forensic science community, fostered in institutions that carry out only scientific agendas. Neither the laboratory nor its budget should be under the supervision of the police department or a prosecutor's office. A 1985 survey found that 79 percent of all laboratories were part of a police or prosecutorial agency.

Yet a more troubling question: How did Zain, Erdmann, and other "dry labbers" get away with it, not once, not twice, but for years?

One answer surely lies with a culture of protective secrecy that silences criticism, encourages nondisclosure of scientific work product, and discourages any admission of errors, much less correcting and accounting for them. Without question, the chief culprit in creating this culture has been the FBI, the most influential and powerful crime laboratory in America. This is an observation made by outsiders and the agency's internal watchdog.

That secrecy and protectiveness has had a corrosive impact on the FBI, according to Inspector General Michael Bromwich. In a scathing report, Bromwich said the FBI ignored its own whistle-blowers and punished some. The agency refused to disclose data or to admit error; it did not discipline agent-technicians who made mistakes, and would not tolerate normal disagreements and criticisms that occur in any scientific setting. In fact, the nation's premier criminalistic laboratory would not apply for accreditation, nor would it open itself to peer review.

The lab director, John Hicks, once wrote to the FBI's counsel, proposing to destroy records that showed the FBI's performance on proficiency tests, rather than surrender them to defense attorneys.

Following the inspector general's recommendations, the agency has applied for accreditation.

In 1989, the FBI held its first international seminar on forensic DNA testing, inviting experts from all over the country. Everyone recognized that DNA would be a fixture in criminal trials. What form should the evidence reports take? The FBI proposed that DNA reports be very much like the ones it issued on other forensic questions: they would declare starkly their final conclusions, with little detail about the methods employed, and not even carry the signature of the analyst responsible for the testing. The invited guests were not so docile. They uniformly voted to require scientists to sign their own reports. Only the FBI representatives voted to support the agency's proposal of silence.

The morning after this vote, Peter was scheduled to deliver a lecture giving a critique of certain DNA laboratories. Buttonholed by two of the top people at the lab, John Hicks and James Kearney, he was ordered not to mention people by name. Peter ignored the instruction.

The FBI's cult of protectiveness has reached far beyond the gates of Quantico—even into the Zain affair.

Zain had been sent to Quantico for a basic serology course in 1977, and the FBI administration later reported that he had "scored well below the class average" on two examinations, and "finished below the passing grade for the course." But, complains West Virginia's Ken Blake, Zain "does have certificates that he completed the course. The FBI issued certificates." Worse still, when two technicians from West Virginia confided to FBI officials during training programs that their boss, Zain, was engaging in questionable practices, there was no serious follow-up.

Finding outlandish fakes of the Fred Zain ilk should have been easy; like a counterfeit hundred-dollar bill, he would be easy to spot. Far more insidious is the everyday fudging, slanting, and concealment of evidence that points to innocence. John Willis of Illinois was convicted in 1992 for one in a string of very unusual sexual assaults: a man would arrive at haircutting salons, have his hair done, then pull a weapon, herd the customers into a room, and attack a woman on the premises. After he left one shop, a quick-thinking victim used a toilet paper wrapper to collect his semen.

At Willis's trial, the state's lab analyst, Pamela Fish, testified that her studies of that evidence were "inconclusive," a seemingly innocuous and fair-minded report. Willis was convicted on eyewitness testimony. After he went to prison, though, there was an odd development that troubled his attorney, Greg O'Reilly of the Cook County public defender's office. This strange crime wave continued. This time, instead of in beauty shops, the assaults took place in bars, in the very same neighborhood. In early 1999, Willis was freed from prison, exonerated by DNA tests on the tissue arranged by O'Reilly, with help from the Innocence Project.

Even before that, O'Reilly discovered that the original lab tests on that same tissue were not "inconclusive" after all.

The raw laboratory notes made by Pamela Fish showed that Willis had been excluded by old-fashioned ABO blood typing as the source of the semen in the toilet paper wrapper. Fish never mentioned this exclusion at the trial; all the jury heard from her was that an unstained portion of the wrapper had shown "activity," making the blood-typing tests "inconclusive."

These observations were not recorded in any of her notes, according to three serologists who provided affidavits to O'Reilly. And though the jurors heard about this undocumented phenomenon involving the wrapper, they never got even a whisper from Fish that her tests of the actual semen stain had cleared John Willis—and those results were explicitly docketed in her lab notes. When O'Reilly learned this and moved to overturn the verdict because of prosecutorial misconduct, the state denied any wrongdoing. His motion was not resolved before the DNA tests exonerated Willis. Fish herself has not commented on these circumstances and is likely to be an important witness in a lawsuit filed by Willis against the state. Indeed, the charges did not slow her ascension in Illinois forensic circles.

The very week that John Willis was released from prison, the lab analyst who might have spared him seven years behind bars was given a new job.

Pamela Fish was promoted to oversee biochemistry for the Illinois State Police crime laboratory.

Fish's misleading testimony in the Willis case, which led to the conviction of an innocent man and allowed a predator to continue roaming the streets, shows why the state should have turned over all of Fish's laboratory notes and data, rather than merely presenting her final report. Her lab notes strongly suggested that John Willis was innocent. Her testimony gave no hint of that. Prosecutors who wish to introduce scientific evidence should be required to disclose all the underlying documentation used to build a final report.

Such reports should say whether any exculpatory inferences can be drawn from the evidence. The names of the technicians who performed the work also should be included; Zain often took the work of others and testified to it himself.

Even with open access to the lab reports and independent institutions, people still can lie and cheat. To weed out such individuals, oversight is needed for the laboratories. For a lab to be accredited in New York State, it must have quality control and assurance programs, and be subject to periodic inspections and spot checking of technicians' data to deter fraud. All lab workers should have access to an independent ombudsman who can mediate disputes over interpretations of data. And lab workers who report wrongdoing should have the opportunity to be given whistle-blower protections.

Finally, that Fred Zain and Ralph Erdmann were able to thrive for years is a backward tribute to the anemic work of defense attorneys in their states. As Public Defender George Castelle of West Virginia points out, if even one defense lawyer had challenged Fred Zain to present his notes during his ten-year reign of error, the charade would have come to an end. Too many lawyers ended up going to law school because of lousy grades in chemistry and biology. A fear of science won't cut it in an age when many pleas of guilty are predicated on the reports of scientific experts. Every public defender's office should have at least one lawyer who is not afraid of a test tube.

6

Snitch

Terri Holland arrived like a college girl wandering the dormitory hall, barefoot, wearing nothing but a very long T-shirt that she hooked over her knees when she sat, catlike, resting her butt on her own folded legs. She was at home in this place, the tiny interview room of the Pontotoc County jail, in the town of Ada, Oklahoma. Her hair was pulled back behind her ears, a great flowing mass that is a light, coppery brown, like the color of a new penny.

Along her arms and hands, the skin was tattooed with flowers and small daggers drawn in deep blue ink. Others, on her ankle and legs, right up to her mid-thigh, were harder for a polite person to get a good look at. The folded legs were exposed to the mid-thigh. She accepted a cigarette, dragged on it, then began to talk.

"Ronnie's going home tomorrow, isn't that right?" she asked.

"It sure looks that way," said Mark Barrett, the public defender who is representing Ron Williamson.

"I am real glad to hear that for his sake, he deserves another chance," said Terri. "Everyone is happy for him. That's good for Ronnie, isn't it?"

In less than twelve hours, Ron Williamson and his codefendant, Dennis Fritz, would be released. It was no secret. By now, the dogs on the street knew it. *Dateline NBC* had sent Alexandra Pelosi, one of the best TV producers in the business, to the town. In little Ada, population 15,630, nowhere was the buzzing louder than in the county jail. Williamson and his codefendant, Dennis Fritz, had been brought back from the state facilities to the tiny county jail in anticipation of their release.

Terri Holland passed Ron in the hall of the jail just a few minutes earlier, scurrying past him to the interview room. He had been dressed in the old-fashioned striped pajamas that make a jail prisoner visible for miles, a human zebra. Williamson—a big lug, a lumpy former athlete, his hair gone white—didn't notice Holland slipping past him. And Terri never said a word to him. In fact, she ducked her head when she saw him coming.

For a woman who sounded so happy to hear that her fellow prisoner was going home, this might have seemed kind of odd. Then again, Terri Holland and Ron Williamson had a history.

Fifteen years earlier, in the fall of 1984, Terri wrote $800 in bogus checks and got caught. In jail, she claimed to have heard Ron Williamson confess to a dreadful murder. After offering this news to the authorities, she was treated to a very soft landing on her bad checks, despite a record of two felony convictions. Holland was a key witness against Williamson at his murder trial in 1987.

And twelve years later, on a hot April day in 1999, they crossed paths in the hallway, their lives once again going in opposite directions. This time, Ron Williamson, proven innocent, was going home. Terri Holland, the snitch who had sent him to death row, was heading back to prison herself for yet another in the string of small-time crimes by which she had defined her adult life.

No wonder she had ducked her head passing him in the hallway. And no doubt she really was glad that Ron was going home. At least he wouldn't be in the prison system to chase her down.

In the study of jailhouse snitches, there is no need to turn to the works of distinguished social scientists or psychologists. The nation's leading authority, Leslie Vernon White, explained the entire process in the late 1980s.

At that time, White was a full-time criminal who never served anything like a full-time sentence. No sooner would he arrive in jail than he would size up the inmate population, like a housewife squeezing tomatoes at the grocery store for the juiciest one, deciding who the prosecutors would most like to hear about. He testified against at least a dozen California inmates, claiming that they happened to tell him the details of the crimes they committed. In one thirty-six-day period, he gave evidence for the Los Angeles district attorney's office in three murder cases and one residential burglary—all arising from what he claimed were fleeting jailhouse encounters during which inmates revealed critical details about their crimes to him. It is unlikely that the archbishop of Los Angeles heard as many confessions as Leslie Vernon White claimed to have heard.

His most spectacular demonstration came in the chaplain's office on the thirteenth floor of the Los Angeles Hall of Justice. White was there to show sheriff's deputies just how easy it was to manufacture "confessions"—even from inmates he had never met. White had testified at the trial of another inmate about the snitch system, revealing many secrets, but the prosecutor's office paid little attention to his description of serial perjuries. The sheriff's office, however, with responsibility for inmates in the county jail, was concerned about his claims, and challenged White.

A deputy provided White with the name of another inmate, the fact that he was a murder suspect, and a telephone. In twenty minutes, White showed his stuff. He made five phone calls and collected enough inside information about the other inmate to claim with credibility that the man had confessed. Posing as a bail bondsman, White called the inmate reception center; as an assistant district attorney, he called the D.A.'s record room, then the D.A.'s witness coordinator, the sheriff's homicide office, and the actual D.A. handling the case. He rang the coroner's office, in the guise of a cop, and learned about mortal injuries to the victim.

With the facts he gathered during these chats, White knew enough about the murder to make up a confession on behalf of an inmate whom he had neither seen nor spoken to. Only amateurs would see that as a handicap.

With the sheriff's deputy still watching in amazement, he then called the court bailiff, and asked that the suspect be brought to the holding tank in the courthouse so there would be a written record that White and the man were once in the same room. The entire performance was tape-recorded and slammed home White's point about people like himself: they could make up any kind of story that would damage just about anyone.

Among inmate informers, White said, the jokes were: "Don't go to the pen—send a friend." Or: "If you can't do the time, just drop a dime." And: "Trouble? You better call 1-800-HETOLDME."

Informants will swarm to a hot case, said White, and the first one there will organize a "booking." That is the term for incriminating admissions that the first inmate will claim to have heard from the target. Then the first snitch will recruit a second one to back up the story about hearing a confession. This corroborates the primary snitch, and allows the second one to "get in the car"—the metaphor for cutting short a jail stay by snitching. The snitches also discussed having access to the "freeway"—the time when they would be able to roam the jail corridors, and thus be in a position to say that they heard someone barking up a confession. This precious morsel of information would be traded with the police and prosecutors for get-out-of-jail deals, or at least extra privileges while locked up.

Another inmate, Sydney Storch, was the "Snitch Professor" who had supplied police with twenty "confessions" he claimed to have heard while locked up. He was a witness in court at least a half-dozen times. In advising another inmate on how to make a good snitch story work, Storch said the truth should not be an obstacle:

"Go for the jugular—you're going to have to be bullshitting a little bit, but you may as well get used to the situation," he said in a conversation that was being secretly recorded. To another inmate who was housed with suspects in high-profile cases, Storch wrote a letter: "You're sitting on a smoking row—used properly, you could cut your time way down. . . . Make sure you call me. I'll do your research."

The "research" involved going to a library and reading back articles about the crime so that the snitch would be able to tell a story that resembled the actual events.

In the swamp ground of snitchery, the footing is treacherously unreliable, prosecutors admit. Master snitch Leslie Vernon White did lead police to several buried bodies that he learned about from other inmates. But he had no qualms about dressing up a story or creating one from scratch. As with virtually everyone else involved in the criminal justice system, snitches come to their work with a rationalization that whatever they do is okay because the victims of their perfidy are all guilty anyhow of something. "Now me and every other [informant] I've talked to have the same policy," said Steve Vulpis, a fellow snitch of White's. "The guy's guilty. Who gives a damn. I want to go home." In that respect, snitches resemble far more respectable people—prosecutors, witnesses, scientists, detectives—who believe that since just about everyone in jail is guilty anyway, a little elaboration on the facts can't hurt. Shave the truth, and it won't bleed.

In the cases of Ron Williamson and Dennis Fritz, the truth hemorrhaged.

On the morning of December 8, 1982, a bricklayer named Charlie Mason was asked by his wife to stop at the apartment of their daughter, Debra Sue Carter, who was not answering her phone. Debra lived in a second-floor apartment. On the landing, her father saw glass, then found the screen door and the front door wide open. He came out a moment later.

"Would you call the police?" he hollered to a woman living downstairs.

"Should I call an ambulance?" she asked.

"No," he said. "Just call the police. An ambulance won't do any good."

He had found his daughter lying facedown, with a blood-soaked washcloth stuck in her mouth. On her back, the words *Duke Graham* were written in ketchup. He rolled her over onto one shoulder. Written on her chest in fingernail polish was the word *Die*. Beneath her body was an electric cord and a belt. The ketchup bottle was found wrapped in a sheet. The following day, the lid of the bottle would be discovered by the medical examiner in the anus of the victim. The crime walloped Ada, a town of fifteen thousand, about two hours southeast of Oklahoma City. The next evening, Glen Gore, a high school classmate of Debra's, told investigators that he had seen Debra at the

Coach Light the night before. A man had been hassling her for a dance, and she implored Glen to rescue her. Gore obliged her by stepping onto the dance floor with her, away from the unwanted attentions of the other man.

Another waitress told the detectives that she had gotten a call from Debra late that night, after their shift had ended and they both had gone home.

"Could you come and get me? There's someone here, and I don't feel comfortable," Debra asked.

For a moment, the friend thought she heard someone putting a hand over the phone. Then Debra said that she'd be waiting for her friend.

Before the other woman could get out the door, the phone rang again. It was Debra, calling to say, never mind, she was okay.

"Is he still there?" asked her girlfriend. "Who is it?"

"Just give me a call in the morning to wake me up for work," said Debra, not answering the questions.

The next morning, Debra's Mickey Mouse phone was found pulled from the wall. She was twenty-one years old, and her stuffed animals were strewn around the room. By day, she worked at the big Brockway Glass factory and the Love's coffee shop. A few nights a week, she worked at the Coach Light. Her father remembered that when she was laid off from one job, she worked in some baby-sitting. She was a spunky girl, he said, full of fight.

She had been killed December 8, 1982, and no one came to talk to Ronald Keith Williamson about the matter until the morning of March 14, 1983, but sooner or later, they were bound to track him down.

Ron Williamson was one of the finest athletes ever to come out of Ada, or the state of Oklahoma. As a boy, he had been a bright, obsessive character, who once had made it his business to learn every fact conceivable about the United States presidents—a topic that dominated all his conversation for months. Later, he switched focus and absorbed every molecule of information about Mickey Charles Mantle, the New York Yankees' star center fielder, the Comet from Commerce, Oklahoma. Ron even set up a shrine in his bedroom and fitted it with Mantle paraphernalia. Mantle had been as near a god as ever rose to life in the state. And no one could say for sure, but Oklahoma might have had the next Mantle in Ron Williamson, big wheel in student government, the star athlete who dated the prettiest girl in town, the one who would go on to be Miss Ada and then Mrs. Ron Williamson. The Oakland A's drafted him in the second round of the 1971 amateur draft; he was picked forty-first in the nation, among 569 high school ballplayers.

Six years later, he came home, a broken man with a broken heart and a broken mind. His arm wore out faster than the patience of the teams he played for, even with his strange habit of calling the front office to complain that a coach or manager had not been giving him adequate playing time. His marriage had crumbled over the years. So had his sanity. Still, he held enough jock charisma, and natural charm, to become a top salesman for Aetna Insurance. But he was too ill for that to last.

He drank too much and consumed fists of Quaaludes. He lost job after job. He was accused twice of rape in Tulsa but was cleared. He moved back home to his parents' house in Ada, and slept twenty hours a day. In the evenings, he would prowl the bars. If it was dark out, he would sleep only on the living room couch, afraid of his boyhood bedroom.

Women feared him. He was big and frequently crude in his approaches. One woman reported that he turned up at her home, unannounced, and demanded sex, and hit her when she refused. She was too afraid to make a police complaint, she said. He was in and out of mental hospitals, alcohol rehab, drug programs. He passed bad checks. Then he took up the guitar, strumming it just about everywhere he went, a new fixation, and through it, he met Dennis Fritz, another lonely man. Ron had been playing outside Love's Store in Ada one evening when Dennis stopped in for coffee. They got to chatting about the guitar, which Fritz also liked to play. Soon, they were a matched set. Where Ron Williamson was a big, blowsy guy, Fritz was trim, short, sensible, and responsible. He taught science and coached at a junior high school. He, too, was on his own.

Dennis Fritz had been married, but in 1975 his first wife had been murdered by a neighbor, who shot her in the back of the head. They had a lovely daughter, Elizabeth, who stayed with her grandmother during the school week while Fritz lived in a trailer near the high school. As small as Ada was, his only social life revolved around the town. He knew few people, and Ron Williamson, the old high school baseball hero, seemed to know everyone. And since Dennis had a car, he served as Ron's wheels. They took trips together, to Tulsa, to Houston, seeking out women in bars, playing their guitars. Inevitably, Ron's eccentricities wore thin on Dennis. By the time Debbie Carter was murdered, the two men had not been out together for an evening for several months.

The Williamson home was about a block from the apartment where Debra died and was even closer for someone traveling by the back alley. When the police came to Williamson's home in March 1983, he said he did not recognize a picture of Debra Carter. He provided hair and saliva samples. His mother, who kept a diary of Ron's wanderings, reported that he had been home by 10:00 P.M. the night of the murder. Williamson took polygraph tests and angrily denied having anything to do with Debra Carter or her murder. Neither the denials nor his alibi impressed the police.

For one thing, Williamson's reputation for vulgar conduct and bad temper with women followed him like a tail of tin cans. Given his pattern of behavior, no doubt due to the torments of his mental illness, it hardly would be a surprise if a hoped-for sexual conquest went awry and turned into a raging murder. Secondly, the Ada Police, working with the Oklahoma State Bureau of Investigation, really didn't know where else to look.

And naturally, when the police investigating the Carter murder targeted Ron Williamson, they also looked closely at the man who seemed to be his only friend, Dennis Fritz.

Fritz was questioned by the police, and told them he had not been in the Coach Light for two or three months before the killing, had never been there with Ron Williamson, and knew nothing about Debra Sue Carter or the murder. In the course of the investigation, law enforcement authorities in Pontotoc County found out that Fritz had a conviction for cultivation of marijuana. This information was relayed to the school, along with the suggestion that the teacher might not have disclosed this conviction when he was hired, plus the news that Fritz was under investigation for rape and murder. Fritz was fired at once. He moved to Kansas City with his mother, worked in construction, then found jobs in Oklahoma to be near his daughter. A year after the murder of Debra Sue Carter, his firing as a science teacher was the only tangible result of the investigation.

The pace would not accelerate in 1984, either. Ron Williamson would spend part of the year in jail for passing bad checks, but he was found not competent to stand trial and ended up in a psychiatric ward. The hairs from the crime scene sat for months in a state laboratory. One examiner had dropped the Carter murder case, saying she was under too much strain from other inquiries. Not until December 1985, three years after the murder, did the state finish its first report on the hair examination. A trained hair man named Melvin Hett concluded that thirteen hairs found around the victim's body appeared to have come from the head and pubis of Dennis Fritz. Another four hairs from the murder scene were linked to Ron Williamson. By itself, though, the hair report was not strong enough to prove capital murder.

Three months later, the police and prosecutor found what they desperately needed: a new witness. Her name was Terri Holland.

Terri Holland kited bad checks, she used drugs, she was a scam artist, and she was a guest in the Pontotoc County jail from September 1984 until January 1985. This turned out to be one of the more remarkable four-month jail stays in the history of Oklahoma.

While she was locked up, she claimed to have heard a prisoner named Karl Fontenot confess to the murder of a young woman—Denice Haraway—who had disappeared without a trace. Everyone claimed there was no deal for Holland's testimony against Fontenot. Still, when she went to court on her own case—bad checks, at a felony level—she was given a sentence that amounted to no more than eleven months incarceration, despite having two prior felony convictions. Karl Fontenot went to death row. Terri Holland went home.

By February 1986, she had passed more bad checks and had moved to New Mexico. Normally, police from a little town in Oklahoma would hardly have the time or the resources to chase a check kiter all the way to another state. Apparently, though, the law in Pontotoc County badly wanted Terri Holland back, so detectives hunted her down.

Once again faced with jail time, Holland had some wonderful news for the detectives, who happened to be the same ones investigating the murder of Debra Carter. A year earlier, while she was locked up in the county jail, not only had she heard Karl Fontenot's confession to the murder of Denice Haraway, but she heard Ron Williamson talking about how and why he murdered Debra Carter. She had neglected to mention this confession because she thought everyone else already knew about it.

During her four-month bit in the county jail, then, Terri Holland had solved the two most heinous murders in the modern history of Ada, Oklahoma, by taking confessions from two complete strangers. As for her new check-kiting case, the district attorney's office proceeded with care. As long as she made restitution, all the charges would be dropped.

Even with the tale told by Holland, no immediate arrest was made of Williamson. There was one big roadblock: None of the fingerprints at the scene matched Fritz or Williamson. Most important, a partial print of a bloody palm had been found on a piece of particle board—and this belonged to neither of the suspects, nor to the victim, whose fingerprints and handprints were taken at the morgue. No matter how strongly the police suspected Williamson and Fritz, they could not ignore the print on the particle board. So by the fourth anniversary of the murder in December 1986, no charges had been filed against anyone.

In early 1987, a book was published that hit the little town of Ada like a cruise missile. *The Dreams of Ada* dealt with the convictions of two men who had been sent to death row based on "dream confessions," in which they told police they had dreamed about the murder of Denice Haraway while sleeping. They were indicted, tried, and sentenced to die before Denice Haraway's body was found. When her remains were found, virtually every detail in their confessions turned out to be wrong. At the trial, Terri Holland had provided important corroborating evidence by claiming that one of these men, Karl Fontenot, had confessed to her while in jail.

The book, by journalist Robert Mayer, threw a ghastly spotlight on the state of justice in Ada, and within a few weeks of its publication, people were lining up to buy it. The book reminded people about the unsolved murder of Debra Carter. In this climate, District Attorney Bill Peterson roared into action. All that stood between Ron Williamson and a capital murder charge was that unidentified palm print on the particle board in Debbie Carter's bedroom. Any defense attorney would simply point to that and say to let Ron Williamson go free, because that's the killer's handprint.

On May 1, 1987, Debbie Carter's body was exhumed, with permission from her father, Charlie. Her hands had been well preserved, and agents from the Oklahoma State Bureau of Investigation were able to retrieve a full palm print. Apparently, the one taken at her autopsy in December 1982 did not capture part of the heel of her hand. Now they had a full print. The mystery was solved: that print on the wallboard was the heel of Debbie Carter's hand, obviously left there during the struggle for her life. The two chief suspects would not be able to hide behind the palm print by claiming it belonged to the killer.

One week later, Dennis Fritz was in Kansas City to do a paint job on his mother's house. Late in the evening, when everyone else was asleep, the phone rang.

"Hello," said a woman. "Is Dennis Fritz there?"

"Yes," said Fritz.

"Is this Dennis Fritz?" she asked.

"Yes, it is," he said.

The phone clicked off. A few minutes later, the Kansas City Police Department SWAT team appeared on his lawn to arrest him for the murder of Debra Sue Carter. He had not heard about the case for nearly five years and had long since assumed that the police were not interested in him. But two Ada detectives, Gary Rogers and Dennis Smith, had flown to Kansas City to assure him that he had not been forgotten. Later, they would question him.

"We know you didn't kill Debbie Carter," said Smith, "but we think you were there and know who committed the crime."

"If you know I didn't kill her, why are you charging me with first-degree murder?" asked Fritz.

"Because you know something about who did," said Smith.

"No, I don't," replied Fritz.

He never budged from that position in the months that followed. And on April 8, 1988, Dennis Fritz went on trial for the murder of Debra Sue Carter, five years and five months earlier.

As the prosecutors went through their opening statement, Dennis Fritz listened glumly. The case against him had come close to collapsing not long after his arrest, when the state was forced to present enough evidence at a hearing to show "probable cause" that Fritz had been part of the rape and murder. The problem was that it barely existed. The hair evidence could not, by itself, do the job—even judges and lawyers know that hair comparisons are not the equal of fingerprint matches.

In the front of the courtroom, District Attorney Peterson was going over the evidence and the witnesses who would be testifying—some of whom were the very people who had salvaged the case against Fritz at the last moment.

"Mike Tenney was a jailer at the Pontotoc County jail," Peterson told the jurors.

Dennis knew the name well. He would not be sitting in this courtroom if it had not been for the mysterious man who suddenly started working in the jail when Dennis was brought there from Kansas City. Tenney visited him in his cell like a long-lost brother, always egging him on about the murder and saying that he might get executed if he didn't help the police.

Now the D.A. was announcing that Mike Tenney had carried evidence out of that jail cell. Tenney and the prosecutor would claim that Fritz had drawn up a scenario about the murder that acknowledged but minimized his role. Peterson told the jurors: "On the second conversation that they had, [Dennis] asked Mike Tenney, he said, what if it happened like this: He said maybe Ron Williamson went to the door, broke in. Then he said, maybe he went ahead and got a little. Ron got carried away and was going to teach her a lesson, and she died. Say it just happened that way, but I didn't see Ron Williamson kill her."

In an odd twist, Mike Tenney had been sent to the jail before he ever appeared on the county payroll, and he did not get an actual job until months later, after he testified against Fritz. Much of the case was like this: constructed not on evidence from the crime scene, but from statements supposedly made afterward, in jail cells, and retailed by jailhouse snitches.

"The hair and seminal fluids corroborated the [snitch] statements," Peterson would say in 1999.

Sure, the prosecution had physical evidence. But it was technical stuff and when you cut through all the murkiness and hedging—"the characteristics are similar to his hair," or "it's consistent with his blood type"—there wasn't much meat to the scientific testimony. Far better were the stories told by the snitches.

In those stories, Fritz would make remarkably clear, declarative statements that revealed his guilt. As a narrative force in the courtroom, these statements were far superior to the scientific evidence. The building blocks of this prosecution would be stories, told by people like Mike Tenney. And then Peterson called another name to the jury.

"James Harjo," said the district attorney, and at the defense table, Fritz winced. Jimmy Harjo had been a barely literate prisoner in the jail who often passed time with Dennis, asking for help writing letters to his girlfriend. And Harjo also had been pulled out for interviews by detectives, who plainly hoped that he would have some dirt to report on Fritz.

Harjo "started asking Fritz questions about that evidence," said Peterson. "They went through it all, and James will tell you that he looked at Dennis, and he said, " 'Well, it looks like you must be guilty.' "

Dennis knew this was coming. Fritz had known that poor Jimmy Harjo was fishing for him to admit something about the killings. In fact, as a precaution, he started asking Harjo after every encounter to sign papers that said, "Dennis Fritz always says he is innocent."

"Dennis came back to his cell," said Peterson, "sat down for a minute, and tears started rolling down his face, and said, 'We didn't mean to hurt her.' And told James that they had removed the incriminating evidence from her apartment and wiped the prints off and took out the beer cans that they had taken to the apartment with them. He asked James never to tell because he had a daughter to think of."

This drama club theatrics, complete with tears, was ridiculous on its face. The apartment had fingerprints everywhere—or so the detectives said. How could the killers just wipe out their own prints following this life-and-death struggle, but none of Debra Carter's? That it was nonsense didn't matter. The district attorney and an Ada detective had found James Harjo after the preliminary hearing, in prison, ready and willing to help prop up the flimsy case against Dennis Fritz.

The next day, when it came time to testify, though, Harjo nearly missed the point.

"I said, yeah, I'll take a Marlboro," Harjo testified. "And he got up, and he went back in his cell, and he came back, and he sat down and gave me that cigarette. I lit that cigarette up, and it was a Marlboro. We was sitting there, and I looked at him, and you could see tears coming down his eyes, and he said, we didn't mean to hurt her. We didn't mean to hurt her.

"He goes, what do you think my daughter would think of me as a murderer? What do you think my daughter would think of me if I went to prison? And I just didn't know what to say."

James Harjo was a small-time burglar who got caught breaking into the same home twice. He saw Fritz, who had gone to college and was a schoolteacher, as an emissary from another world. The prosecutor gently tried to move Harjo to the subject of the case.

Q: Did he say anything at all about what had happened that night? Did he tell you?

A: He said they was drinking beer, and they was drunk, and they took their beer cans out and wiped everything down.

Q: And did he ever tell you when he said "we" who he was talking about?

A: Be Ron Williamson.

The next witness was far smoother. Mike Tenney, at age thirty-five, was hoping to hook onto a real paying job in law enforcement. He had arrived at the jail as a "trainee" just in time to meet the new man in the cell, Dennis Fritz. The trainee was a fastidious memo writer. Alone among the jailers who spent eleven months with Fritz before the trial, Tenney had collected notes of incriminating statements.

"Okay. It was on August the second," Tenney began. "Mr. Fritz said he needed to talk to me and to come back to his cell when I got the time. And we were talking about him making some kind of deal, and he said, well—"

"Could you speak up just a little bit?"

"Okay. Let's say it happened—it might—let's see, let's say that it might have happened this way. Maybe Ron went to the door and broke into Carter's apartment. And then, let's say I went ahead and got a little. Ron got a little bit carried away and was going to teach her a lesson. She died. Let's say it happened this way. But I didn't see Ron kill Debbie Carter, so how can I tell the D.A. something I really didn't see."

"Was that the end of the conversation?"

"That was the end of the conversation."

This version had slight but consequential differences to the one Tenney had given months earlier. Then, Tenney had said that Fritz was talking about a hypothetical situation in which he would have cut a deal—if he had anything to deal with. And that was just how Fritz described the conversation.

"Mike would come back and talk to me about a deal and the death penalty. And after several, several times, I just told him, I said, look, Mike, I said, if I was guilty and if I had of been up there and Ronnie had broken and went ahead and got a little—I used the word, expression, 'got a little'—and I was there, I told him, do you think that I would be going through all of this and going before a jury that was picked for the death penalty? Don't you think I would try to make some kind of a deal, ten- or fifteen-year-old deal. You know, short of the death-penalty type of thing. . . .

"If Ron Williamson had of been in there, and if I had knowledge of this, I would not hold back that kind of information for anybody for any reason whatsoever."

"At any time, did you ever tell Mike Tenney that you were guilty of this charge?" asked the defense attorney.

"No sir, I never told Mike that. I always told Mike Tenney I was innocent."

One of the slight surprises at the trial was the behavior of a witness who had spoken to the detectives on the night after the murder. Glen Gore, a deejay and bartender himself at another club, had told the detectives at the beginning that Debbie was being pestered by a guy in the club, and to get away from him, she had hailed him down.

"Glen, save me—this guy's bothering me," she said, according to Gore.

That pestering man, Gore told the cops, was Ron Williamson—Dennis Fritz's sidekick. Gore had been scheduled as the first witness at Fritz's trial. Suddenly, the prosecutor reported that Gore was refusing to take the witness stand, would invoke his Fifth Amendment rights, and didn't care if the judge gave him a contempt citation. By then, Gore was in prison himself, doing forty years for kidnapping and assault on a live-in girlfriend, so the prospect of six months for a contempt charge wasn't likely to faze him.

Eventually, the district attorney prevailed on Gore and he testified. While Gore remembered seeing Ron Williamson at the Coach Light on the night of the murder, he was not able to say that Dennis Fritz had been there. In fact, no witness saw Fritz in the club or ever saw him with Debbie Carter under any circumstance. It made no difference.

After the jury came back with a guilty verdict, the question of penalty—death, or life without parole—had to be decided. The verdict, for Fritz, was life.

Just after it was read, there was a commotion in the courtroom.

DEFENDANT: Ladies and gentlemen of the jury, I would just like to say to you—
THE COURT: Excuse me.
DEFENSE LAWYER SAUNDERS: Dennis, you can't do that.
THE COURT: Mr. Fritz.
THE DEFENDANT: My Lord, Jesus in heaven knows that I didn't do this. I just want you to know that I forgive you. I'll be praying for you.

The trial of Ron Williamson was far more raucous. He had been on and off the medication for his mental problems. His attorney, Barney Ward, was experienced, but he was trying his first capital case, and he was blind, and he was afraid to be alone with his client. Ron Williamson was out of control, and he didn't care who knew about it. More than once, Ward tried to quit. "I'm too damned old for it," he said in court. "I don't want anything to do with him, not under any circumstances." He was being paid $3,600 for the entire case, and he bitterly resented every minute consumed by his mad client.

And this time around, Glen Gore adamantly refused to testify. Instead, the judge ordered his previous testimony be read to the jury.

Williamson's defense lawyer had more on his mind, though, than a few indisposed prosecution witnesses. Barney Ward worried that his client could turn on him. "I arranged to have my son sit behind me during the trial with instructions to bring him to the ground if he made any sudden move toward me," he would say later. "On the whole, I found my representation of Mr. Williamson to be an extremely unpleasant experience, and I was glad to get this case over with."

The greatest outrage in the trial, by everyone's standards, came when the remarkable Terri Holland testified. To the lawyers and judge, Ron Williamson behaved disgracefully. For the battered man sitting in the dock, though, the scandal was the stories that this woman was allowed to tell.

Q: Ms. Holland, did you ever hear him describe or talk about any of the details of Debbie Carter's death?

A: He was telling—I guess in the bullpen, the guys back there—that he—he said he shoved a Coke bottle up her ass and her panties down her throat.

At that, Williamson shouted from the defense table. "You are lying. I ain't never said nothing like that in my life. I did not kill this girl, and I call you a liar."

MR. WARD: Be still.

THE DEFENDANT: I don't even know what you're—I mean, you're going to pay for that.

The prosecutor let those chilling words settle on the courtroom, then he continued. He had to fix a slight problem with Terri Holland's testimony.

The victim had been violated with a ketchup bottle, not a Coke bottle; also, she had been gagged with a washcloth, not her panties. The assistant district attorney did quick repairs.

Q: Ms. Holland, let me ask you about the details you were just relating. As far as your memory goes, are you sure about the objects that he stated that he used. You said "Coke bottle."

With that, Williamson's lawyer jumped up. He knew that the prosecutor was trying to undo the damage of wrong details being provided by the snitch. He objected. Before the judge could rule, though, Holland realized her mistake and spoke. "He said a Coke bottle or ketchup bottle or bottle—"

Attorney Ward was disgusted, but there was nothing he could do. The prosecutor went on with her examination.

Q: Did he ever tell why—you said that he killed—
A: He wanted to sleep with Debbie Carter.

"You're a liar," Williamson yelled.
"Shut up," said Ward.
"She's a liar. I ain't going to sit for it. I didn't kill Debbie Carter, and you are lying."
"Ronnie, come on, sit down," said Ward.
The commotion lasted for another few seconds.

Q: Ms. Holland, can you recall if he ever said why he did what he did?
A: Because she wouldn't sleep with him.

"You're lying, damn it, tell the truth," howled Williamson. "I never killed nobody in my life."
The judge called a recess, and from then on, Williamson spoke only when he testified, denying every last word of the charges. And when the jury read out the death verdict, Ronald Keith Williamson never said a word.

Actual innocence

Debra Carter had been dead nearly six years, and at last, the town of Ada had some justice. Two men were paying.

———

At age thirteen, Elizabeth Fritz was banned from seeing her father in prison. The person issuing the ban was her father, Dennis. "She should not experience this," Fritz told his mother. The visiting room was often a scene of desperate intimacies, including sexual liaisons, and the atmosphere was far too degrading for a child. By mail and by phone, Elizabeth strongly supported his innocence, and since he never gave up hope that one day he would be vindicated, he adopted the no-visit policy. Elizabeth agreed.

To others, he said: "I do not want to become institutionalized."

———

Death row in Oklahoma is part of the Oklahoma State Prison H-Unit in McAllister. That unit is entirely made of cement. The cells have no windows. Two cement slabs protrude from the wall for mattresses. Nothing may be hung on the wall. Cement shelves are provided for personal items. The inmates are locked down twenty-three hours a day, and brought into a "yard"—actually, another room, with openings in the wall twenty feet up—for an hour a day. Only four or five inmates can fit in the yard at any time, but because of Ron Williamson's disintegrating sanity, he went alone. His fragile state made him the object of sport for a few of the more sadistic guards.

"Ron," came their taunting voices on the intercom. "This is Debbie Carter. Why did you kill me?"

"I did not kill Debbie Carter," Ron would scream from his cell for hours on end. "I did not kill Debbie Carter. I am an innocent man."

During the investigation into Carter's death, an alcoholic drug addict named Ricky Simmons walked into the Ada Police Station and said he had information about the murder. "I killed her," said Simmons. He was insane, addled with drugs, and knew no details of the murder. On death row, Williamson wasn't too fussy. "Ricky Jeff Simmons confessed to the murder of Debra Carter," Williamson would bellow. "I am an innocent man."

The cases of Fritz and Williamson were appealed through the state courts in Oklahoma. In August 1994, Williamson's final appeal was denied. One morning, a prison guard tapped on Williamson's cell and told him he was going to the warden's office. Because of his erratic behavior, he was escorted by two or three guards. Inside the office, the warden sat at the head of a long table. Williamson was told to sit at the other end.

The warden said he had a duty to carry out. The corrections officers stood on either side of Williamson, his hair now stringy, his face a gaunt skeletal mask with pasty white skin stretched across it.

"You have been sentenced to execution by lethal injection and such sentence will be carried out at twelve-thirty A.M., the twenty-fourth of September, 1994."

The prison had received no stay of execution. He would be moved to the holding area near the death chamber and was asked to provide a list of five people who would be allowed to visit. His sister, Annette Hudson, would be sent a form, asking what the funeral home should do with his body.

Ron Williamson had always had his own cell. But now he was moved into a disciplinary cell, which was double locked, with two doors. Not that he had suddenly become harder to handle; the disciplinary cell was slightly more soundproof, and it muffled the screams that Williamson now hurled at the world almost twenty-four hours a day. In Oklahoma, the execution date normally is set sixty days after the last appeal has been denied, and the warden formally notifies the prisoner thirty days beforehand. By some quirk, though, the Williamson date was set thirty days after the appeal, and so the warden immediately had Ron brought to his office to be read the death warrant. Because of the quick date, Janet Chesley, his appellate attorney, was caught short and did not have a chance to visit him in prison and warn him about the sentence.

Also, she wanted to tell him that there was one more chance. She was going to ask a federal judge to issue a writ of habeas corpus, finding that the conviction had been unconstitutional and seriously flawed. By the time she brought this news to him, he was beyond consolation and in a total psychic breakdown. His hair, a salt-and-pepper mix, seemed to turn snow white in a matter of weeks. He was forty-one, and looked twenty-five or thirty years older.

Chesley and others worked around the clock to draw up their brief.

They argued that his trial had been flawed by poor defense work and illegal prosecution tricks. The defense, after all, had not made an issue of Ron's competency to stand trial, even though his medical records showed severe mental illness, as did his behavior during the trial. The prosecution had built its case around his alleged confession to the jailhouse snitch, Terri Holland—but had not revealed a two-hour videotaped statement in which Ron denied the murder and never wavered for an instant. It was a scandalous piece of sharp lawyering by District Attorney Peterson, the defense argued. And no one, during the trial, had gone into the remarkable fact that snitch Terri Holland was working off her bad checks for the second time by implicating an inmate in a murder confession. The hair evidence was too unreliable, lacked scientific grounding, and could not be used as the basis of an execution.

On September 17, Ron was moved to a special holding cell for condemned prisoners with less than a week to live. Two days later, the federal court for the eastern district of Oklahoma issued a stay of execution so it could consider the arguments raised by Williamson's attorney. Five days before the date of his scheduled death, Ron Williamson was moved back into the "regular" death row cells. His wailing did not stop. One year later, to the day, U.S. District Court judge Frank H. Seay signed an order issuing a writ of habeas corpus, saying that the state should grant him a new trial or cut him loose. Williamson plainly was mentally ill; both the prosecution and defense clearly had failed in their duties to see that he had been competent for trial. The hair evidence was patently unreliable. The state had not turned over the two-hour videotape of Ron denying anything to do with the murder. And, the judge said, the snitch testimony bothered him.

"Another troubling aspect of this case concerns the motivation of one of the State's most important witnesses, Terri Holland," wrote Judge Seay. "Holland's testimony provided the only evidence of straightforward admissions of guilt by [Williamson]."

A federal appeals court agreed that Ron Williamson should have a new trial. His new attorney was Mark Barrett of the Oklahoma Indigent Defense System. Barrett moved to have Williamson declared incompetent and sent to a psychiatric facility. Williamson objected, but the attorney prevailed. In the psychiatric hospital, a dentist noticed a growth on the roof of his mouth and sent him for tests. A cancerous growth was removed. He climbed back toward mental health.

Disappeared into the prison system, Dennis Fritz had no contact with Ron Williamson. He had neither law nor lawyers on his side. The state courts ruled that he received a fair trial, that a jury had heard the lab people talk about his blood type, the hair experts about his hair, the snitches about his confession, and him talking about his own innocence. There were no procedural flaws. The jury's verdict was sovereign. The appeals court put the case and life of Dennis Fritz into dead storage.

He hit the prison library and became his own lawyer.

Please test my DNA and the DNA from the crime scene, he asked one state court after another.

Your case is no longer before the court and since we don't have jurisdiction, we don't have the authority to order the district attorney of Pontotoc County to do anything about a DNA test. Or so a judge ruled in two or three seconds flat.

Fritz went to federal court, the refuge of prisoners who believe a state has gone deaf to American justice.

You have not yet exhausted your appeals in the state courts of Oklahoma, the federal court ruled.

If Dennis Fritz learned anything in prison or in life, it was how to take a punch. Starting with the jury verdict, he had lost about seven consecutive court decisions. Nothing about death row can be counted as an advantage, but at least Ron Williamson had access to capable and dogged legal help in his appeal. Dennis, as a life-term prisoner, had no right to counsel in his quest for DNA tests. Nor could he have the tests done.

Around that time, Williamson's attorney, Janet Chesley, suggested that Dennis write to the Innocence Project in New York. Not long after that, she won the new trial for Williamson. It was 1995, and DNA tests were the gold standard in every courtroom in the country. The prosecution would have to do the tests for the new Williamson trial. Those results might help Fritz, too.

Now Ron's new attorney, Mark Barrett, teamed up with Fritz's new lawyer, Barry, and students from his Innocence Project. They started negotiations for new DNA tests on the old evidence. The district attorney took the position that the DNA of Dennis Fritz would not be tested against the old evidence. Fritz was not the one getting a new trial, Williamson was. Fritz didn't have a right to the tests.

Barry was prepared for this argument, because he had heard it before, and not only in Oklahoma. In most states, prisoners had no legal rights to DNA tests. Within a few weeks or months after their convictions, the case is considered closed. These policies flew in the face of common sense and fairness—after all, a guilty prisoner would get no benefit from the advanced tests, and an innocent one would merely be reaching for justice—but the laws were ironclad. In most localities, he and Peter had gotten around the laws by schmoozing, publicity, and cajoling. Often, the prosecutors had no objection.

In time, Barry convinced Peterson that Dennis Fritz should be included in the new tests, whether or not he had the legal right to them.

Mark Barrett, meanwhile, began to prepare for the second trial of Ron Williamson by interviewing the witnesses who had testified for the prosecution. Barry had a piece of advice for him when he was going to visit Glen Gore.

"Bring along a swab," said Barry. "Maybe he'll give you a DNA sample."

———

Glen Gore was waiting when Mark Barrett and his team arrived at the prison in Lexington, Oklahoma, on February 10, 1999. Dressed in the prison-issue blues, his black hair neatly groomed, he cordially greeted his visitors.

"I've been expecting you," said Gore.

"Is that right?" said Barrett. "Why?"

"I saw the deal back in 1985," he said.

"What deal was that?" asked Sara Bonnell.

"What the federal judge said," replied Gore.

He had gotten the year wrong, but he had the right decision and showed excellent judgment about its importance. Judge Frank Seay's 1995 decision granting Ron Williamson a new trial specifically had mentioned Gore. The judge said that Gore had not been investigated thoroughly as a suspect, either by the prosecution or the defense. He was the last person seen with Debbie Carter. A witness told people that Gore had been in the parking lot of the Coach Light arguing with Carter and that he had shoved her into her car. His hair and blood were taken for comparison to the crime scene evidence but were not properly examined by the state. All this, the judge said, were points that a vigorous defense attorney would have brought out.

Most important was Gore's history of violence. Judge Seay noted that he had attacked the woman he lived with and endangered her child. One week after he was named as a witness against Williamson, he had made a plea agreement, and charges of kidnapping, assault, and battery were dropped. The victim's family had written to the state judge who was sentencing Gore on the reduced charges, saying:

"We want you to be aware of how dangerous we feel this man is. He intends to kill our daughter, granddaughter, and ourselves. This he has told us.

"We have gone to great lengths to make our daughter's home burglar-proof, but all failed. To go into detail of all the times he has attacked her would make too lengthy a letter.

"Please give our daughter enough time to get the child raised before he is out of prison and the terror starts again, so the little one never has to live through that again."

They were powerful words, but Barrett and his companions felt no sense of menace on that February day in the visitors' room. Gore joked with them about Bill Peterson, the district attorney, a man he loathed for sending him away for forty years. He recalled how he came to testify against Williamson and Fritz.

"The D.A. told me he'd go after me if I didn't stick it to Ron and Dennis," Gore told the attorneys. He had looked at pictures in a photo lineup but hadn't been able to identify Williamson or Fritz. He wasn't sure that Williamson even had been in the bar that night, despite his testimony.

"Peterson told me, 'If things don't go right, we are coming after you,'" Gore claimed.

Although Peterson has not made himself available to comment on

Gore's account, it should be remembered that the D.A.'s accuser was, after all, in prison for forty years because of prosecution by Peterson.

"Would you be willing to take a polygraph on this?" asked Barrett.

"Sure, no problem, I'd do that," he said. "I offered to do one for the police, but they never took it."

"How about a saliva sample that could be tested for DNA?" asked Bonnell.

"What for? They already took that," said Gore. "Everybody has to give it in the prison."

"You know that the DNA has been tested for Fritz and Williamson," said Barrett.

"I read about that," said Gore.

"And you know the results came back negative—it wasn't their DNA at the crime scene," said Barrett.

"I read that, too," said Gore. "Do you think they're going to come after me?"

"Do you think your DNA could be on her?"

"It could be," said Gore. "I danced with her that night. Five times."

"Well, the DNA they have from her body wouldn't have gotten there from just dancing," said Barrett. "They have DNA from the semen."

"Oh," said Gore, who seemed surprised. He excused himself and got another inmate, a man named Ruben, who served as a paralegal and jailhouse lawyer. While he was away, Sara Bonnell spoke to a guard, who gave her a Q-Tip and an envelope.

"Glen," said Bonnell. "Would you give us a saliva sample?"

She held out the Q-Tip.

"I did not authorize that," said Gore, annoyed. "I did not agree to that. You went ahead and got that without my consent."

He grabbed the Q-Tip, snapped it in half, and proceeded to clean his ears with it. Then he dropped the two pieces into his pocket.

"You're trying to make him the main suspect," said Ruben, the prisoner paralegal.

"He probably already is," said Barrett. "Did you have sex with her?"

Gore wouldn't say. Barrett leaned over.

"Are you saying you've never had sex with her?" asked Barrett.

"I'm not saying that," said Gore.

"Even if it was consensual sex, if she went along with it, it would be better to tell now," said Barrett. "Because if you did, that semen is going to match up with your DNA."

"I didn't do it," said Gore. "I can't help you."

With that, he turned and strode out. The lawyers picked up their belongings and left. In the hallway, Gore was pleasant. He wouldn't mind seeing Mark again, but it would be better if it took place at his work site.

"Where's that?" asked Barrett.

Gore explained that he had a day job in the town of Purcell, at the Public Works Department. He made another nasty remark about the district attorney, then left.

Snapping that Q-Tip might postpone the reckoning for Glen Gore, but it couldn't protect him. The state maintained a data bank of DNA collected from all convicted prisoners, and Gore's was in there, somewhere. When plans were being made for tests of the old evidence from the Carter crime scene, Barry suggested a kind of DNA test known as STR.

"That's what is in the state data bank," he explained. "If we get STRs from the crime scene, Gore's STRs already are on file in the data bank."

Barry and Mark Barrett then lobbied Mary Long, the state's DNA expert, to run the DNA from the murder scene through the prison data bank. A few weeks later, the lab report came back. The semen found in Debbie Carter's vagina, her anus, and on her underwear matched with Glen Gore's DNA. There was no trace of Dennis Fritz or Ron Williamson. At the request of District Attorney Peterson, the information was sealed. Before Peterson would agree to let the two men go, the prosecutor wanted the hairs tested.

When Dennis Fritz heard this, he panicked. He told Barry that he understood DNA, having taught science, and knew the possibility of tampering with the semen evidence was virtually nil. But hairs? The detectives had plucked dozens of hairs from his body. As Dennis saw it, if they could send a spy into his jail cell to collect a phony confession, what would stop them from planting a few of his hairs in the crime scene kits?

This was hardly paranoia on Dennis's part, Barry realized. He consulted with experts and put together an intricate, subtle plan that would detect if any of the sample hairs taken from Dennis or Ron had been stuck into the crime evidence.

Before the hairs found in and around Debra Carter's body were tested, each shaft would be "washed" with sound waves that could shake off microscopic bits of dried blood or other biological material. The "washing" would be collected, and it, too, would be DNA tested. Those results would be revealing. If no one had monkeyed with the evidence, then the biological material on the hair washings should include DNA from the victim. After all, they had been collected from under her bloody body and from a rag stuffed in her throat. For instance, if a hair "found" on the rag was linked by DNA to Dennis Fritz, then the biological wash that came off it should have Debra Carter's DNA. If the wash had some other DNA on it, then Barry could make a strong argument that it had been taken from Fritz and planted in the evidence kit. It was an elaborate protocol, and all parties agreed to it. In the end, though, not one of the hairs was linked by DNA to either Fritz or Williamson. Two were tied to Glen Gore.

The road back to the public works yard in the town of Purcell, Oklahoma, takes drivers past little houses where men sell tin cans from their porches. At noon on April 14, 1999, Jim and Alexandra Pelosi of *Dateline NBC* rolled into the yard in a rented car.

"We're looking for Glen Gore," said Jim.

"Glen? He's out brush-hoggin' somewhere," said Ben Hudson, the yard boss.

"Brush-hoggin'?" asked Jim.

"Cuttin' grass along the road somewhere," said Hudson. "He'll be back in about thirty, forty minutes for his dinner."

The reporters bought sandwiches, then came back. Still no Gore. They were led out to a site three or four miles from the yard, where several men were working on a new road, including one who wore a shirt that said INMATE on the back. But there was no sign of Gore.

"He must be back in the yard," said a man named Billy.

"We were just at the yard," Pelosi answered.

Glen Gore, it turned out, had vanished. He had read stories in the *Ada Evening News* about Dennis Fritz and Ron Williamson getting out of jail within twenty-four hours. He also read right through a veiled reference in the story to another unnamed "suspect" implicated by those same DNA tests.

That morning, he had simply walked away from the work site when he heard that two people who looked like lawyers wanted to speak with him.

———

That same afternoon, the lawyers at the Pontotoc County Courthouse in Ada were feeling behind-the-scenes friendly, relaxing and chatting with Bill Peterson. No one had anything to fight over. By agreement, Dennis Leon Fritz and Ronald Keith Williamson would be freed the next morning, twelve years after their arrest for the murder of Debbie Carter.

Peterson's assistant, Chris Ross, was entertaining the visitors from the defense side, including Barry, Mark Barrett, and Sara Bonnell.

Dressed in jeans and a plaid shirt, Ross had a clipped, sarcastic manner that matched his buzz-cut hairdo, along with the impressive beer belly that often besets former athletes. He reminisced with Judge Tom Landrith about Ron and the case. The judge remembered Ron growing up as a star athlete. The judge had also known him as the broken-down mental patient with a drinking problem and had represented him on intoxication charges. This was not unusual; Ada is a very small town.

When Barry asked Ross about the reliability of the jailhouse snitches in light of the DNA, Ross asked, "Do you mean Terri?"

"Yeah," said Barry. "Terri Holland. What about her?"

"Well," Ross said, grinning. "We like to say she has a C-spot."

"A C-spot?"

"Yeah, you know, C-spot. For confessions."

Everyone guffawed. She had taken confessions on the most spectacular murders in Ada's recent history, the killing of Debra Carter in December 1982 and the murder of Denice Haraway in April 1984.

"That's her C-spot working," said Ross.

———

Across the street, in the county jail, Ron Williamson was smoking cigarettes, talking with Dennis Fritz for the first time in twelve years, and chatting with Jim.

"You really do go out of it when you are on death row," said Williamson. "The only way I realized it was Christmas is that they gave us two desserts."

"I have been in Hades, because mine was a lesser-security prison," said Fritz. "Ronnie on death row was in hell."

Fritz had more salt than pepper in his hair, which looked blown dry and pushed back on his head. A neatly trimmed and well-spoken man, he stood about five feet, eight inches, about 150 to 160 pounds.

Williamson was about six feet, one or two inches, a man at once gangly and lumpy, with Stan Laurel hair that had gone to white and sat flat on his head. The traces of the athlete's grace were lost beneath the overgrowth of age, paunch, and worries. Most of his molars had surrendered to hard living and cancer of the mouth. Only his front teeth remained. When he was not speaking, his tongue seemed to be hunting for his missing teeth. He took most of his breaths through his mouth.

Both he and Fritz were dressed in old-fashioned, horizontally striped prison pajamas.

"The stripes are running the right way," said Williamson. "Just the wrong people are in 'em."

They do not joke about Terri Holland. The C-spot gag, had they heard it, would do nothing for them. She had stolen years from their lives, simply because Ron had been in the jail for bad checks with her fourteen years earlier.

"An out-and-out liar," said Williamson. "They put me right across from the girls' bullpen. They never put any of the male prisoners across from the girls' bullpen. She'd ask about the murder case all the time. Then they'd pull her over to the city police department, find out what I said."

———

In the judge's chambers, Barry inquired about the jailhouse "trainee," Mike Tenney, who in his first days on the job managed to hear Dennis Fritz speaking about the case and later gave several renditions of their conversation. The one he volunteered at trial was incriminating. When pressed, he conceded that Fritz always had maintained his innocence.

Even so, Tenney's sudden arrival in the jail was extraordinarily convenient, coming at the very time that the prosecution needed witnesses to buttress the case against Fritz. It so happened that Prosecutor Ross had his worries about Tenney, too.

"I always was suspicious of him," volunteered Ross. "He was so eager he created problems. I had a case where someone was picked up by three officers besides Tenney. We had the guy red-handed. Then Tenney almost screwed up the case by claiming the defendant blurted out a confession as he was being arrested. No one else there heard the confession."

––––––

Just before supper time, Mark Barrett and Barry learned that Glen Gore had escaped from his work-release assignment. They visited the jail and passed the word to the two men.

"He ran?" said Fritz. He could not believe it. Here he was, known as innocent for months, living in a high-security prison while the man who was implicated in the murders was free to walk away from a sweetheart job on a road crew.

Fritz broke into a broad grin. Williamson fell over, cackling.

"He's showing his guilt right there," said Fritz.

"If he wasn't guilty, he wouldn't run," said Williamson, simply.

Gore surrendered a week later. Described by D.A. Peterson as the "prime suspect" in the killing of Debra Carter, he had not been charged with the murder as of early October 1999. However, he was no longer permitted off the grounds of the prison.

The following morning, the two men dressed for court and were walked separately across the lawn in handcuffs. All the local TV and radio stations followed them as first Fritz, then Williamson, were escorted into the building.

Strangely, Dennis Fritz knew his daughter perhaps better than most fathers, having had nearly daily contact with her by phone and mail. Of course, he had not seen her for twelve years. But he knew about her schooling, and her friends, and her career as a manager for one of the leading telecommunication companies in the world. He could read her mood by one note in her voice.

For all he knew, though, nothing could prepare him for the vision that awaited him when he stepped into the courtroom on that spring morning. Elizabeth Fritz was dressed elegantly, a beautiful young woman with brown hair and a smile like a sunrise. His knees shook. His daughter. Shakespeare had written a sonnet:

> *Thou are thy mother's glass and she in thee*
> *Calls back the lovely April of her prime.*

He looked at her, then sat so his knees would stop shaking.

Later, at the press conference, Dennis was eloquent in his thanks to the people who had helped him. "My daughter has made my life whole, has kept me a whole person," he said.

The questions then turned to Ron.

"How do you feel, Mr. Williamson?"

Ron paused. Time had collapsed on death row. He had counted the seconds. A week had lasted an entire year.

"How do you feel, Mr. Williamson?" he was asked again.

"About what?" replied Ron.

———

Because of tales told by jailhouse snitches, Ron Williamson was nearly murdered by the state of Oklahoma and Dennis Fritz was imprisoned for twelve years. So were thirteen other men ultimately freed through DNA exonerations, some 21 percent of the Innocence Project cases. In no instance did the snitch admit to making up stories.

Under recent federal sentencing guidelines that make "cooperation" the only passport out of long, mandatory-minimum prison terms, snitch culture has been chiseled into the life of the American federal courts. That seems an odd response at the same time that dozens of men like Ron Williamson and Dennis Fritz are being freed from long sentences or death row.

In Canada, the country was shaken by a single, spectacular wrongful conviction case based on phony snitch testimony. Guy Paul Morin, twenty-three, was accused of [...] [mur]dering and sexually assaulting his next-door neighbor in 1983. The [...] evidence came from two jailhouse informants. When his con[...] [...]rned in January 1995 because he was proven innocent [...] [...]on reviewed the case and laid down new rules f[...] [...] [n]ow, before a snitch can testify, a high-level [...] [...]ust satisfy themselves that the tale can be c[...] [...] [oth]er inmates. The committee also must determine w[...] [...] [T]erri Holland, is a recidivist. In court, the testimony is pr[...] [...]ble, and the prosecutor must show the judge that it is worth hea[...] [...] [...]re it can be presented to the jury. Finally, all deals with the informant must be written, and all conversations either videotaped or audiotaped.

Not an iota of reliable evidence would be blocked if such rules were adopted in the United States. And the Ron Williamsons of the world would not sit outside an execution chamber, watching the days of their lives run down.

Junk Science

On the last day of May in 1991, a fine-looking black Lincoln Continental pulled into the Dallas Gun Club at 8:55 A.M., and young Tim Durham slid out of the driver's seat, popped open the trunk, and hauled out a handsome set of shooting hardware: a .410 rifle, a .28, and a well-worn ammunition pouch. By the time his father, Jim, managed to lift himself out of the passenger seat, Tim already had carefully piled the gear on the ground. Watching from the door of the club with no small amount of relief was James Little, who had been fretting over the Durhams' arrival for the start of the Pan American Skeet Shooting Competition.

"Jim!" hollered Little. "I thought you'd never get here."

"I apologize for being late," said Durham. "We ran into traffic."

Strictly speaking, that wasn't true. Tim had slept in that morning while his parents were visiting with their hosts in Dallas, and everyone had lost track of the time. James Durham was glad to have Tim along. At age seventy-four, he was still an avid shooter, but every year it seemed that the guns weighed just a few more ounces, and the trunk of the car seemed another few inches deeper. Tim came to the skeet shoots not only to tote his father's stuff but also to referee. Tim was a short man, just five feet, four inches tall, but he was broad in the chest and shoulders. He had the early workings of a red beard, and that morning, a few people would remark on Tim's new growth.

For the Durham family, skeet shooting was the hub of their social life. Many of their friends were shooters, and their calendar was blocked around skeet tournaments. To make this event, the Durhams had driven nearly five hours the day before from Tulsa, Oklahoma, to Dallas, staying with old family friends, Jess and Jean Spoontz. Everyone had gone to dinner the night before at a branch of the Olive Garden restaurant chain, and the Spoontzes' daughters would be dropping by later that day to catch up with Tim and his parents. There would also be a small celebration for Tim, as he was turning twenty-nine the next day.

The morning shoot ended shortly after 10:00. James Durham gave Tim his gun and ammo bag, his protective eyeglasses and ear plugs, and said they would meet inside the club. It was a warm morning, and he wanted a cold drink. Inside, though, James Durham met other people in the skeet game, and as a leader in his district, he had to sort through some squad problems before he got to his beverage. Tim joined his father in the discussion, and then they headed back to the Spoontz house to have a bite of lunch before the afternoon shoot.

As the men arrived home, Jean Spoontz and Eleanor Durham were heading out to treat themselves to facials. Tim was hungry, and Jean suggested that he heat up the leftovers they had brought home from the Olive Garden the night before. She showed him their microwave, then dashed out with Mrs. Durham for their appointment. At noon, the door opened. It was Cynthia Spoontz, a daughter, who worked a few minutes away, popping in to say hi to Tim and have a bite.

"I heard there was some spaghetti and garlic bread for lunch," she said.

"Well," he said, pointing to his now-empty plate, "there's some garlic bread."

Cynthia ribbed him about scarfing down the food, and they laughed. Later in the day, the Spoontz family, their husbands, and the Durhams all relaxed in the hot tub.

That same morning, many miles away, another girl had dressed for her family's swimming pool. It was the last day of school for Molly M., and her mom had dropped her off at home after they picked up report cards. Molly was a very sensible girl for an eleven-year-old, and she would be fine in the family's big home in a safe, very wealthy neighborhood in Tulsa.

Around 10:30, a man came to the front door, and Molly told him to go around to the back. The front door had been chained from the inside, and she didn't have the key to open it.

She opened the door and saw a short man, dressed casually. He was there to do yard work, he said. Well, her mom and dad weren't home, explained Molly. Did she know the time, the man asked. Molly turned to look at the clock, and then he was in the door and pouncing. In the next few minutes, she would absorb as many details as she could. He was a red-headed, pock-marked pedophile who carried her to the basement and assaulted her. Finally, he left, and at 11:10, she called 911. Upset, she was still able to give her parents and the police a complete description of the red-haired man. He was around her mom's height.

The outrage of a crime against an innocent child, inside her own home, in a fine neighborhood would qualify as news in any town. The Tulsa newspaper and TV stations played the story big, and the failure to solve the crime remained an open wound. The case stymied police. About ten weeks into it, a Tulsa detective got a tip at his own kitchen table. His wife worked in the probation department and said she knew a short, red-headed man who fit the description. This man had been involved with drugs and alcohol, and had a record of petty crimes. His father was a rich businessman who owned an electronics store, Radio Inc. The son was on probation. His name was Timothy Durham.

Molly M. looked at his picture in a photo lineup but wasn't sure. They brought her back another time. Looked like him, she said, and she initialed the back of the picture.

In January 1992, Tim Durham, now going to school in Utah and off drugs and drink, was arrested by the Tulsa police and brought home to face charges in the rape of Molly M., seven months earlier.

That he had a formidable alibi—at least eleven witnesses could put him in Dallas, more than three hundred miles away, around the time of the attack on Molly—was a tripping hazard that the prosecution could step over, and neatly.

No matter what those witnesses said, the district attorney's office said, it had evidence that would prove Timothy Durham had raped Molly M. And unlike the alibi witnesses, who were just a bunch of Durham friends and older people who really had no idea where they had been on a particular morning, months earlier, the D.A.'s evidence would come from forensic laboratories and would qualify by the customs of the courthouse as "scientific."

Hair first was used as evidence in a courtroom in Berlin in 1861. Two decades later, an expert testified in a Wisconsin criminal trial that he had examined a hair from a crime scene and found that it matched one taken from a suspect. When the Wisconsin Supreme Court was asked to review the case in 1882, it warned that "such evidence is of a most dangerous character" and reversed the conviction. That was a minor setback for the hair experts. They got microscopes, marched into courts in every state, and said they could see the truth on their slides. They emerged during the age of invention, when humankind's appetite for marvels was satisfied more through the secular channels of science and technology than through the mystic forces of religion and ritual. Sherlock Holmes was a hero. Hair experts found clues in the fragments of life shed by everyone and ignored by most. They could see the invisible but still speak like scientists.

The hair people rode into courts on the shoulders of the fingerprint men, who persuaded courts in Britain and the United States that fingerprints were unique, based on patterns of fine ridge details, combined with loops, arches, and whorls. At the time, the declaration that these make one-of-a-kind blends for each human was a guess, and a good one, as shown by a century of experience and millions of individual fingerprints in a national data bank. Not so for hair analysis.

Under a microscope, an individual shaft of hair appears two inches wide. With this perspective, the examiner identifies the hairs as coming from one of three racial groups—Caucasian, Mongoloid, or Negroid—and from a body region—scalp, pubic, or limbs.

In theory, that is the start of an arduous comparison of crime-scene hairs—the "unknowns"—with "known" hair samples plucked from the victim and the suspect. If enough characteristics are the same in two hairs, examiners will say they "look alike" or are "consistent" or "similar." Hair examiners tell about hundreds of hours examining individual hairs, a job of such exactitude that previously it was reserved in the Bible for the divinity. ("But the very hairs of your head are all numbered," Matthew 10:30.) In fact, hair experts as a group were neither godlike nor particularly scientific.

The weakness of the field is well established. For instance, hairs pulled from the same head might not match one another. The hair examiners cannot agree on criteria for comparisons. Some people have "featureless" hair that is hard to distinguish. With all the uncertainty about matching criteria, no one has been able to set up data banks for hairs, like the ones for fingerprints. That's also why no one can plausibly claim to know if the characteristics of a particular hair are rare, common, or somewhere in between.

In the early 1970s, the U.S. Law Enforcement Assistance Administration (LEAA) sponsored a proficiency testing program for 240 laboratories that provided evidence in criminal cases. The labs botched many kinds of tests: paint, glass, rubber, fibers. But by far, the worst results came from hair analysis.

Out of ninety responses for the hair survey, the proportion of labs submitting "unacceptable" responses on a given sample—either by failing to make a match, or making a false match—ranged from 27.6 to 67.8 percent.

On five different samples, the error rates were 50.0 percent, 27.6 percent, 54.4 percent, 67.8 percent, and 55.6 percent. In short, there was little difference between flipping a coin and getting a hair analyst to provide reliable results. The hallmark of the scientific process is that results are reproducible; given the same tests, with the same materials, and the same procedures, two labs should come up with identical results. LEAA found that not even the mistakes were consistent. Perhaps most revealing is that these were open tests. That meant the lab directors knew ahead of time that they were being tested, like the chef in a restaurant who knows that an influential food critic has reservations for that evening. A far more rigorous gauge would have replicated real-life conditions by having the samples submitted blindly, slipped into the laboratory as if they were just evidence from another case.

If DNA technology is at one end of the spectrum—having been tested and proved, not only in crime scenes, but in laboratories and in clinical medicine—then hair evidence is on the other end. And hair is only one of the forensic sciences with shaky underpinnings. Some could have come right out of a carnival sideshow.

In Florida, Juan Ramos was sentenced to the electric chair for a murder—based in large part on evidence from a Pennsylvania dog handler who swore that his German shepherd could pick up scents months and years after a crime. According to the dog, Ramos's scent was on both the victim's blouse and the murder weapon, which the dog had sniffed five days after the fact. A judge later asked that the dog be tested on other evidence that was five days old. The dog flunked. Ramos's conviction was overturned, and he was acquitted at a new trial. Other cases built on testimony from the superdog with superschnoz were overturned in Virginia, Ohio, and Arizona.

From Mississippi came Michael West, a forensic dentist and inventor of the West Phenomena. With a pair of yellow goggles and carrying a blue laser light, West claimed to be able to visualize tooth marks, cuts, and scrapes on the skin of crime victims that no one else could see. Asked what his margin of error was, West replied: "Something less than my savior, Jesus Christ."

His first application of the blue light came in 1990, during the investigation of the stabbing deaths of three elderly people in central Mississippi. Two weeks after the crimes were committed, West examined the hand of the prime suspect. With his light, he claimed to see indentations in the suspect's palm that matched exactly with three exposed rivets on the knife used as the murder weapon. He took photographs, he later testified, but they were overexposed. No one has ever been able to duplicate West's work. The suspect was freed after two years in jail, when a judge ruled that the West Phenomenon was not admissible evidence.

In another case, West said that thanks to his blue light, he could match a man's teeth to bite marks found on the skin of an elderly rape and robbery victim. He declared a perfect match, using his signature phrase: "indeed and without doubt." But DNA tests of the attacker's skin, taken from fingernail scrapings of the victim, excluded the man whom West had implicated, indeed and without doubt. His repeated use of that phrase offended even professional forensic societies that have tolerated their share of phony or dubious scientists. West was suspended for one year from an association of forensic dentists, and he resigned from the American Academy of Forensic Scientists when an ethics committee voted to expel him.

How could such junk science prevail in matters of life and death? Often, the horror of a violent crime will open the door to uncritical acceptance of "novel" techniques that produce no reliable evidence. When these techniques are brought into court, typically as evidence against poor defendants, the defense simply does not have the resources or expertise to mount a difficult challenge.

More important, the legal standard for scientific evidence, the "Frye Rule," created a witless echo chamber: If one court allowed hair evidence, a second court would not make an independent judgment on its admissibility. And if one hair expert testified that he or she had followed the techniques practiced by other hair experts, then that usually was good enough for the courts. Indeed, deafened by the reverberations of previous Frye rulings, the courts would simply ignore new data, like the LEAA proficiency tests that showed hair experts should not be trusted.

Not until 1993 did the U.S. Supreme Court take steps to block junk science. In *Daubert v. Merrell Dow Pharmaceuticals,* the High Court said that federal judges would have to serve as gatekeepers for evidence that purported to be scientific. Fundamental questions about reliability, the Court said, must be asked: Has the expert's test been replicated? Is there an error rate? Have the methods been published in peer-reviewed journals? "Scientific methodology today is based on generating hypotheses and testing them to see if they can be falsified; indeed, this methodology is what distinguishes science from other fields of human inquiry," the Court said in its decision.

————

In 1995, U.S. Judge Frank Seay's decision to free Ron Williamson of Ada, Oklahoma, rested heavily on the unreliability of hair evidence. Applying the standard from the *Daubert* case, he wrote, hair evidence shouldn't be used in court. "As with eyewitness identifications, erroneous conclusions can increase when the examiner is told which hair sample is from the suspect in the crime," he noted. His decision to grant Williamson a new trial was upheld by the 10th Circuit Court of Appeals, although the appellate judges balked at his ban on hair evidence. Instead, they relied on another of his findings to overturn the conviction, namely that Williamson had not been effectively assisted by his trial lawyer.

Vindication for Judge Seay's view of hair evidence would not be long in coming. In 1999, new technology, mitochondrial DNA tests, proved that the hair experts in the Williamson case were even worse than anyone suspected. The tests were performed on the seventeen hairs that had been taken from the crime scene and "matched," in the terms used by the district attorney, to Williamson and his codefendant, Dennis Fritz. The results? All seventeen were misidentified. Not one originated with Fritz or Williamson. The error rate was a perfect 100 percent. In fact, a pubic hair identified as Fritz's actually turned out to be from the victim, Debra Carter. Not only were the prosecution "experts" from the Oklahoma State Bureau of Investigation dead wrong. Even the analysts hired by the Fritz and Williamson defense couldn't get it straight.

The most stunning error involved Glen Gore, the prosecution "witness" who implicated Williamson. Mitochondrial DNA tests in 1999 linked Gore to two hairs found around the victim's savagely beaten body. Fifteen years earlier, the state hair examiners said they had checked Gore's hair. He was excluded as the source of what appears to be his own hair. The prosecution put him on the witness stand, and he helped send one innocent man to death row and another to prison for life.

After a century of expert testimony about microscopic hair comparisons, DNA tests had exposed the field as lethal nonsense: 29 percent of the wrongful convictions studied by the Innocence Project included evidence from hair analysis.

––––––––––

The Durham family hired one of the top lawyers in Tulsa, but Tim and his attorney did not get along with each other. Little Molly M., now thirteen years old, made a strong witness. She pointed to Tim and said she was now certain that he was the man who had come to her door on the last day of school in 1991. While her sincerity was not in doubt, there was enough uncertainty in her early identifications to throw a shadow on her reliability.

In came Carol Cox, the prosecution's hair examiner.

"I look for very common things that are easily overlooked . . . things that normally people would overlook and leave at the scene," she explained. The proof is in front of our eyes, if only we look. She went through the hairs collected from the daybed, from the carpet, and from a vacuum used at Molly M.'s home. She looked at the hair under her microscope, seeing, she told the jury, a kind of "elongated rope." Her mission was to see if twenty-five characteristics in the "known" hair—that is, in the samples provided by Tim Durham—matched with the "unknown hairs," those collected at the crime scene.

During her testimony, she never quite got to twenty-five characteristics matching—but she did produce a few showstoppers. In describing how she fixed the hairs on slides for the microscope, she mentioned that an unknown Caucasoid head hair "was fairly hard to mount" because it "tended to straighten a little bit more" than one normally finds with Caucasoid head hair. She felt that the mysterious hair was more round than oval, making it more difficult to handle.

Durham's hair acted the same way, she said. Assistant D.A. Sarah Smith pounded this point.

Q: When you say they were particularly hard to mount, because normally hairs curl up and these straightened out, have you ever had that occurrence before in known Caucasoid hair?

A: No, I haven't.

Q: Never?

A: Not yet.

Cox agreed there is no science on the books or in the journals about the characteristic she claimed to have seen. No one published studies on this trait. For all the examiner knew, this "straightening" could have been caused by the humidity in her lab. Making it seem like an extremely rare event gave her testimony a powerful charge.

She also reported seeing a "reddish-yellow hue" and said that among "the red-headed population, maybe a third of the people would have that." Or maybe not. There is no reliable library of information on these shades within colors.

"Would you go so far as to say it's unusual to find these hues?" asked the prosecutor.

"I have seen it in less than 5 percent of the hairs I have examined," replied Cox. "These particular hairs were especially light. I have not found any pubic hairs as light as these before."

There was something else she had never seen before: the tips of the pubic hairs had been cut, as if shaved by a razor. This was such a remarkable fact that Hair Examiner Cox did not even mention it in her written report. In fact, no prosecution expert mentioned it—until a former girlfriend of Durham's was found who revealed that Durham had shaved his pubic hairs. On the witness stand, the hair examiner reported that she, too, had noticed cuts on the pubic hairs.

"How many times in your training and experience have you received male pubic hair that's been cut on the end?" asked Prosecutor Smith.

"This was the first time," replied Cox.

If it was so remarkable a finding, why had it not appeared in her original report, before the ex-girlfriend appeared? Cox just didn't write that kind of thing down.

The next scientific testimony showed no immediate signs of junkiness. Dr. Robert Giles, a molecular biologist with a Texas laboratory known as GeneScreen, gave testimony on DNA test results. He was brought on with all the fanfare due an expert who was bringing the most modern and discerning technology to the courtroom: DNA tests. Dr. Giles's lab tested patches of Molly M.'s swimsuit three times. The first two times, the only DNA he found was Molly's.

On the third try, though, he came up with something else: a faint dot on his DNA board, indicating a match with one of Tim Durham's genetic markers. Lots of people had those markers—at least one man in ten. Still, it was a small enough group for Dr. Giles to come to court and give his considered opinion that Durham belonged in the pool of suspects.

He conceded on cross examination that the "faint" result was something that took some expertise to see—namely, the expertise that came with being Robert Giles.

"I can't say that someone could walk in and pick up this particular [DNA] photograph and make the same call that I would make," Giles testified. "I'm making that call based on the fact I've been doing this for several years. I have been involved with gene amplification from its very beginning. . . . I have experience in knowing how to make these particular calls. There is some art involved in that, but that's why I'm trained as a scientist to do what I do."

In her summation, Assistant D.A. Smith came back to the DNA tests and the hair. True, the test couldn't narrow it down to any fewer than 10 percent of the population. But how many people in that 10 percent were short men with red head hair and light red pubic hair that had been cut with a razor?

Could eleven alibi witnesses be wrong? Sure they could, said Smith—either purposely or unintentionally mistaking the date of the skeet shoot in Dallas for the day of the crime. Too much scientific evidence said Durham was there, he raped the girl, he ruined her. Assistant D.A. Smith pointed out that her scientist performed three DNA tests on the same evidence.

"Why do you think they did that test again?" Smith asked rhetorically. "[Dr. Giles] said, 'Yeah, we tried something different.' . . . He told you there was a faint 1.1 [Durham genetic marker]. He didn't hesitate. He didn't qualify his results or anything else. He just told you the results."

As things turned out, Dr. Giles didn't quite tell all his results. Those would not come out for several years—long after Tim Durham had been found guilty, based on DNA evidence and on hair analysis, of raping Molly M. The full truth would not emerge until Tim began serving a sentence of 3,220 years. An appellate court later cut the sentence by 100 years.

———

Durham's cause was taken up by a pair of scrappy Oklahoma lawyers, Richard and Sharisse O'Carroll. They fought their way through the evidence and realized that the prosecution's strongest card was the DNA test. The lawyers contacted Barry at the Innocence Project. In short order, they came to a conclusion: The tests by GeneScreen were riddled with quality control problems that, when ignored, turn solid science into junk.

Dr. Giles's DNA test had, indeed, shown a genetic marker consistent with one of Tim Durham's. That was the "faint" dot that he reported seeing only in his third and final test. But his report was incomplete. Giles did not mention that an additional marker also showed up in one of his earlier tests. That marker could not have originated with Tim Durham or with Molly M. Years later, Dr. Giles said the marker was an artifact that was safely ignored. But his failure to mention it was called "misleading" by other experts, including Dr. Bradley Popovich of Oregon Health Science University. Said Popovich in an affidavit: "It is simply not objective science, nor acceptable science, to ignore such obvious data in one's work product." This was not the only time the lab had come under fire. Prosecutors in California had complained about GeneScreen's work. And in an Indiana murder case, the lab reported finding sperm cells on a swab taken from the mouth of a victim. The cells actually were yeast. Lab officials blamed a weak microscope.

When the Innocence Project arranged to have Tim Durham's DNA retested by Dr. Edward Blake at the Forensic Science Associates laboratory, the results conclusively excluded Durham as the source of the sperm. The prosecution conceded that the Blake results were valid. In fact, so did Giles.

Durham was released in December 1996 after doing five years. Junk science had ruined him, topping the eleven alibi witnesses who swore they saw Tim Durham three hundred miles away.

Once, while in jail, Durham was pulled from a bed and kicked until his ribs were broken, a punishment administered to him by other inmates for molesting a child. As he lay on the ground, cowering, he could hardly begin to explain that he, too, was a victim, of a court system unwilling to scrutinize any evidence coated with a veneer of "science." As his face was pounded into the floor of a filthy jail cell, he could not protest that too many crime labs have long served as arms of local police and prosecutorial agencies rather than as independent forces. With his nose mashed and bleeding, there was no way he could argue that what passes for science in a courtroom could never pass muster in a clinical laboratory, and that, indeed, patients would be slaughtered by their doctors if courtroom science was practiced in medical settings. Tim Durham could only cover up and hope for the clubbing to end.

The protections for the next Tim Durham should come from a mix of reforms, both in laboratory and at the bar:

• Like medical labs, all the disciplines in crime labs should be subjected to regulatory oversight and should meet standards of professional organizations.

• These labs should submit to external blind proficiency testings, in which samples would be sent in just as with any ordinary evidence. Labs should be rated on their ability to come up with valid results.

• In court, the scientists should provide, as a matter of course, information about known error rates for a procedure, and whether any controls failed.

• The defense bar and the prosecution agencies must inspect underlying data from science reports, to ensure that testimony is not distorted by either side.

• The crime labs must be independent and not rely on the prosecution or the police department for their budgets.

• The labs should be regulated. One good model is the New York State Forensic Science Commission, which oversees the twenty-two crime labs in New York and the state's DNA data bank. The Commission can shut down labs that don't meet standards, and it has required them to become accredited by the American Society of Crime Lab Directors. Many lab directors have been glad to answer to the commission because it provides them with a buffer of independence from local law enforcement agencies. The Commission consists of representatives from the judiciary, prosecutors, crime labs, police departments, and the defense bar. The statute creating the Commission was drafted with help from Barry and Peter. They serve, by appointment of the governor, as representatives of the Speaker of the State Assembly and the state defenders' organizations.

———

After he came home, Tim Durham chose to stay in Tulsa, work in the family business, and ponder how he would clear his name. How do you unring a bell? He has learned disturbing information since his trial. Another little girl, a neighbor of Molly M., was attacked a month earlier by a man with a similar description: short, red-haired. That girl was shown Tim's picture but did not identify him.

Moreover, Tim learned that a man with an uncanny resemblance to him had surfaced in Tulsa, just around the time of the two attacks. The man, like Tim, was five feet, four inches tall and had reddish-brown hair. His name was Jess Garrison. He was paroled in March 1991 from a conviction for a sexual assault on a child. He moved into Broken Arrow, a community next to Tulsa, in April 1991, when the attacks began.

When Tim was arrested for the attack on Molly M. in December 1991, Jess Garrison disappeared. He hanged himself in an abandoned warehouse. One day, Tim Durham hopes, he will be able to dig up Garrison's body and test his DNA.

Broken Oaths

*[A district attorney] may prosecute with earnestness and vigor—indeed,
he should do so. But, while he may strike hard blows, he is not at liberty
to strike foul ones. It is as much his duty to refrain from improper
methods calculated to produce a wrongful conviction as it is to use every
legitimate means to bring about a just one.*

Justice George Sutherland, for the majority,
Berger v. United States, 1935

For an innocent person, the two most dangerous words in the language
of the law are "harmless error." These are the magic words that appellate
courts use to absolve police officers and prosecutors of misconduct.

In Suffolk County, New York, a detective destroyed his original notes
and dictaphone recordings in a rape investigation because the victim's "times
were off." The courts upheld the guilty verdict—even though the convicted
man had tried to mount an alibi defense based on the time of the incident. The
appellate judges reasoned that the victim had made a very strong identification

of the defendant. The result would have been the same, the judges decided, even if the detective had not destroyed his notes. Therefore, destruction of the notes and tape was "harmless error." Harmless to everyone except the defendant. He was proved innocent and released; his alibi was true; none of those who had altered records to change the time of the crime was punished.

The victims of a rapist at a mall in West Virginia were secretly hypnotized to enhance their recollection of the attacker's face. Hypnosis of witnesses is so dangerously suggestive that the practice is forbidden in many states, but the lawyers for Glen Dale Woodall were never even told that it had taken place. Harmless error, said the court. Woodall was sentenced to two life terms without parole, plus 335 years to be served after the life sentence. This innocent man served four years.

In Oklahoma, a Tulsa prosecutor didn't bother to mention until the eve of Tim Durham's trial that a second child had been attacked in a crime very similar to the one Durham was charged with. That other child didn't pick Durham out of a lineup, so there was no sense letting his defense know about it. Harmless error, said the state's higher courts. Durham, an innocent man, was sentenced to 3,220 years.

In Virginia, a victim told police that she didn't get a good look at her rapist but that she did see his car. The report of her conversation never was turned over to the lawyers defending Edward Honaker—although the prosecution case was based on the victim's identification of Honaker. It so happened that he drove a different color car than the one she described as being used by the rapist. His conviction and life sentence also were affirmed by higher courts.

In Chicago, two college students were assaulted by two "black strangers" near the campus of the University of Chicago. On May 6, 1986, the two victims identified Donald Reynolds as one of the attackers while a police officer was questioning him in the street. A photo lineup was created that included Billy Wardell's picture, since he was a friend of Reynolds. One of the two victims selected Wardell's photo and later identified him in a lineup. The other victim failed to make an identification. Given the location of the crime near the prestigious school, it was a very hot case.

Meanwhile the rape kits, trace evidence, fingernail scrapings, and plant material, along with clothing seized from Reynolds and blood samples from both men, were sent to the Chicago Police Department's crime lab. Analyst Maria Pulling reported that Reynolds matched none of the trace evidence. She signed the report and forwarded it to the front desk of the lab for delivery to the prosecutor and the defense. But the exculpatory report was never delivered to the defense. Ten years later, the volunteer counsel, David Gleicher and Kathleen Zellner, obtained DNA exonerations of both men; full pardons were granted by the governor. That was when Pulling first learned the case had gone to trial. When she found out that her report had been concealed, she was astonished.

The myth of harmless errors is everywhere, not just in courthouses. In Boston, an eleven-year-old girl riding in a car with her mother thinks that she sees the man who raped her the day before. They call the police. Marvin Mitchell was confronted by several police officers, including Trent Holland. Mitchell wore a full mustache and goatee. The girl had said the rapist was clean shaven.

Mitchell was frisked and then arrested by officer Holland for public drinking. His picture was taken. The girl later was brought to look at an array of pictures and selected Mitchell's.

"What were you wearing yesterday?" Officer Holland asked Mitchell.

"Gray pants," Marvin would recall responding.

The officer filled out the incident report and left blank the box about statements made by the suspect. Mitchell would face rape charges. Four months later, at a pretrial conference, the commonwealth prosecutor reported having no oral statements from Mitchell.

Nearly a year afterward, the case was ready for trial. Suddenly, the prosecutor informed the defense lawyer that she had just spoken to Officer Holland who, it turned out, did get a statement from Mitchell after the arrest. Asked what he had worn the day before, Mitchell supposedly replied, "pinkish pants." This happened to match precisely the girl's description of her attacker.

When Officer Holland took the stand at trial, the defense lawyer objected. If Mitchell really did say that he had worn "pinkish pants," he had not been given his Miranda warnings. The judge, smelling a rat because the damning statement suddenly had emerged sixteen months later, agreed that it looked like Mitchell had not been read his rights.

The next morning, the prosecutor presented Holland's partner, Officer Robin DeMarco. Without so much as a single note to refresh her recollection, DeMarco recalled that sixteen months earlier, during a discussion in the booking room with other officers, several of them were saying how frequently people wear the same clothes for several days.

Mitchell, who supposedly overheard their conversation, spontaneously announced, "I didn't have these clothes on yesterday. . . . I had pink pants on." Because it was a voluntary statement, the Miranda warnings did not have to be given. The judge admitted the statement. Mitchell was convicted. He served seven years in prison before his new lawyers, David Kelston and Noah Rosmarin, arranged DNA tests of semen on the girl's clothing. Marvin Mitchell was cleared.

Officer Holland had been accused of misconduct eighteen times as a cop, but the police department's internal investigation failed to substantiate the charges, so he was never disciplined. One judge accused him of committing perjury. On another occasion, he was accused of planting drugs on a witness to coerce false testimony. When his "pink pants" story was referred to the district attorney, he declined to investigate it.

———

"Harmless error" is the lie that the criminal justice system tells itself. For 63 percent of the DNA exonerations analyzed by the Innocence Project study, misconduct by police or prosecutors played an important role in the convictions. Lies, cheating, distortions at the lower levels of the system are excused at higher ones. Even when an appellate court is sufficiently perturbed to reverse a guilty verdict, nothing happens to the people who broke their oaths and the law in pursuit of conviction.

Since 1963, at least 381 murder convictions across the nation have been reversed because of police or prosecutorial misconduct. A study by Ken Armstrong, the legal affairs writer for the *Chicago Tribune,* found that not one of the prosecutors who broke the law in these most serious charges was ever convicted or disbarred. Most of the time, they were not even disciplined.

Then came the case of Rolando Cruz in Chicago—combining a crime of the darkest horrors with a cocky, disagreeable suspect and a team of police and prosecutors so fully convinced of their righteousness that they were willing to do anything to get their man. That these elements merged to result in a wrongful conviction is not startling. What happened afterward, though, was unprecedented.

———————

Little Jeanine Nicarico had the flu one February morning in 1983, so her parents decided that she should stay home from school. The family lived in Naperville, Illinois, a middle-class bedroom community of Chicago. Her dad, Tom, was an engineer who worked downtown. Pat, her mom, worked at a school near their home. At age ten, Jeanine could stay home by herself but was not old enough for her parents to let her pass the whole day alone. So her mom dashed home in the mid-morning to check on her. Then she came back at noon to fix her lunch. Then Mom went back to school.

A few minutes after 3:00, Jeanine's older sister, Kathy, came home. She found the front door kicked open and the frame ripped from its hinges. Jeanine was gone. The police rushed to the scene. Crime-scene investigators found a bootprint on the front door and different footprints outside a rear window. The multiple footprints would become important later, when they were used to support a theory that more than one person had been involved in the crime. Someone had cased the house through the rear window and spotted the little girl home by herself. The parents just wanted their daughter back. Two days later, her body was found six miles from home, on a dirt trail in the woods. She was naked. She had been sodomized. She had been killed with a blunt instrument. The world shook.

The days stretched on with no arrest, then months went by, and finally, the police picked up a tip. Alejandro Hernandez, also known as Crazy Alex, had heard about the reward. He knew who killed the girl. The police put him in a room, brought in a box of money, and told him to talk. He mentioned the name of Rolando Cruz, a well-known punk in the area with a record of criminal trespass and petty offenses. On a slippery deck, Cruz became a rope for the desperate detectives. Cruz claimed that he heard on the street that Jeanine had been killed in a certain house, gave the address, and the detectives used his information to obtain a warrant. Later, Cruz said that he was shot at because he was helping the cops, and he was moved into a motel, where he dined on the detectives' expense accounts.

Crazy Alex, meanwhile, offered the police a full roster of suspects. Among those he nominated were a man he knew only as Ricky, and an acquaintance named Stephen Buckley. The "Ricky" never was found, although a bunch of Rickys were stopped, questioned, and released when they provided solid alibis. Buckley gave police his boots for comparison with the print on the front door. Cruz and Hernandez apparently did not shut up about the case—and soon became the targets themselves. On the eve of the Republican primary for the DuPage County state's attorney, Cruz, Hernandez, and Buckley were indicted for the murder of Jeanine.

During preparation for the trial, the sheriff's criminologist, John Gorajczyk, studied Buckley's boot and the footprint and decided they didn't match. When he verbally reported the findings, his boss, the sheriff of DuPage County, told him to keep his mouth closed and not to write a report, Gorajczyk would later testify. The prosecutor then tried another cubbyhole of footprint experts—the Illinois State crime lab. The best he could get from that lab was a statement that a comparison was "inconclusive." Finally, he sent the boots to a renowned shoe "expert" in North Carolina, a crackpot who claimed that not only could she say the footprint came from Buckley's boot, she also could detect the height and race of the person who left the footprint.

On the eve of trial, the prosecutor said he had just learned of an amazing development from two detectives. Months earlier, they said, Cruz had recited a dream to them about the murder of Jeanine. In it, he described a vision in which her nose had been broken and her face had hit the hard ground with such force that it left an indentation. Here was the most potent piece of evidence yet for the trial—and not a single piece of paper contained any record of the conversation. Even though Cruz allegedly made the statement in May 1983, the detectives had no written reports on it. After supposedly hearing this confession, they let Cruz walk away. Nor did they testify about it when they appeared before the grand jury. And no one asked Cruz about the statement when he testified before the grand jury. More than a vision, the statement was nearly a miracle.

At the trial, the defense attorneys tried to block testimony about the dream statement but were unsuccessful. The jury could not reach a verdict on Buckley and his boots; Cruz and Hernandez, however, were both convicted of murder and sentenced to die. There was a problem, though. The Illinois state Supreme Court said the two men should have been tried separately. So their convictions were vacated and the cases sent back for new trials.

When Cruz was tried again, the new jury also heard about his "vision" statement, and the result was the same: conviction, plus a death sentence. Hernandez, however, fared slightly better: conviction, with an eighty-year term.

Behind the scenes at the Hernandez trial, there was a development that few knew about. All along, the prosecutors had presented a theory that the murder of Jeanine had started as a burglary; that several men had come to the house, looked in the window, and saw her alone. That's why the bootprint on the front door and the different shoe print beneath a rear window were so important.

When a crime technician arrived at the courthouse to testify for the state, he pulled aside one of the prosecutors and relayed some news: representatives from the Nike shoe company said that the prints at the back window had been made by a woman's shoe, perhaps size six or five and a half. Either size was too small for Cruz or Hernandez. The prosecutor put the technician on the witness stand and carefully avoided any mention of shoe size or likely gender. In fact, the defense was not told about the Nike analysis.

While Cruz and Hernandez were being tried, another critical development was unfolding. A pedophile and murderer named Brian Dugan had been arrested in other sexual assault cases, not far from the scene of Jeanine's murder. In an attempt to avoid the death penalty, he volunteered that he had murdered five people, including Jeanine Nicarico. Cruz and Hernandez were not involved, he said. Later, DNA tests would confirm that Dugan had attacked the child and showed no evidence that Cruz or Hernandez participated. With the case crumbling, the police and prosecutors in DuPage County pressed on. But two investigators in the sheriff's office quit in disgust. When Cruz and Hernandez appealed their convictions, the prosecution was supposed to be represented by Mary Bridgid Kenney in the attorney general's office. She declined to argue that the convictions should stand and resigned on principle. The convictions of both men were thrown out because of mistakes in procedures and admission of evidence, and not because of any misconduct. For a third time, the DuPage officials prepared to try Cruz.

By then, Cruz was being helped by a new private investigator, John Eireman, who was working with Larry Marshall, a professor at Northwestern University Law school, and Tom Breen, a chain-smoking former prosecutor who describes himself as a "dyed-in-the-wool Republican from the North side of Chicago." Said Breen of his outlook on life: "I believe in the system. I don't want to see problems in the system. I was relatively sure that the system would do the right thing." At least, that was his outlook until he dug into the case of Rolando Cruz.

For the third trial, the state again introduced the Cruz "vision" as evidence. All along, the prosecution had faced the problem of not having any written record of a statement that Cruz vehemently denied making. At the first two trials, the detectives had told juries that someone else was aware of the Cruz statement: their supervisor, a lieutenant. But he had not been called as a witness. Before the third trial, though, the defense summoned the lieutenant to a court hearing. Yes, said the lieutenant, his men had phoned him at home for advice about the Cruz statement. He corroborated the investigators. This was not what the defense had hoped he would say. The prosecution promptly listed him as a witness for the actual trial.

On the night before he was to testify, though, the lieutenant appeared at the prosecutor's office. He had searched his mind, checked his records, and now realized that he had not been home that night. He actually had been in Florida on vacation. He didn't get the call from the investigators.

For Judge Ronald Mehling, that was enough. The case was a bench trial, meaning that the judge, and not a jury, would give the verdict. After Judge Mehling heard the lieutenant admit that he had lied, perhaps inadvertently, about the phone call, the judge wanted no more testimony. He held a picture of Jeanine Nicarico up in the courtroom. For twelve years, longer than the little girl's entire life, the state of Illinois had pursued Rolando Cruz, with highly suspicious testimony and outright fakery. The case was over.

"This kind of misconduct is tolerated because the prosecutors are seen as the good guys," said Professor Marshall, an aggressive and successful advocate for the wrongly convicted. "It's legitimate to bend the rules and the truth when you have a 'greater good' as your goal."

What followed was perhaps as remarkable as the twelve years of litigation that preceded it. A special prosecutor was assigned to probe the handling of the Nicarico case, from top to bottom. After months of inquiries, three prosecutors and four sheriff's office investigators were indicted for perjury and obstruction of justice. Most of the case centered around the "vision" statement they claimed had been made by Cruz. The seven were tried in the spring of 1999. The accused cops and prosecutors argued that the failure to mention the dream statement in their reports was mere sloppiness by the officers and not an element of a sinister conspiracy to obstruct justice with lies. At the end of the state's case, the judge dismissed charges against two of the three prosecutors. And when the remaining defendants presented their case, there was one last strange development: Even though not a syllable about the vision statement appears in any of the grand jury transcripts, five grand jurors were called as witnesses for the law enforcement officials. All five remembered there had been some "mumbling" about such a statement during the grand jury proceedings fifteen years earlier. The defense lawyers reminded the jurors that Cruz had filed a civil rights lawsuit seeking millions of dollars. The message to the jury was clear: conviction of the law enforcement officials would amount to a ringing endorsement of Cruz's claim and could cost local taxpayers a small fortune. Thanks to the resurrected grand jurors, and the belligerent testimony of Cruz, all of the officials on trial were acquitted on June 4, 1999.

Criminal prosecution is an extreme remedy for misconduct. The prosecution of the DuPage officials was a singular event, done at great cost and turmoil, and unlikely to be repeated. A more realistic approach would narrow statutes that grant broad immunity from civil suits to prosecutors, even when they intentionally misbehave. Naturally, government officials should be permitted to carry out their duties without fear of being hit with lawsuits every week, but it is possible to balance this concern with the rights of victims of misconduct.

Under the current setup, a prosecutor can't be sued for knowingly allowing perjured testimony or for deliberately covering up evidence of innocence. It hardly needs to be said that willfully violating the constitutional rights of citizens is not part of the prosecutor's duties. Lawsuits for intentional misconduct could deter the most outrageous practices, while not interfering with conscientious officials.

The Department of Justice has claimed for years that its federal prosecutors are exempt from the ethical rules established by state bar associations. The department was forced to change that stance when a Republican congressman from Pennsylvania found he had no avenue to complain about his tormentors—the federal prosecutors who had hounded him for a decade in a kickback investigation. The congressman slipped a rider on a spending bill that forces federal prosecutors to abide by local ethics rules. It became law in April 1999.

The congressman may find that the ethical governance of the bar associations has little impact on prosecutorial misconduct. Nearly all disciplinary action by bar associations arises from abuse of client funds—typically, money that was given to an attorney to be held in escrow for a home purchase. In circumstances where life and liberty are at stake, though, most state bar associations are ill-equipped to review the ethical behavior of prosecutors, and they almost never do so. One positive step would be to create panels that would specifically examine complaints against prosecutors.

Beyond rules and lawsuits is leadership. Respect for law and order has been the battle cry of politicians for ages. No greater terror exists than the accusation that a politician coddles criminals. In the 1988 presidential campaign, George Bush destroyed Michael Dukakis with a commercial about Willie Horton, the convict who used a prison furlough granted by Dukakis to commit rape. The lesson was not lost on President Bush's son, Texas governor George W. Bush.

In 1985, a Houston woman was raped in her bed. She described the intruder as a "white male, age thirty-five." She also described him as "a white male, but he had an unusual color of skin. It was a honey brown color, but he was not black." Four months later, she spotted Kevin Byrd in her neighborhood. He was the rapist, she said. Kevin Byrd, however, was black, and unmistakably so. At trial, the victim and prosecution managed to persuade the jury that her attacker was black, and that her repeated use of the word "white" in the police reports was an error by the detectives. The same error was contained in the report she signed. The jurors believed her and convicted Byrd.

Twelve years went by, and Byrd's cause was taken on by a leading Texas defense attorney, Randy Schaffer. He arranged DNA tests on the rape kit that showed Kevin Byrd to be innocent. Then came the amazing performance of George W. Bush.

On July 25, 1997, the district attorney joined Schaffer in petitioning the Board of Pardons and Paroles for a gubernatorial pardon of Byrd on the grounds of actual innocence. Three days later, the judge who presided at the trial, Doug Shaver, and the sheriff, Tommy Thomas, sent similar pleas to the board. The board acted swiftly and unanimously recommended that Governor Bush pardon Byrd.

The governor denied the pardon and suggested the whole matter belonged in court. The governor's spokeswoman pointed out that the victim still believed Byrd was her attacker. The Bush political calculus was clear: Duck not only the tough calls but any that might carry the slightest risk of having a crime victim get on TV and call you an accessory to rape. A few weeks after Bush's denial of the pardon, the defense attorney got a letter in the mail from the governor. Randy Schaffer opened it eagerly, hoping for good news from Bush. He found, instead, a fund-raising pitch.

"I took his letter and sent it back, and where he says, 'I need your help,' I wrote, 'I need your help: Will you pardon Kevin Byrd?,' " said Schaffer.

Not long afterward, with the national press covering the Byrd follies, Bush reversed himself and signed the Byrd pardon. Kevin Byrd was the fifteenth person to be pardoned by Bush. He was the first African American to receive one. The governor said that mentioning race was a disgrace.

Sleeping Lawyers

We set our sights on the embarrassing target of mediocrity. I guess that means about halfway. And that raises a question. Are we willing to put up with halfway justice? To my way of thinking, one-half justice must mean one-half injustice, and one-half injustice is no justice at all.

Harold Clarke, Chief Justice of the Georgia Supreme Court

Convicted murderer Dennis Williams had been given all the rights a person had coming. He had a trial. He had twelve jurors. He had a lawyer. He could march himself right into the death chamber, the Illinois Supreme Court ruled on April 16, 1982. In particular, the court said that his defense lawyer had met all the constitutional requirements for competency. These standards are written in highly technical legal jargon, but laypeople can understand them by thinking of a "breath test." If a mirror fogs up when placed beneath the lawyer's nostrils, he or she is not ineffective, as a matter of law.

Of the seven judges on the Supreme Court, one complained that Dennis Williams had not gotten a decent day's work from his attorney. Justice Seymour Simon said that it didn't make sense for one lawyer to defend three men on the same charge, as had happened in the Williams case. Plus, the standard for competent lawyering in a capital case had to be better than simply the breath test. "If the court can safely reduce every attorney to the level of a novice," he wrote, "we may as well all take the novice; he's cheaper."

The defense lawyer, Archie Weston, had sat quietly as the prosecution systematically excluded blacks from the jury, finally creating a panel of eleven whites and one black woman. The defendants were four black men from the Ford Heights section of Chicago, charged with kidnapping a white couple from a suburban gas station, murdering the man, gang-raping the woman, then murdering her. For starters, the lawyer might have taken more care with the jury selection. Then came the trial, and the *Kojak* issue.

An important prosecution witness said he turned off *Kojak,* played a guitar piece for forty-five minutes, then saw the four men running into an abandoned building where the bodies were later found. He put the time at 3:00 A.M. Anyone who checked the time *Kojak* ended would have known something was wrong. That night, the episode had finished airing at 12:50 A.M.—so even forty-five minutes later, after the witness finished his guitar recital, the victims were still alive. They were last heard from at 2:30 A.M. If the four men were seen in Ford Heights at 1:30 or 2:00 in the morning, they hardly were available to kidnap the couple in Homewood at 2:30 A.M. But the defense attorney didn't make mention of the timing problem.

And then there was the Caucasian hair collected from the backseat of Williams's car. The state's lab expert said three of the hairs matched the victims' hair. Weston didn't talk to any other forensic experts. Years later, it would be shown that the hair was nothing like the victims'.

In all, it was an uninspiring performance by Attorney Weston, but lawyers have gotten away with much worse. Weston was well liked among his peers, considered to be a man who took on the problems of too many clients who couldn't pay—making it necessary for him to carry a caseload that was unmanageable. He did a lot of volunteer work as the head of the black bar association. The majority of judges on the Illinois Supreme Court decided that Dennis Williams could die. "A defendant is entitled to competent, not perfect, representation," wrote Justice Robert Underwood. Of course, different tactics might look better in hindsight, but no case would ever end if every move made by a losing lawyer were subject to scrutiny by appellate courts.

And so the matter of Dennis Williams might have rested until he was executed—except for a critical development. A few weeks after the court voted six to one to affirm his conviction, the justices were presented with disciplinary cases of lawyers who had broken the rules. Justice Simon, who had been the sole vote against upholding the Williams conviction, was an old-line Chicago politician who had risen to the bench from the ranks of ward captain, alderman, and president of the Cook County Board. Among his gifts was the ability to remember a name. When he heard that a lawyer named Archie Benjamin Weston was in hot water for mishandling his clients' business affairs, the justice paid attention.

In 1978, the same year Dennis Williams was tried, Weston had been accused of mishandling the estate of an elderly woman. Within days of Williams's conviction for first-degree murder, a civil judge removed defense attorney Weston as administrator of the estate and held him in contempt. A $23,000 judgment was entered against the attorney. After he failed to pay, his home was seized and sold at a sheriff's auction. In Illinois, the conduct of lawyers falls under the jurisdiction of the State Disciplinary Commission, which opened an investigation and subpoenaed Weston's financial records. When he ignored the subpoena, the commission initiated disbarment proceedings.

Justice Simon privately called an investigative journalist named Rob Warden, who had been covering the Williams case, and met him for drinks at the City Tavern. The judge wanted to make sure he had his facts lined up—that the Archie Weston now in trouble with the bar association was the same fellow who had represented Dennis Williams. The very same man, Warden told the judge.

When Weston appeared before the Illinois Supreme Court, pleading to save his law license, Justice Simon asked Weston why he had failed to defend himself before the Attorney Registration and Disciplinary Commission, which had leveled the disbarment charges against him.

Well, said Weston, at the time of the disciplinary proceedings, he was hard up and under so much stress that he had not been thinking straight.

When the court retired to consider the fate of Counselor Weston, Simon convinced his colleagues to investigate the dates to see whether the trial of Dennis Williams coincided with Weston's fall from grace. Justice Simon knew the score. And faced with evidence that a man sentenced to death had been represented by a lawyer in the midst of a personal collapse, the Illinois Supreme Court began a slow, spectacular reverse somersault. The judges sent for the prosecution and new defense lawyers from the Williams case.

First, they asked the state's attorney and the Williams appellate lawyers if it mattered that Weston had been falling apart when he was fighting for Williams's life.

Of course, said Williams's new lawyers.

Absolutely not, said the state's attorney. Unless someone could show big errors in how Weston handled the trial, it didn't matter that he was going bankrupt, no more than if he were actually psychotic and hallucinating for eighteen days.

Finally, the Court ruled. Sure, Archie Weston may not have been Clarence Darrow, but the justices would not describe his performance "as actual incompetence or as of such a low caliber as to reduce the trial to a farce or sham." Still, the court reversed the conviction of Williams and ordered a new trial, concluding that under "the unique circumstances and sequence of events in this capital case, which will rarely, if ever, be duplicated, that the interests of justice require that Dennis Williams be granted a new trial." Nearly in the same judicial breath, the justices also disbarred Archie Weston.

Old-fashioned Chicago politics, it turned out, had saved the life of Dennis Williams, an innocent man. The case would linger for years. Williams and his three codefendants would be proven innocent, primarily through the extraordinary efforts of journalists Warden, Margaret Roberts, a Northwestern University journalism professor named David Protess, and Protess's students. Along the way, the licenses of three other defense lawyers for the Ford Heights Four were either suspended or revoked.

Speaking to the American Bar Association in 1996, a member of the U.S. Supreme Court remarked on the importance of a capable lawyer.

"Recent development of reliable scientific evidentiary methods has made it possible to establish conclusively that a disturbing number of persons who had been sentenced to death were actually innocent," said Justice John Paul Stevens.

He could have been speaking of the case of Dennis Williams—or many of the people who were freed from prison through DNA testing. Studies by the Innocence Project found that 27 percent of the wrongfully convicted had subpar or outright incompetent legal help.

Such as Frederick Daye of San Diego. Sorry to impose on your busy schedule, Daye wrote to his appeals attorney. But he was wondering about something. It had been two years since the attorney had taken his case, and he had not heard a word. Daye was serving long, hard time time for rape, of which he was innocent. Another man, also convicted of being involved in the same rape, signed a sworn affidavit saying that Daye had had nothing to do with it. The postconviction attorney had been provided with a sheaf of legal research, all the trial transcripts, briefs, and, of course, the statement exonerating Daye. So naturally, Daye wondered if there had been any developments in those two years.

It turned out that the postconviction lawyer didn't have the first idea about how to handle the new evidence, so he did nothing. And by the way, even if he had figured out the procedure, he had managed to lose the files. At the same time, the court was preparing to destroy the evidence from the rape case, which would have eliminated Daye's ability to prove that he wasn't part of the rape.

That Daye was stuck with such an incompetent is revealing. Originally, he had a very capable lawyer named Carmela Simoncini who took his phone call at Appellate Defenders Inc., a not-for-profit corporation that has a contract with the state of California. While she was allowed to collect the documentation and conduct legal research, Simoncini was prohibited by the agency's contract with the state from appearing in court to argue "collateral" issues, such as newly discovered evidence of innocence. Instead, she had to farm out that portion of the case to a private attorney.

After Simoncini prepared the research, she waited in vain, as did Frederick Daye, for the appointed counsel to tell a court about Daye's new evidence. When Simoncini learned that the case evidence, including the original rape kit, was about to be destroyed, she went to court and had it saved. She also filed other papers that, in effect, seized the case. In short order, Frederick Daye was freed—proven innocent by both the affidavit from the real criminal and DNA tests.

When Daye was released, news reporters in California contacted the negligent attorney. Was he concerned that the two years of needless delay might expose him to a legal malpractice suit? The attorney just about shrugged. He himself had just filed for bankruptcy.

For the innocent, the importance of competent, aggressive counsel cannot be overstated. But two prongs of public policy have worked to undercut this. First, by failing to find fault with even the worst examples, the courts have ratified the performance of incompetent, slovenly, indifferent, or drunken attorneys. The attorney who amiably escorts his or her client into prison, or even the electric chair, is protected from judicial sanction.

Second, the pockets of excellent advocacy—typically, the attorneys provided after a capital conviction for complex appeals work—have been defunded by an act of Congress.

In the famous case of *Gideon v. Wainright,* the Supreme Court said every defendant, rich or poor, was entitled to an attorney. For the most part, the systems of "indigent defense" that have emerged in the last thirty years make no pretense of complying with *Gideon's* mandate of supplying counsel to improve the defendant's chances of receiving a fair trial. The poor person is often assigned a lawyer who lacks the knowledge, skills, or even the spirit to defend a case properly.

In too many states, serving as counsel to the indigent is a fast way to join their ranks. For instance, in Mississippi, the maximum fee for non–death penalty cases is $1,000, plus a token amount for office overhead. In certain rural sections of Texas the limit is $800. In Virginia, $305 is the most a court-appointed counsel can receive for defending a client in a felony punishable by less than twenty years. A kid selling sodas on a summer weekend at Virginia Beach would make more money.

The result, in Texas, has been attorneys in capital cases who slept through most of the trial. Those lawyers passed the mirror test: they were breathing, if a bit loudly. In Kentucky, an attorney who gave his business address as Kelly's Keg, the local watering hole, was assigned to a capital case. He had no experience. His home was decorated with a big neon beer sign. He missed the testimony of important witnesses because he was out of the courtroom. He came to the trial drunk. When police searched his home, they found garbage bags hidden under a floor containing stolen property. The court said that his behavior did not adversely affect his client.

Traditionally, some of the brighter public interest lawyers have risen to the infinitely challenging work of death penalty appeals. There is less room for them now. One plank of the Republican Party's wildly popular 1994 Contract with America called for hard limits to appeals in death penalty cases, a goal embraced by President Bill Clinton. Consequently, those sentenced to death must act as their own attorneys at critical stages of the postconviction process. "Many of those poor people, particularly the illiterate or the mentally retarded, are no more prepared to file and litigate a postconviction challenge without a lawyer than a passenger can be expected to fly the Concorde to France without a pilot," said Stephen Bright of the Southern Center for Human Rights.

For close to twenty years, most postconviction work for prisoners sentenced to death was carried out in each state by capital resource centers, offices where experienced lawyers litigated on behalf of the condemned. Many politicians saw the resource centers as frustrating the public will for death sentences.

The attorney general of South Carolina ran for office on a promise to replace the electric chair with an electric sofa, to speed up executions. He kept his word: In 1995, he campaigned to end the funding for the capital resource centers. From the perspective of the defendants, the resource centers had been a source of vigorous and successful advocates. At least four innocent people were freed from death row due to the efforts of resource center attorneys. And between 1976 and 1991, the resource centers indeed gummed up the works: those attorneys were able to obtain reversals on constitutional grounds in 40 percent of 361 capital judgments. Now, under the Clinton-

Gingrich scheme, when the stakes for the accused get higher, the ranks of counsel are thinner.

Money alone is not enough. To ensure high-quality defense services for the poor, performance standards should be enforced in every jurisdiction, with sanctions for individual lawyers or public defender organizations that fail to meet them. Clients lose their liberty or lives due to the ineptitude of their assigned counsel. The lawyers themselves are rarely punished.

Among the more remarkable revelations of the DNA era has been the attitude of defense counsel, both in private practice and in the publicly funded legal-aid offices. When the Innocence Project contacts lawyers to let them know that their old cases had been reopened and the client exonerated, many lawyers expressed shock. The defense attorney who presumes a client is guilty may be right a majority of the time. But that presumption makes him or her useless when an innocent person comes along.

David Shephard, a young airline worker in New Jersey falsely accused of rape, was advised by his attorney to accept a plea to reduced charges. She had lobbied hard for the plea bargain and thought it was a fair deal. By Shephard's account his counsel was so angry at David for his refusal that she would not communicate with him for the rest of the trial, even failing to prepare him for the witness stand. She also did not call the one person who was with Shephard at the time he supposedly committed the crime. Around the time of Shephard's exoneration, the attorney was the head public defender for the state of New Jersey.

The public defender sent word through an aide that she always believed in Shephard's innocence but did not give her view on how she had handled the trial.

In Oklahoma City, Robert Miller was cleared by DNA of raping and murdering two elderly women. The same test implicated a confessed rapist. But Miller's counsel from the public defender's office pressed him to take a plea even after the DNA results excluded him. He declined but was not freed for five years.

In September 1982, Steven Toney was arrested, based on a photo identification, and charged with dragging a woman from her doorstep in St. Louis and raping her. He insisted that he was innocent. Toney claimed he repeatedly asked his public defender, Stormy White, to have the semen tested for ABO bloodgroups, and that she refused. "I don't recall that," said White, "but we tried to show that the prosecution could have done more tests and didn't, and that was because they were afraid that it might ruin their case."

After he exhausted his state appeals, and without the aid of a lawyer, Toney wrote to a federal judge requesting that the evidence be preserved for DNA testing. The prosecutor opposed him, and the judge refused to order the tests. Finally, Rebecca Stith was assigned to the Toney appeal. Accepting Stith's arguments, a panel of federal appellate judges faulted the state and district courts for failing to allow the tests, and also for not exploring the effectiveness of his trial counsel.

"Toney has raised substantial claims that his counsel provided ineffective assistance by failing to exhaustively pursue the issue of mistaken identity and by failing to obtain the requested blood tests," three judges from the U.S. Court of Appeals for the 8th Circuit ruled in 1996.

Fourteen years after his conviction and imprisonment, Toney was able to have the evidence tested. The DNA exonerated him and he was freed. White, now a senior public defender in St. Louis, said that during the trial, she had fought for him as an innocent man. His menacing behavior, perhaps born of frustration, frightened the jury during the trial, White recalled, and a water pitcher had to be removed from the table. The victim had given powerful testimony. In 1999, White said she was not persuaded that Toney is innocent and has doubts in general about DNA tests, though she noted that her views could be a way of coping with the psychic weight of his conviction. As for Toney's claims that she had not been an effective advocate, White said that he had not complained about her representation until after he had lost his first round of appeals. "It always bothers you when someone makes that appeal," said White. "But a guy's gotta do what a guy's gotta do."

The number of capable public defenders is astonishingly high, but so is their burn-out rate. No wonder. Start with the overwhelming caseload. The prosecution is backed with far more resources and enjoys a base of public support for its cases. The typical indigent defendant is seen as a pariah and the defense lawyer as close kin. With an infusion of financial support that would put their salaries on a par with local prosecutors, continuing legal education, and a more flexible work plan, cynicism and pessimism could be defeated. No less than the public and prosecutors, the defense bar needs to absorb the revelations of the DNA era, especially the exclusion of 25 percent of the prime suspects in the laboratory. What was good enough for government work no longer should pass, whether in the private sector or the public defender's office.

In 1984, a man named Ed Honaker paid for the lethargy of his attorney. Accused of rape and kidnapping, although he was one hundred miles away at the time, Honaker faced the typical state criminalist, who testified that he had looked at the slides of the rapist's semen and was able to detect sperm. Honaker's court-appointed lawyer, for tactical reasons, never mentioned one fact to the serologist: Several years before the rape, Honaker had had a vasectomy. He could not produce sperm. The serologist later swore in an affidavit that if he had been told about the vasectomy by either side, he would have testified Honaker was not the rapist.

In prison, Honaker contacted the Reverend Jim McCloskey and Kate Hill of the Centurion Ministries. With help from the Innocence Project, they obtained DNA tests that cleared Honaker. He served ten years of a life term because his trial lawyer shot blanks as an advocate.

Race

If we accepted McCleskey's claim that racial bias has impermissibly
tainted the capital sentencing decision, we could soon be faced with similar
claims as to other types of penalty.

Justice Lewis Powell, for the majority,
McCleskey v. Kemp, 1987

On the day Calvin Johnson, Jr., was to go free, the heat of June fell in a numbing blanket on Jonesboro, Georgia, just as it had for all the time that there has been a Jonesboro, a Georgia, or warm days in June. Nothing moved. The flags of the Confederacy dangled, limp in the dead air. The hum of air-conditioning rose from the old rail depot, now converted into a center for tourists. Jonesboro likes to boast that it is the town where *Gone With the Wind* really happened.

The Confederacy lost a pitched battle there in 1864, giving Sherman a clear road to the sacking of Atlanta. As a little girl, the author Margaret Mitchell sat on the porch of the Fitzgeralds' ancestral home in Jonesboro and listened to tales of the antebellum South. Later, she would render them again as the lore of a lost, gracious civilization, populated by Brett and Scarlett. Every day, pilgrims in search of Mitchell's mythical Tara unload from their cars and buses at the Jonesboro rail depot. A local costumed as a plantation gentleman leads them from the hazy present into the imagined past.

On June 15, 1999, as tourists gathered in front of the glass cases that display the crumpled bullets and belt buckles salvaged from the fields, another costumed man was across the street from the rail depot. He, too, had become tangled in the snares of history. Calvin Johnson, Jr., was wrongly convicted of rape in 1983. He waited in a cell on the second floor of the Clayton County Courthouse.

By that day in the middle of 1999, and not a moment sooner, all sides agreed that a terrible mistake had been made. Later that afternoon, Johnson knew, the judge would make it right. Send him home. Just one problem. He was wearing a bright red jumpsuit that had been issued to him by the state prison that had been his custodian all those years, and here he was, sitting in the Clayton County jail in Jonesboro, Georgia. He couldn't ball up that jumpsuit and leave it in a *county* laundry hamper when it belonged to the state. He would have to go back in the van to Hancock State Prison, return the state's property, and be processed out of the institution. Maybe tomorrow.

Standing at the cell bars, Johnson explained the snag to a visitor. His tone was calm, the topic disappointing, but he quickly put it aside. His moment of freedom would come, today or tomorrow. Too many times, in the early years of incarceration, his own rage and bitterness had risen in a tide. No more. He was glad for the visit. For six months, Peter had been a New York voice on the prison phone, explaining the tests that were being done, the arguments made, the motions filed. He had arrived in Georgia that morning to move formally in court for the release of Johnson, so for the first time, lawyer and client were face-to-face.

A month from his forty-second birthday, Calvin Johnson was as handsome as a movie star and as fit as a center fielder. He smiled easily, even when relaying the distressing news about his incarceration being prolonged by the jumpsuit.

"We'll do something about that," promised Peter. "Soon as I leave here, I'll visit with the district attorney and make some calls."

More than the inane snarl with the jumpsuit, Johnson seemed troubled, oddly enough, by the space he occupied on that steaming morning. By all appearances, it was just another big cell in a county jail, metal shelves bolted on the wall to serve as bunks, an unshielded toilet in one corner. Places just like it had been his home for thousands of nights.

"This is where they brought me the first night I came in here," Johnson said. "When I was waiting trial, I stayed right here. It brought too much back. Things I had put away."

————

If high school yearbooks ran a contest for the graduate least likely to go to prison, Calvin Johnson, Jr., would have been an easy winner. He came from a powerfully ascendant family. His father, Calvin Johnson, Sr., was born and raised in a small tobacco farm community called Oine in North Carolina, the same place his clan had lived since they were brought in chains to North America as slaves. Johnson Sr. was reared in a place and time of total segregation, sanctioned by law. He served in the U.S. Army after World War II in Europe, and came home to find that his seat was still at the back of the American bus. He would have none of it. With the GI bill, he took himself to college, then law school, and he met JoAnn. They married and moved to her home town of Cincinnati, Ohio. Johnson Sr. became a state senator. "We were a young, black, middle-class family on the rise," said Johnson Jr., the family's second child and only son.

In 1970, the family moved to Atlanta. Once the capital of the segregationist South, by the late 1960s the city was being transformed. Whites were moving into the suburbs. Blacks were moving into political power. The city had its first black education commissioner. Johnson Sr. had a chance to develop housing. The family settled into the Cascade Heights neighborhood, the center of the African American power structure in Atlanta. Johnson Jr. played football at Southwest High School and was a member of the drama club.

All the Johnson children—Judith, Calvin, and Tara—were expected to go to college, just as both their parents had done. Calvin chose Clark College, close to home, but moved out and began to earn his keep while he studied. He worked at WSB Radio and TV as a newsroom assistant, delighted to be learning the ropes. At school, he held part-time jobs in the communications department office, and he met a film student from a sister school, Morehouse, which shared some facilities with Clark. The film student, named Spike Lee, had a brassy New York attitude, Johnson decided. Not that he was hiding his own plumage. Johnson drove a canary-yellow Trans-Am. He also met a young woman, Kyra Loney, and they fell in love. To keep up, he needed more money than he could earn from the minimum wage jobs at school and in the newsroom. He turned to the biggest employer in the metropolitan area—Delta Air Lines—and found work paying more than $9 an hour; he stayed with the airline after graduation.

From a distance, his father scented trouble. He was not fond of his son's companions or his beverage, which was serial beers. The fears were not misplaced. Johnson Jr. also had developed a taste for marijuana. His car was pulled over one evening just after he purchased a $5 bag. The arrest set off a train of events that amounted to slow-motion panic. In his lifestyle, Johnson basically spent every dime as soon as he made it, so he could not handle a fine. He could not afford a lawyer. He did not want to ask his family for the money and bring down the wrath of his father. To serve time, instead of paying a fine, meant he would have to give up his job. His actual brain never entered the picture, apparently. He broke into a house, was arrested for burglary, and was charged with possession of a concealed weapon, a pocketknife he used at work.

"That was it for me—that was my mistake," Johnson said. "That was what I did wrong, and I am responsible for that." That was not the view of the police. He became a chronic suspect. A white woman was raped in her apartment, and Johnson briefly was identified as the attacker; but the charges were dropped. The victim in that case said her attacker was uncircumcised; Johnson had been circumcised as an infant. For the burglary, he was sentenced to eight years and served fourteen months because the prisons were overcrowded. He returned to the world in December 1982.

He and Kyra Loney resumed their marriage plans. He immediately took a job at a courier service depot. He lived in the College Park section of Atlanta, just as he had before the first case.

In the early hours of March 9, 1983, a white woman in the Yorktown Condominiums was wakened by a man sitting on her back and pulling on her shoulders. Louise Lewis felt a belt tighten around her neck until she passed out. When she came to, he was putting a towel on her head.

The terms of the attack were specific. Using hand lotion as a lubricant, he violated her anally and then vaginally, ejaculating twice. Before he left, he switched on the light, and she saw a black man of medium build, with prominent eyes, and wearing army-type khakis. He covered her head with a pillowcase, stole some money from a wallet, and left.

Two weeks later, the police showed her an array of six photos. She identified one, Calvin Johnson, Jr., as the rapist, but when she went to a lineup, she picked another man. Still, Johnson was indicted for the rape.

What appeared to be a classic case of cross-racial misidentification was about to become a unique, small-scale laboratory experiment in social science.

––––––

The trial had to resolve one major question, namely, the accuracy of Louise Lewis's identification. Johnson was mounting an alibi defense, so the credibility of his witnesses would be stacked against her certainty. Ms. Lewis had, after all, only a fleeting chance to view her attacker. But she was quite sure Calvin Johnson was the man.

"I saw everything," she testified. "I know he was black and didn't talk like a southern black. And he didn't talk street jive. He was smooth and soft-spoken."

That would be a good start on a description of Calvin Johnson, reared in Cincinnati, college-educated, with his major field of study in communications. She was asked to point out the man who had attacked her.

"Him," she said, sending her finger toward Johnson. What about the lineup? Hadn't she picked out someone other than Johnson then? Indeed, she had.

"Why did you do that?" asked the district attorney, Robert Keller.

"I was just—wouldn't allow myself to look at him fully in the lineup," said Lewis. "I went in and I looked, but I—as I continued looking, I just refused to let myself look at him anymore, and I just picked another person."

Later, she said, she saw Johnson during a court proceeding, and confirmed that he was the man who attacked her.

"How do you know today that that's the same person that attacked you on March 9th?" asked Keller.

"I know. I know it's him. I know it's him. There's no—I might have been wrong in this, or I even—I was right in this one—I could have been wrong, but I know I'm right. I know that's him."

"What about that man today causes you to remember or positively say that he's the one?" asked the prosecutor.

"I know that's him. That's his face, his eyes, the whole thing," said Lewis. "That's him."

"What about his eyes?"

"That's him. I mean, they're very predominant, you know, they stick out," she said.

The testimony of Lewis was backed by another white woman who lived in the same condominium complex. A black man, shortly before the rape, had attempted to enter the neighbor's apartment. Like Lewis, the neighbor had picked Calvin from the photo array but selected someone else at the lineup.

Then came another, powerful witness: a third white woman who lived just a few miles from Lewis. Two days before Lewis was attacked, this woman was wakened by a man tying a belt around her neck. She, too, had been assaulted anally, by a man who used hand lotion during the crime, and then placed a pillowcase over her head. This victim did not identify Johnson from his picture—but did select him at the lineup. And she, too, had a white neighbor who saw a mysterious black man. This neighbor had taken a shower, then found a strange black man in her apartment. He fled.

Given that these two crimes shared unusual details—the same physical description of the suspect, the use of the belt, the hand lotion, and the pillowcase—and took place just a few miles and two days apart, the prosecution was allowed to bring the second victim as a witness in the Lewis case because it was a "similar transaction."

As it should happen, though, the two crimes could not be tried in the one courthouse. Lewis had been attacked in Clayton County; the rape of the second victim took place in her home, just over the border in Fulton County. To testify against Johnson, the second victim came to Jonesboro, the county seat. Her testimony, every bit as searing as Lewis's, seemed to come to the ordinary conclusion.

"Any other direct?" asked the judge.

"No, sir, Your Honor," said D.A. Keller.

"You can step down, miss," said the judge.

"Thank you," she said.

"Call your next witness," the judge ordered the prosecutor.

At that moment, the second victim had taken a few steps from the witness box and was crossing in front of the defense table. Suddenly, she lunged at Johnson.

"You stupid bastard!" she screamed, flailing at him.

Immediately, court officers restrained her. The defense attorney, Akil Secret, asked the judge to declare a mistrial but was denied. Nearly two decades later, a juror would recall that moment as a window that suddenly opened, showing him the victim's cast-iron certainty. Calvin Johnson was the man.

The Johnson defense was not complicated. He testified and said he was not the man who broke into Louise Lewis's home and raped her. He had been away. He had worn a beard for a few years, and the victims and witnesses all had described a smooth-faced man. His boss from Courier Dispatch said that Calvin wore a beard, just as his photo ID card from work showed. He had spent the day of the attack at Kyra Loney's house, a Sunday, then come home around 2:00 in the afternoon. Kyra said he was at her house. So did her mother.

JoAnn Johnson, Calvin's mother, remembered the Sunday because it had been pouring early. When Calvin came home, she had some plans to make a meeting with the sorority she advised at a local college, but she was not feeling well. Instead, she said, the family watched football on TV.

"Was there anything particular you remember about that day?" asked Johnson's defense attorney, Secret.

"Well, they watched some football games," said Mrs. Johnson. "Herschel—what's his name, Herschel Walker—I watch the games sometimes, but anyway, Herschel Walker was playing his first pro game, and so they sat and watched that that day."

Practically the whole state had stopped that day. Herschel Walker, a college track and football star, had won the Heisman Trophy while playing for the University of Georgia.

Johnson's whereabouts in the afternoon and early evening were important because of the testimony from the neighbor who said he was the black man who had tried to enter her home then, well before the attack on Louise Lewis.

As for the evening and the night, Mrs. Johnson said that because she was suffering from high blood pressure and diabetes, she had become a fidgety sleeper, disturbing her husband's rest. For two weeks, she had taken to a couch for the night, so that Johnson Sr. would get a decent rest before rising early for work.

"Where were you the rest of this night?" asked Secret.

"On the couch, at the den, watching television," said Mrs. Johnson.

"Did Calvin leave the house any that night?"

"No, he did not."

"Is there any way he could have left the house without your knowing it?" asked Secret.

"No way," said Mrs. Johnson flatly.

It was possible, of course, that Johnson's fiancée, her mother, and his own mother, had agreed to stitch serial lies together, creating an alibi that would cover him. Harder to explain was the description of the rapist as clean-shaven, and the work photo and testimony from his boss indicating that Calvin wore a beard. And one other piece of evidence could not be ignored.

At Lewis's house, a single hair was recovered from her bed sheet, the prosecution said. The state crime lab had examined it, declared that it was a "Negroid pubic hair," and said it was completely unlike any of the hair plucked from Calvin Johnson's scalp, eyebrows, chest, or pubis.

Moreover, Louise Lewis said that she had never, in the six months she lived in that apartment, entertained any black guests, male or female. The defense had called the criminalist with The Georgia State crime lab who gave evidence that the hair didn't come from Johnson. The defense position was clear: the only black man to enter that apartment was the rapist, and he had left behind the pubic hair.

On cross examination, District Attorney Keller could not ignore such an important piece of evidence excluding Johnson.

"Can you tell me exactly where it came from?" asked Keller.

"No, sir," testified the criminalist, Raymond Santamaria.

"Can you tell me whether or not that hair could have come from Louise Lewis if she used a public rest room and transported that hair onto the bed sheet?" asked Keller.

"That would be a possibility," said Santamaria.

"If the sheet was laundered at a public facility, could the hair have originated there?" asked Keller.

"Yes," said Santamaria. "That's another possibility."

"If blacks had lived in that apartment six months earlier and the sheet touched the floor and the hair had been on the floor, could it had [sic] gotten on there?" asked the prosecutor.

"Yes, sir," said Santamaria.

Calvin Johnson, Sr., sitting at the trial, could hear in these questions a faint echo of the nightmares of race mixing that haunted the Jim Crow South of his youth: white women carrying Negroid hairs into their homes from public toilets, or from laundromats where the sheets of black people freely mingled with the linens of the whites. He had watched the trial from start to finish. He had seen four white women testify that one black man, his son, was responsible for two ghastly crimes. He had heard four black witnesses, including his wife, testify that Calvin was elsewhere and wore a beard, unlike the clean-shaven rapist.

The defense lawyer, Secret, and Calvin were the only blacks in the front of the courtroom. The judge, his clerk, the court stenographer, the prosecutors, and every single member of the jury were white. The jury panel had been chosen from the rolls of Clayton County. Two black people who originally sat in the box had been excused by Prosecutor Keller, who used his "peremptory" challenges to strike the blacks from the jury. At that time, the prosecutor was not required to explain why those two jurors did not belong.

"Cut and dried," said Calvin Johnson, Sr. "The judge, the jury foreman, the jury, the prosecutor, the same people. Just didn't have the same name or gender. Same county people, same set-of-mind people. I heard the prosecutor, Keller, saying in the hall, 'This one is going to be easy.' He was right."

The jury was gone forty-five minutes. Calvin Johnson, Jr., was guilty on all counts. A few weeks later, he stood before Judge Stephen Boswell.

"Mr. Johnson, is there anything you desire to say before sentence is pronounced, or why sentence should not be pronounced on you?" asked the judge.

"Yes, sir," said Calvin. "I would like to say one thing to you, Judge Boswell, to Mr. Keller, and to the detectives involved, Detective Storey, Detective Harper back there, with God as my witness, I have been falsely accused of these crimes. I did not commit them. I'm an innocent man, and I just pray in the name of Jesus Christ that all this truth will be brought out, the truth will eventually be brought out. That's all I have to say to the court in Clayton County, here today, Judge."

Judge Boswell sent him to prison for life.

A year later, he was tried in Fulton County. The prosecution offered him a deal: If he pleaded guilty to this second rape, the sentence would run alongside the time he already was serving. Backed by his family, which was carrying his legal expenses, Calvin Johnson, Jr., declined.

If anything, the Fulton County case was much stronger than the first one had been in Clayton County. For example, when Johnson took the witness stand to deny the charges, the prosecution was allowed to point out that he already had been convicted of an identical rape that took place just a few miles and days away. And second, there was no "Negroid hair" found on the sheets of the second victim that the defense could claim belonged to the rapist and not to Calvin. Otherwise, the evidence was identical in all respects to the first trial. The Fulton jury deliberated overnight. They came back with a verdict of not guilty. Not only was the result different this time, so was the composition of the jury. The people who made the decision, the second jury, included five whites and seven blacks.

Calvin Johnson returned to state prison and joined the lifers who worked at the hardest duty. Almost immediately, he was back on a brush-cutting crew, in waters up to his knees, with snakes wriggling past, under the guard of correction officers with shotguns. They were known as the Bossmen.

———

During most of the twentieth century, rape was a capital offense in many states, meaning the offender could be executed. This sentencing option was rarely exercised when white men were convicted; however, it was almost universally employed when a black man was found guilty of raping a white woman. In the early decades of the century, the newspapers would report delicately that a "Negro male was hanged for the usual crime." Of those executed for rape, 90 percent were black.

"By 1977, Georgia had executed 62 men for rape since the Federal Government began compiling statistics in 1930," wrote U.S. Supreme Court Justice Thurgood Marshall in 1987. "Of these men, 58 were black and four were white."

The state had "operated openly and formally" separate systems of justice for white and black. "The criminal law expressly differentiated between crimes committed by and against blacks and white, distinctions whose lineage traced back to the time of slavery," Marshall wrote.

Nationally, blacks were more than half the prisoners condemned to death, though they committed far less than half the crime. So intolerably random were the execution schemes of Georgia and other states in the southern "Death Belt" that the Supreme Court struck down the death penalty in 1972, in the *Furman v. Georgia* decision. The Court invited the states to create new programs that were less arbitrary. By January 1977, when Gary Gilmore was executed by firing squad in Utah, most of the states had revised their death statutes. The exercise of the death penalty remained intrinsically tied to racial considerations: In Georgia, studies through the 1980s showed that those who killed white victims were 4.3 times more likely to get the death penalty than those who murdered blacks. Blacks who kill whites are nineteen times as likely to be executed as whites who kill blacks. Similar results were found in nearly every other state. And the death penalty was only one of many laws that appear race-neutral on the books, but in practice are far more harshly administered on black suspects.

In the 1990s, an antidrug law in Georgia called for "two strikes and you're out"—that is, after the second felony drug conviction, the prosecutors could seek life sentences. Of those serving such sentences, 98.4 percent were black. Under the law, the prosecutor had absolute discretion on whether to seek this stiff penalty. Prosecutors sought the life sentence for just 1 percent of the eligible white defendants, but invoked the provision against 16 percent of the black defendants.

In law, probation is used to provide a second chance. White criminals in Georgia "were 30 to 60 percent more likely than blacks to get probation instead of prison time" for serious crimes, according to a study by Bill Rankin of the *Atlanta Journal-Constitution*.

In New Jersey, black motorists who speed on the New Jersey Turnpike are five times more likely to be stopped than white drivers. Along the I-95 corridor that runs from New England to Florida, similar results prevail. In Maryland, blacks make up 77 percent of the people stopped and searched by the state police along I-95—but make up only 17 percent of the drivers who use the highway. In New York, six dozen black males who rode their bicycles without bells were not only stopped and given summonses but actually were forced to spend a night in jail.

Every contact with the criminal justice system, no matter how trivial, can mushroom. "We cannot pretend that in three decades we have completely escaped the grip of a historical legacy spanning centuries," declared Justice Marshall. "We remained imprisoned by the past as long as we deny its influence in the present."

In Illinois, two black men, Billy Wardell and Donald Reynolds, were convicted of sexually assaulting two students at the University of Chicago. Bad enough that they had attacked the women, said the judge. "You were going to have some more fun, with some white girls," the judge said, sentencing them to sixty-nine years in prison. Both men were later proven innocent.

The Innocence Project study of DNA exonerations found that 40 percent of the sexual assaults or murders involved black men and white victims.

That's triple the rate at which such crimes actually take place: The Justice Department reports that 15 percent of sex murders involve black assailants and white victims.

————

In the early years of his prison stay, Calvin Johnson fell apart. He became, he said, an emotional time bomb, full of bitterness and self-pity. His family kept up its visits. One Saturday, his mother JoAnn arrived home, plainly distraught from having seen her son in such tatters. Calvin Johnson, Sr., was furious. He got in the car and drove to the prison himself.

His son saw his father approaching and tried to make himself scarce. The father demanded to see Calvin. He was blunt.

"I told you," he said, "back in school, back when you worked for Delta, I told you not to mix up with that marijuana. You look in the mirror. Ninety-nine percent of the time, somewhere down the line, you caused your life to take the path it did. You hadn't got mixed up with the marijuana, you wouldn't have been caught up in this thing.

"Don't ever put your emotions ahead of your mother's, and go crying on your momma's shoulders."

This was harsh medicine. Calvin rode out the tempests of rage and self-pity. He took up religious studies. His fiancée visited for a while, but finally, he told her to go ahead and live her life. She was ready for children, and he would not be their father. Every month, from the family homestead in North Carolina, his great-aunt Sally Bett Patilla sent him five dollars out of her Social Security check. He worked with weights and cut his natural athlete's physique to sharper turns.

A life sentence in Georgia meant that he could apply after seven years for parole. To be eligible, he would have to go through the prison sex-offenders' program. He declined. He was not a sex offender. His parole application was turned down.

Three years later, he decided to take the first part of the program. The second part required him to sign a statement of responsibility for his crimes. He refused and was thrown out of the course.

"If you don't participate, they'll never let you out," a counselor told him.

"I sure wouldn't feel right," said Johnson, and that was the end of it. His family was scraping together money for another lawyer to make his case at the parole board. He told them to stop. Neither he nor they would pay blackmail for the stolen years.

He was moved to a medium security camp, but the experience was disturbing. Most prisoners were on short stays, going home. Every week, it seemed, someone else was leaving. That was hard to watch, and because the other inmates had not settled in for long hauls, their behavior was wilder. Calvin asked to be transferred back to the more stable facilities where the convicts were doing longer time.

By 1994, he had heard and read about DNA tests. With help from James Bonner, a lawyer with Prisoners' Legal Counseling Project at the University of Georgia, he filed a motion seeking a new trial and DNA tests. The negotiations with the Clayton County district attorney's office were tortured. After a year, the prosecutors agreed to the tests, and the evidence was shipped to a laboratory called Genetic Design, in Greensboro, North Carolina.

The rape kit arrived at that lab in October 1995 but did not contain a sample of Johnson's blood to use as a reference point in the tests. It took another year to draw a tube of blood from Johnson at Hancock State Prison. While this was dragging on, a new commissioner of the state's Department of Corrections was appointed. Wayne Garner, an undertaker, had no experience in running prisons, but he was a crony of the governor, Zell Miller, and had plenty of notions about how to run prisons.

"One third of state prison inmates ain't fit to kill," Garner declared. As recounted by Atlanta civil-rights attorney Stephen Bright, the undertaker/corrections commissioner did the following:

"He fired the system's academic and vocational teachers two weeks before Christmas in 1996. He had previously fired seventy-nine recreation directors and seventy-four counselors. He changed the name of all but one of the department's facilities from 'correctional institution' to 'state prison.' He eliminated hot lunches for prisoners and placed inmates in ninety-day boot camp programs on a diet of sandwiches and water three times a day. He announced he would require inmates to walk four miles a day."

Dressed as a commando in all black, Garner led raids on prison cells in supposed searches for drugs and contraband. The raids turned into blood-baths, and inmates were awarded $283,500 in compensation after lawyers from the Southern Center for Human Rights filed actions.

Directly affecting Calvin Johnson was another maneuver by Garner and the governor: they defunded the Prisoners' Legal Counseling Project, leaving Johnson with no legal representation. It was a terrible moment to be abandoned.

Even after his blood sample was, at last, sent to the laboratory, nothing seemed to happen. The laboratory was in a state of turmoil. The technician handling Johnson's case took another position. Three months later, the lab was acquired in a corporate takeover. That took up most of a year. Eventually, in October 1997, the evidence was shipped to a forensic laboratory in Research Triangle Park in North Carolina. Only a small portion remained—two slides, each containing a low count of sperm and a wooden Q-Tip stick stripped of its cotton by earlier testing. Working with one slide, the technicians were unable to find enough DNA.

By then, in early 1998, a childhood friend of Johnson's, Kim Stewart in Cincinnati, had read about the Innocence Project. She sent Calvin the address.

With a shrinking body of evidence, Peter instructed the lab to stop its work. Only one slide remained, and he did not want it to be burned up in another futile test. Instead, he shipped it off to Dr. Ed Blake, the forensic scientist in California known for his ability to find the merest trace amounts of DNA. The evidence arrived in California in July 1998, four years after Calvin first applied for the tests. Where others had seen only a bare wooden stick, Blake found a few wisps of cotton embedded in the wood. These contained a minute amount of biological material, from both the victim and the rapist. From those fibers and the remaining slide, Blake was able to profile the sperm DNA left by the rapist. It was not Johnson's.

In November 1998, Peter contacted Robert Keller, who was still the Clayton County District Attorney. Keller allowed that he was impressed with the results but needed time to have his experts review it and to locate the victim. Months passed with no action. In April 1999, the prosecutor advised Peter that he would not consent to Johnson's release until one more test was done. He wanted the Negroid pubic hair discovered on the victim's sheets tested. He viewed it as very significant evidence.

Years earlier, when a lab looked at the hair under a microscope and said it was nothing like Johnson's, the district attorney had taken a much different position. Then, Keller was busy suggesting that the solitary hair had come from a public toilet or from the laundromat. After all, the victim said that no black person ever had visited her apartment. Now, the prosecutor wanted to test the hair he once had argued meant nothing.

Peter asked Dr. Blake, who had received all the evidence in the case, to locate the hair. Later that day, Dr. Blake telephoned Peter in great excitement. Sure enough, he discovered the slide containing the "Negroid" pubic hair from the sheet. But instead of a single pubic hair, there were actually three Negroid pubic hairs. They had been found on the victim's sheet and now were mounted on a glass slide.

This was explosive. Keller and the state criminalist had contrived all kinds of scenarios to explain how one black pubic hair, not Calvin Johnson's, could have found its way onto the victim's sheet. The jury had been misled. The transcript shows how:

Q: Did you retrieve any hairs from the sheet?
A: Yes, sir.
Q: Did you determine from your examination of that hair whether or not it was—what part of the body it came from?
A: There were several hairs, several Caucasian head hairs and a Negroid pubic hair.
Q: And of course, it did not match the victim's hair?
A: The Caucasian head hairs from the sheet did match the victim's known head hair. The one Negroid pubic hair did not match the known pubic hair of Calvin Crawford Johnson.

Perhaps, had the jury known the truth—that there were three Negroid pubic hairs recovered from the sheet, none of them from Calvin Johnson, the prosecutor's story about public bathrooms and integrated laundries would have been laughed at.

That was a lost moment, sixteen years earlier. The DNA results, when they came on June 11, were unequivocal. The DNA in the hair matched that in the sperm cells. The hair was from the rapist. So was the sperm. None of it was Johnson's.

————

JoAnn Johnson knew the DNA tests might set her son free. The family had fallen on hard times since Calvin had been sent away. They had spent a good deal of money on his legal bills, and she had suffered from heart ailments. Still, when the time came to pay for the DNA tests, she reached into her retirement savings. A few months later, in February 1999, she had a stroke. She was in a long-term-care hospital in June when he was due to get out.

At 2:03 P.M. on June 15, 1999, Judge Matthew O. Simmons said: "Mr. Johnson, you are free to go."

Calvin hugged Peter, his sisters, and then his father, who walked away with a knotted-up tissue in his hand. The father had spent every day since February in the hospital, feeding his wife.

Johnson emerged into the hazy afternoon sun, greeted by TV cameras and reporters wanting to know how he felt. He mentioned that he was looking forward to soaking in a bathtub, after sixteen years of prison showers. He kept his voice even, and a bright smile rode across his face. He would not be drawn into criticism of the district attorney, although privately, he had confessed to anger at the memory of certain moments in the trial.

"When he started saying, 'Maybe the hair came from a laundromat,' I said, 'He doesn't care about me, about my life. He just wants to get a conviction,'" said Johnson Jr.

The black alibi witnesses had been rejected, and the white identification witnesses accepted. An all-white jury had convicted him in forty-five minutes, and then a jury of seven blacks and five whites had tried harder, thought longer, and came back with a not-guilty verdict. To explain an inconvenient piece of evidence, the prosecutor had summoned the mewling ghosts of segregation: a white woman could catch Negroid hairs from the toilet seat.

The father had been hard on Calvin in prison for having gotten into the trouble that had made him a chronic suspect. Yet Calvin Sr. reflected, on the day of his son's liberation, on how much his son had suffered from the visions of an era that many supposed has been erased from American life.

"I grew up in total segregation. When my kids came up, they had no idea about that stuff. Legally, on the books, you were equal to whites. Socially, when my kids were coming up, they were defined as black and not equal to whites," said the elder Johnson.

He finished speaking and loaded into the car with Calvin and his two sisters, off to the hospital for the reunion with the ailing JoAnn. As they left town, they passed an old Confederate cemetery, laid out in the shape of a Confederate flag. The casualties of the Battle of Jonesboro, 1864, are buried there.

It took all of a century after that war, Thurgood Marshall once observed, to liberate blacks from the legal structures of American segregation. He warned that the practices of racism would survive its legal extinction. And indeed, racial laws and customs, once so stark, have been worn down by time. Yet like the writings on a tombstone from a bygone era that can be rubbed into high relief, those fading days are legible once again in the prison years of Calvin Johnson, innocent man.

11

The Death of Innocents

The boys sat on the edge of Becky's Pond as if time, under the rising July sun, had no end. Jackie Poling and his friend Chris Shipley were just a few miles from downtown Baltimore, in a little semirural development called Fontana Village, but the two boys could have been Huck Finn and Tom Sawyer, measuring the summer of 1984 by the fish in their bucket. Chris, ten, had brought his fishing pole and had come up with two blue gills. Jackie, not quite eight, had worked only a string and raised a turtle up from the mud. With a careful hand, he had lifted the turtle into one palm and solemnly inspected the wise old eyes. He was very proud. He put the turtle into the bucket and went back to fishing his string.

The glory of his trophy still was busting from Jackie when the man wandered past the pond. He glanced at the boys and might have kept going, but Jackie called to him.

"Hey, mister," yelled Jackie.

The man stopped. One of the boys would remember that he had curly blond hair and a mustache.

"I want you to look at my turtle," said Jackie proudly. The man walked back, good-naturedly, to inspect the boy's treasure.

"What kind of turtle is he?" asked the man, who was wearing a muscle T-shirt and shorts.

"That's a stink-pot snapping turtle," said Chris.

Then they heard a voice singing out their names. "Chris, Jackie."

It was Dawn Hamilton, the girl who lived behind the pond. She was walking down the path. Chris knew her well; she was nine years old that summer.

"Did you see Lisa?" asked Dawn.

"No, she wasn't here," said Chris.

Lisa was a cousin, and Dawn lived with her. As the eldest kid in the house, she was sort of responsible for the little ones. Her aunt Sissy had sent Dawn to find Lisa, who had wandered into the woods, which was forbidden territory, because Sissy was afraid the kids would fall into the pond.

"Jackie, did you see Lisa?" she asked.

"Nope," said Jackie. "Want to see my turtle?"

"I have to find Lisa," said Dawn. "Could you please help me look for her?"

Chris still had his pole in the water. "Nah," he said. "I'm fishin'."

The curly-haired man spoke. "I'll help you find her."

"Thanks," said Dawn.

"What's her name?" he asked.

"Lisa," said Dawn.

They wandered along the path into the woods and passed close to a house. A woman in her yard saw them passing by. She heard Dawn yelling: "Lisa! Lisa! Lisa!"

Then she heard the man say to Dawn: "Lisa and me is playing hide-and-seek. Come on, let's go find her."

Five hours later, Dawn Hamilton, a girl who smiles from her photograph with a front tooth missing, was found facedown in the woods. Her skull had been crushed. Her underwear and pants were flung over a tree branch. She had been raped and then violated with a stick. A sneaker imprint appeared on her neck. In a few weeks, she would have started fourth grade.

Quite a while later, a defense lawyer would speak to a jury in Baltimore County:

"Just because the state seeks the death penalty doesn't mean that their evidence is strong," said Leslie Stein. "In fact, it is no comment on their evidence at all. It is merely a comment on the kind of crime that was committed. . . . I want to remind you of one other thing: that awful facts, ghastly evidence, is not a substitute for proof."

The case against the man accused of murdering Dawn Hamilton was weak in the classic soft spots. The boys didn't identify him at the lineup. Neither did the last person to see Dawn alive, the woman who noticed the girl and a man walk into the woods for hide and seek—at least, she didn't identify the suspect until after she saw him on TV, in handcuffs. And the results of a special forensic psychiatric test were "reanalyzed" to make them seem incriminating, when the suspect, in fact, should have been cleared by the test.

If Kirk Noble Bloodsworth had been accused of robbing a bank, there is a reasonable chance the prosecutors would not have taken the case to trial. The evidence against him was that weak. And yet, it is easy to see how the jury convicted him. With such gruesome facts, the barrier to conviction dropped considerably. Almost anyone might have voted for Kirk Bloodsworth's guilt, if only as a way to speak for Dawn Hamilton's life.

The day after she was killed, the *Baltimore Evening Sun* featured two pictures of Dawn Hamilton on the front page. In one, she was smiling out from a school picture, missing a front tooth. In the other, she was not visible, contained inside a zippered black body bag toted by two men wearing short-sleeve shirts in the hot July sun, across a disorderly bramble. A number was set up for information. The police assigned an artist to make a composite sketch, based on the descriptions given by Chris and Jackie of the man they saw at the pond. The story led all the news. A $1,000 reward was offered. The hotline rang, scores of times. *NO SOLID LEADS FOUND IN GIRL'S KILLING*, the *Sun* reported two days later. Ten detectives were assigned to the case. On August 3, the hotline had received 286 tips. A woman said the sketch in the newspaper looked very much like a man who worked at Harbor to Harbor, a furniture importing company not far from the scene of the murder. The man's name was Kirk. She gave no other information.

At Harbor to Harbor, the detectives spoke to the owner, who said that Kirk Bloodsworth had shown up at the door a month earlier, desperate for any work at all. He had grown up on Maryland's Eastern Shore, the son of a waterman, had gone to Bible academy, had done a turn in the Marine Corps. She never had a better worker. In fact, Kirk had been so strong and fast and willing to put in long hours that the owner thought about opening a second store in Ocean City, on the Eastern Shore, with Kirk as manager. He was delighted by the idea. On the evening before the murder, he had worked at the store until 10:30 P.M. A week afterward, he just stopped showing up. No call, no forwarding address, nothing.

The detectives went to the home address he had given at work and found his wife, Wanda Bloodsworth. She had met Kirk in a bar earlier that year; two months later, they were married. It had been difficult. They often fought. She had two children from a previous marriage, and she brought them to live at the shore but then decided to go back to Baltimore with the rest of her family. Kirk had followed a few days later, hitchhiking a ride and arriving in Baltimore over the Fourth of July weekend. Of a half-dozen somewhat dissolute adults living in their little house, Kirk was the only one working. This led to more arguments. One day, he just disappeared. She had filed a missing person's report, suggesting he might have gone back to his hometown on the shore, to Cambridge, Maryland, where his father had a business.

By now, the newspapers were reporting that the detectives had consulted the FBI's famous Behavioral Science Unit, known for constructing engrossing profiles of killers based on the manner and place of death. Before the detectives drove to Cambridge to speak with Bloodsworth, the profilers had suggested a simple test. The detectives should clear the room and place a few artifacts from the murder scene on the table, to gauge his reaction. So they stopped in town, bought a pair of panties and blue shorts, like the ones Dawn Hamilton had been wearing, and then picked up a big rock in the parking lot of the police station. These were placed on a table in the interview room.

In Cambridge, Bloodsworth said he would speak with the detectives, under one condition: that they not force him to go back to Wanda. They agreed. At the police station, one of the detectives waited near the table while the other escorted Kirk inside.

He said nothing about the rock and clothing, and as the profilers had instructed, they were quickly stashed out of sight, behind a TV, to avoid implanting them in Bloodsworth's mind.

"I wasn't even sure he saw them," one detective would say later.

Indeed he had. After the detectives took a few Polaroid snapshots and agreed to take one back with a note to Wanda, they let him go. Kirk said he couldn't be certain where he had been on July 25, the Wednesday of the murder, because it was his regular day off. He might have been around the house until noon. He wasn't sure. The night before, he had gotten off work at 10:30 after a twelve-hour shift, and he and his wife had gone to a bar where they once again had a spat. She went to stay with her mother. He could tell the detectives one thing. He had never been to Fontana Village and had nothing to do with the murder of Dawn Hamilton.

The detectives brought the Polaroid pictures back to Baltimore and showed them to the two boys in a photo array. Jackie couldn't pick anyone. Chris thought Kirk Bloodsworth looked like the man but said the hair color was wrong—too red. Still, it looked like him. That was enough. From sources in Cambridge, the cops heard that Kirk was telling friends about the rock and the underwear he had seen in the interview room. He was one good poker player, the detectives decided. They got a warrant and drove out to Cambridge to arrest him.

When they got back to Baltimore, Kirk Bloodsworth was furious. He had nothing to do with this crime. They tried to calm him down.

"Listen," said one detective, "when we go outside, there's nothing we can do about it, there's gonna be a ton of press out there, taking pictures of you. You want a jacket or a blanket to cover your head?"

"I'm not hiding from anyone," snarled Kirk. "Let the whole world look at me. I didn't do anything wrong."

The detectives called a few of their witnesses. They told them not to watch TV that night because they had made an arrest in the Dawn Hamilton murder, and a lineup would be held. It would be better not to see the suspect until the witnesses came to the police precinct. The witnesses ran to switch on the news. Kirk Bloodsworth, with his proud head of red hair, stalked out of the police station in the company of the detectives. He did not bow or flinch but just kept going.

————

Little Jackie Poling came to the lineup the next day with his mom; his best friend, Chris Shipley; and Chris's mom. The detectives drove them in a police car. The boys were very afraid. At the Bloodsworth trial, Det. Robert Capel described the ordeal:

Q: How was Jackie acting at this time?
A: Extremely nervous. As a matter of fact, when he was asked if he wanted the men in the lineup to say or do anything, "Yes," he said, "yes, I want them to leave."

Jackie picked Number 3, a police officer filling out the six-person lineup. Nearly a month later, his mother would call the police and explain that Jackie had been too afraid to name the real killer. He had whispered this to her when they left the police station and had told her that the real one had been Number 6. She couldn't really explain why she had waited so long to tell the investigators, but it didn't seem to matter all that much.

The lineup experience was, if anything, even worse for Chris Shipley, two years older than Jackie and better able to name his fears.

"After you walk through these (curtains), you can see the full lineup room," Detective Capel would testify. "And as we just got through the curtains, Jackie froze, I mean, excuse me, Chris froze, and his mother helped him and he continued to the podium.

"Detective Ramsey asked him if he could make an identification, and Chris just shook his head."

Outside the room, though, Chris regained his composure and told his mother he could pick someone. She called Detective Capel over.

"He said that he knew all the time that it was Number 6, but he didn't want the man to hear his voice because the man could tell it was him because it was a little kid's voice," Capel testified.

In the trembling of the boys, the lineup itself felt like an extension of the crime: an act of continuing terror against small children. And so did the trial.

The two boys, clearly frightened, came to court to give testimony. They talked about the man they saw at the pond that day and how he was now sitting in the courtroom. The neighbor came to court and said she had seen Kirk Bloodsworth leading Dawn Hamilton to the woods for a game of hide-and-seek.

Detective Capel also would explain the behavioral test in which the rock and the underwear were left in view of Bloodsworth at the police station to see if he would react to them. If he responded visibly, that was a sign suggesting guilty knowledge.

Q: Did Mr. Bloodsworth have a reaction?
A: Yes, very definite.
Q: And what was his reaction?
A: It was not an immediate reaction, but it was a long-term reaction. He remembered everything we put on that table, although we removed it.

In fact, the scenario had been devised to trigger an immediate response, in front of the detectives, and Bloodsworth showed none. That Bloodsworth had spoken about these items later to friends did not seem all that shocking. After all, he never had been arrested, and the police were targeting him in a terrible case and had intentionally shown him what looked like pieces of evidence.

However feeble, it was the prosecution's attempt to corroborate the identifications made by the boys. And that was just about the entire prosecution case. The defense pulled together some alibi witnesses who felt that Kirk probably had been around his own home at the time of the murder but whose ability to distinguish one day from the next seemed to depend on a script.

The jury went out and cast an eleven-to-one vote for guilt on the first ballot. Within two hours, it was unanimous. On March 22, 1985, a judge sentenced Kirk Bloodsworth to die. He was twenty-four years old.

———

At this writing in mid-1999, twenty-five years have passed since the U.S. Supreme Court put aside its reservations about the fairness, cruelty, and reliability of the ultimate penalty, and began again, in Justice Blackmun's words, "tinkering with the machinery of death." In that time, 553 people have been executed, a number that includes defiant murderers and people who used their last breaths to protest their innocence.

In that same period, another eighty condemned men and women have been released from death row, and ultimately had their convictions vacated forever. For every seven executed, one innocent person is freed, not only from death row but from incarceration. Despite this chillingly high rate of error, courts at every level are being pressured to shut their doors to death row appeals, just as more and more windows are opening to reveal capital mistakes.

Between 1973 and 1993, an average of 2.5 people were freed from death row every year. In the next six years, that rate nearly doubled, to an average of 4.6 condemned people set free annually. And yet, increasingly, the courts do not listen to claims of innocence.

In thirty-three states, any claim of innocence based on new evidence must be brought to court within six months of the final appeal. Only seven states permit the motion at any time. As a result, most prisoners can get state relief only by making executive clemency applications to governors, a process more attuned to political winds than the nitty-gritty details of investigations based on molecular biology. Pardons are considered acts of mercy, not a method to determine actual innocence.

Historically, the relief valve for state prisoners was the federal courts. This was all but shut down by Congress under its 1996 Anti-Terrorism and Death Penalty Reform Act. In its zeal to achieve finality in death-penalty litigation, Congress eviscerated the great writ of federal habeas corpus, the mechanism used for almost two hundred years by state prisoners who wanted a federal court to review the justice of their state convictions. The 1996 law gives condemned prisoners six months after their state appeals to ask for federal intervention, and sets a one-year time limit for all other cases. This "reform" legislation also requires federal courts to presume state courts are right about many things that state courts often are wrong about. Everyone agrees that it is a terrible thing for an innocent person to be imprisoned. Far worse, though, would be for a politician to take a moderate line on crime.

Prisoners who want to prove their innocence through DNA tests must run this gauntlet of state and federal time limits to get access to evidence and to a day in court. Only two states, New York and Illinois, have statutes that give inmates time and money for postconviction DNA testing. Elsewhere, it's up to the local district attorney. And whenever a prosecutor does not consent, the Innocence Project has had to fight long, expensive, and maddening battles. The project has filed suits that seek to establish a constitutional right to prove actual innocence that would override deadlines. Congress and state legislatures could pass laws like those in New York and Illinois. As for prosecutors and courts, a 1999 Justice Department study sent them a clear message: Don't stand in the way of tests that might prove innocence.

Seven men on death row got past the procedural hurdles and established innocence with DNA tests. They include Ron Williamson, the former minor-league baseball player from Ada, Oklahoma, and Rob Miller, the man whose "dream" statement was claimed to be a confession. The crimes had smacked into their communities like tidal waves, saturating the public in coverage by the news media. Three others were in Illinois, including Rolando Cruz and Alejandro Hernandez, condemned for a murder of a young girl, very much like that of Dawn Hamilton.

Dennis Williams was sentenced to death in 1978 and again following a retrial in 1987 for the rape and murder of a couple kidnapped from a gas station on the east side of Chicago. Williams had been convicted with three other men—nicknamed the Ford Heights Four—but he was the only one to receive a death sentence. Once again, the police were feeling the heat—and when other suspects turned up, after the initial arrests, they were ignored.

Twenty years later, journalism students from Northwestern University, led by their professor, David Protess, reinterviewed the other suspects and obtained confessions from them. These were backed up by DNA tests.

Ronald Jones, a down-on-his-luck ex-con from the south side of Chicago, was accused of the 1985 rape-murder of Debra Smith, twenty-eight, the mother of three. Jones gave a signed confession after ten hours in custody, when, he says, he was beaten and brought to the abandoned building where the murder took place. His "confession"—that he killed Smith after she took ten dollars for sex and wouldn't perform—didn't make much sense since Smith was not known as a prostitute, and had left her fiancé at home while she went out to buy fried chicken. In 1994, five years after the conviction, the trial judge who sentenced Jones to death refused to approve sensitive new DNA testing. Instead, he mocked Dick Cunningham and Gary Pritchard, attorneys working with the Capital Litigation Division of the state appellate public defender, for continuing to believe in Jones's innocence. Nonetheless, with some help from the Innocence Project and a ruling by the Illinois Supreme Court, Jones finally obtained the tests. They showed that the semen on Ms. Smith's body didn't originate with Ronald Jones. In May 1999, he became the twelfth inmate in twelve years to be released from the Illinois death row.

———

In 1994, Kirk Bloodsworth also joined their number. The panties of Dawn Hamilton, it turned out, had been stained with semen, then flung into a tree. A test of the semen by Dr. Edward Blake at the Forensic Science Associates laboratory in Richmond, California, showed that Bloodsworth could not have been the source. He was released from prison, given a pardon by the governor, and awarded $300,000 in special compensation by the state.

All this, simply because the ejaculate of a murderer had been captured on a child's underwear.

Over the years, debate about the current death penalty scheme in the United States has covered its cost, inequities, usefulness as a deterrent, and the fundamental moral issue of retribution. Layered and sophisticated, the arguments can be ignored by no serious person. Yet the revelations of the DNA era transcend them. No less than someone accused of a barroom brawl or gas-station stickup, the person charged with capital murder faces a system that relies on eyewitnesses, confessions, forensic experts, snitches, defense lawyers, prosecutors, and police officers. Historically, the fallibility of these parties has been given lip service, then ignored in the backwash of emotion that follows a terrible killing.

Now, with DNA, it is possible to see that these errors, rising from human nature, are not abstractions but authentic sources of torment to those falsely accused and wrongly convicted. In capital cases, such errors condemn the innocent.

A semen stain the size of a dime saved Kirk Bloodsworth; he owes his life to the depravity of a murderer. Suppose the killer of Dawn Hamilton had "merely" murdered her, and not added sexual assault to his crime; there would have been no semen on Dawn's panties to find, no sperm cells barcoded with the murderer's DNA and not Kirk Noble Bloodsworth's. But for that, the state of Maryland, under authority granted it by the U.S. Supreme Court, would have murdered an innocent man.

"I have never in my history have ever had a violent act, especially on a child," Bloodsworth told Judge J. William Hinkel, who was about to sentence him to die. "Giving me a life imprisonment or the death sentence does not serve justice properly in my opinion."

He struggled to tell the judge, without insulting him, that the trial had been all wrong.

"I think this has been a travesty of misjustice all the way around, not to put the Honor on the spot or anybody else in this Court. They have to do their job. Somebody told them what to do, and then it comes down the line.

"All's I'm saying, Your Honor, I did not commit this crime on July the 25th, 1984. If I had have, it would have been stated from the start. Thank you."

Judge Hinkel spoke about the legalities. Then he got to the crime.

"The most terrible of all crimes, murder, rape, sodomy . . . was committed upon the most helpless of all our citizens, a trusting little girl. The torture that she endured and the horror that was visited upon her is beyond my mere words to describe or express."

Having presided at the trial, the judge knew the prosecution's case was translucently thin. Yet the crime was horrible. Could he do less?

"Therefore," said Judge Hinkel, "it is the judgment of this Court that the Defendant be committed to the Division of Correction for the purpose of carrying out the sentence of death as to the first count."

The courtroom erupted in cheers from the family and friends of the dead girl. The sound shot into Bloodsworth like an ice pick. He was alone now. The world wanted him dead. "That's when I realized this was no longer a dream," Bloodsworth would recall, "but there was a real possibility I would be executed, although I was completely innocent. It was the loneliest feeling I ever had."

That was March 1985. On June 28, 1993, Kirk Bloodsworth walked out of the courthouse, free and clear. The state's attorney, Sandra O'Connor, said she had nothing to apologize for.

"We did nothing improper," said O'Connor. "The evidence against the defendant was extremely strong, and we took it to trial."

A famous study, *In Spite of Innocence,* by Hugo Bedau and Michael Radelet, documents 463 cases of wrongful capital convictions in this century. Some involved legal innocence, in which a person who participated in a crime was charged incorrectly with the murder. Others involve actual innocence.

"The bottom line," said Michael Radelet, "is we're making all these God-like decisions without the God-like skills. But people don't want to be bothered by that."

Less than a month after he was released from prison, Kirk Bloodsworth was asked to speak at a hearing in the U.S. House of Representatives on a proposal that would shorten the appeals process in capital cases.

"Speaking as a person who is supposed to be dead," said Bloodsworth, then thirty-four, "I believe the death penalty should be abolished, period. Because you can't be sure."

Starting Over

The big man dialed another number, and began to wonder whether he was just listening to a tape, with the same dialogue replayed over and over again.

"I was recently released from prison," David Shephard began, "and I am looking for a job."

"All right, we have some programs that can help you with job skills and placement," said the woman on the phone. "We will need to take some information. How long were you incarcerated?"

That was easy. "Eleven years, five months," said Shephard, "minus one day."

"Do you have a place to live now?"

"Fortunately, I am staying with my mother; she has a room for me," said Shephard.

"What were your crimes?" asked the woman.

"I didn't really have any," said Shephard. "I was not guilty."

"Then what were you in prison for all that time?"

"They said I kidnapped and raped a woman," said Shephard, "but they let me out early. A DNA test proved I didn't do it."

"So you're on parole or probation?" asked the woman.

By now, Shephard knew where the conversation was going. This was the fourth call he had made to people who held contracts to place and counsel convicts after their release.

"No, I'm actually innocent," said Shephard. "I have an order from the judge that says, 'The arrest and conviction which is the subject of this order shall be deemed not to have occurred.'"

"Then I don't know what help we can give you," said the woman, "because we deal with ex-offenders. Technically, you're not an ex-offender if the conviction is 'deemed not to have occurred.' All our programs are for people who were guilty. Were you working before you were arrested?"

"I worked at Newark Airport," said Shephard.

"Will they take you back?" she asked.

"The place went out of business three years after I went away," said Shephard. "My brother was working for them. Do you have some groups that I could attend, like for support?"

"I'm sorry," said the woman. "All our groups are for people who are participating in the programs. So you wouldn't be eligible for that."

"All right," said Shephard, knowing his cause was lost.

"Contact the state employment agency," said the woman. "You can find a job. They have postings. You don't even have to say you were arrested, because the whole thing was canceled. You'll be all right."

"Thanks," said Shephard, hanging up the phone. It wasn't all right. He had gone hunting for jobs. They had a place on the application that asked for employment history. What was he supposed to write down he had been doing for the last eleven years? Working in the prison laundry? Running a numbers racket while in Yardville? That wasn't going to cut it.

On a lark, he wrote to the office of the governor of New Jersey, Christie Todd Whitman, explaining his situation. Someone sent a letter back saying that they couldn't do anything for him, but maybe he should try the Department of Corrections. Which would send him to one of the ex-offender programs, and he would be back where he started, no conviction, no job, no work history, no money.

The whole thing had started at work, on a bitter cold New Year's Eve in 1983 twelve years earlier. The job, guiding planes along the ramps at Newark International Airport, had been a good one—Shephard was making $11.75 an hour, nice money for a kid who was just nineteen years old and had dropped out of high school. That morning, the staff had been told to go to a classroom inside a hangar at the airport to collect their paychecks. Normally, they had to line up outside a trailer where the timekeeper worked. At least they wouldn't be standing in the wind.

David Shephard seemed to have life right about where a young man would want it. He had a girlfriend, she was expecting, and they were going to get married. He had a good job. And he had picked up his paycheck; he was taking home more than $700 because he had worked some overtime.

When he left the classroom with his pay envelope, two white men in suits stepped up to him.

"David? We'd like to have a word with you," said one.

They were detectives from Hillside, a small town a few miles from the airport, and they wanted to talk about a stolen car. Would he mind coming to the police station?

"No problem," said Shephard.

David Shephard had never set foot in a police station in his life. When he arrived in Hillside, he suddenly found that he would be in the custody of the state for a long time to come. A week earlier, on Christmas Eve, a twenty-one-year-old white woman had been seized at a mall in Woodbridge, New Jersey, driven to Hillside, and raped repeatedly by two black men. During the attack, one man referred to the other as "Dave." A week later, her car was found near the terminal building at Newark Airport where Shephard worked. Her purse was found in the trash. The company had agreed to line up its employees and point out the two black men named Dave. The victim had been watching.

Shephard was questioned for most of the day, fingerprinted, photographed, then locked in a cell. He was the only one in the jail cell. Late in the evening, he heard voices over the loudspeaker.

"Shephard. Why did you rape that white woman?"

"Shephard. You shouldn't have done that."

"We're going to get you."

"Wait till midnight, when all the sirens are blasting. We'll get you."

A few minutes before midnight, the lights in the cell area were turned off. Alone in his cell, in the dark, Shephard could hear a door opening and the footsteps of several people approaching. He climbed off the bunk and into the farthest corner of the cell.

"We're gonna get you, Shephard!" said someone.

Suddenly, over the loudspeaker, another voice barked: "Leave the prisoner alone. Leave the cell area at once."

"Shit!" said one of the voices in the hallway.

A moment later, sirens from police cars and fire trucks and ambulances wailed into the sky. The new year was starting. In another hour, Shephard would have the company of a solitary man who had been arrested for public intoxication. Never had he been so happy to see a drunk in his life. The next morning, he was moved to the Union County jail. There, he was given a short course in survival. While playing cards through the bars, another inmate stole his cigarettes. Shephard's cell mate, a career criminal nicknamed Dego, told him: "You have to do something, or you'll have no peace."

That night, David beat the thief with a metal dinner tray until the tray bent. The whole tier was locked down for three days; forty-eight inmates, but no one ratted him out.

At the county jail, where he spent eighteen months, he found himself an outsider among people who knew one another well, a reunion of old acquaintances who were catching up on the latest gossip and news. They spoke of who controlled the action. Who ran food rackets. Who controlled drugs. Who was in charge of the yard. Shephard thought they were talking about their neighborhoods and what was going on back home, but then he realized it was all about state prison. That was their world, and he was sure that it would never be his.

The trial was short. The woman said Shephard was one of the two men who attacked her. His family testified that David had gone to work that day and had come home as usual on the bus. The bus driver said Shephard was a regular passenger, but he couldn't remember if he was on board Christmas Eve, as opposed to any other night. In private conferences, Shephard's attorney urged him to take a plea bargain that would give him a ten-year sentence. "It appears that you did this crime," he recalled being told by his attorney, who later would become the chief public defender for the state of New Jersey. She insisted she believed in his innocence, but by David's account, that was their last conversation. They didn't even speak to prepare Shephard before he swore on the witness stand that he was not guilty. He was sentenced to twelve to sixty years.

At the state prison, he was interviewed for the sex-offenders' group therapy but was told that he was not eligible because he was in denial. A guard urinated in his food. "Rapist doesn't need to eat, and if he wants to, this is how he will eat," he remembers the guard saying. He created a story: He actually didn't rape anyone but had robbed a group of people and forced them to take off their clothes. He had touched one person, so the cops inflated the charge to rape. That version of events improved his stature inside, where rapists were considered no more than something stuck to the shoes of murderers and robbers.

He fought. He smoked pot. He was set on by four guys one day in his room, after he took a shower. He fought them off with a Bic pen. A prisoner Shephard knew went to bed with a plastic bag tied around his neck, then pulled the covers over his head so the guards would not see him suffocating. After three years, Shephard established a sports-betting ring and soon had prisoners and guards as his customers. He read about DNA tests and wrote a brief himself, applying for a writ of habeas corpus. The judge assigned Diane Carl, from the Union County public defender's office, to assist him. He was released April 28, 1995.

———

Back home after eleven years and four months, Shephard discovered that he was carrying some bags that were not easy to drop. He would not visit Newark Airport, because he had been arrested there; he wouldn't ride a bus or train, because of the crowds. Freed during the first warm breaths of spring, he spent hours sitting on his mother's porch, often falling asleep there.

His mother found him there one night. "David," she said gently. "Come on inside."

"Guess I can't get enough of the outside," he said sleepily.

He found a job, eventually, through a friend who worked for the mayor of Newark. He cleaned City Hall. The take-home pay was about $10,000 less than what he was getting with overtime at the airport, but he was glad for the work. In the evening, he would take a long walk home. His girlfriend Erica, and their son, Lamar, nearly a teenager, he would see on weekends. He opened a bank account, and wondered about the plastic card with the black magnetic stripe on the back. He did his banking only during teller hours because he had watched two ATM cards be quickly swallowed by the machine and he was too embarrassed to ask for help.

One morning, he went to work and had another payday surprise. His check was $150 short. He went to the payroll department.

"That's a garnish on your wages," said someone there. "Nothing we can do about it."

The New Jersey Department of Social Services had provided welfare for Lamar for one year while Shephard had been away. He had been deemed a deadbeat dad for having failed to pay child support while he was in prison. With interest, the amount owed for the one year was $18,000. As with crime, no politician ever got in trouble for being too harsh with welfare recipients.

He visited a lawyer, Paul Casteleiro, in Hoboken, New Jersey, who was known for bringing lawsuits on behalf of people whose rights had been violated. Like everyone who meets Shephard, the lawyer was impressed by his openness, his lack of bitterness, and the way he had landed on his feet. Shephard brought the trial transcripts and reports with him. Casteleiro would review them.

Shephard got a call a few weeks later. "Bad news," said the attorney. "There is no one to sue."

The victim was wrong and had made an honest mistake. The police had relied on her identification, and properly so. Given that evidence, the prosecutors had sought an indictment, and a jury had found him guilty. They honestly thought David Shephard had raped the woman; DNA tests that would contradict the eyewitness had not yet been invented. That Shephard spent eleven years, four months, three weeks, and six days in the custody of New Jersey was a consequence of human error, not malice. The state had carried out its responsibilities with due regard for all his rights to a fair trial, a free lawyer, and the right to appeal.

Couldn't he sue the Hillside Police Department for wrongful arrest? No, because the detectives had "probable cause"—the victim's identification—to believe Shephard was the rapist when he was nabbed. How about malicious prosecution? Again, the rules don't make that possible for Shephard or most wrongly convicted people—they would have to show that a district attorney proceeded without probable cause, and with actual malice towards the defendant. Even in cases where prosecutors plainly violate important rules, such as the requirement to let an accused person know evidence of innocence, once a grand jury has voted an indictment, the prosecutor and the state enjoy broad immunity.

Unless Shephard could prove that the victim had identified him in bad faith—knowing that he had not done the crime—she, too, was immune from a lawsuit.

Millions of dollars in payments were made to Glen Dale Woodall, William Harris, and other innocent men in West Virginia, but only because of the depraved and reckless behavior of Fred Zain, the pseudo-serologist who manufactured results to make them look guilty. Just about that level of outright corruption or fraud has to be shown before most states will compensate the wrongly convicted. In West Virginia, for instance, the highest award before the Zain convictions were overturned was $35,000.

Similarly, in Illinois, the four men wrongly convicted in the Ford Heights murders settled their civil rights lawsuit for $36 million, a staggering sum that reflected the state's exposure to charges of police and prosecutorial misconduct.

If David Shephard had tripped on a cracked sidewalk and broken his leg, or if he had used a shampoo that made his hair fall out, he would have had a better chance of winning a lawsuit than he would for having been ordered at gunpoint by the state of New Jersey into a prison between the ages nineteen and thirty.

Only sixteen states have laws that compensate the wrongly convicted. Most are so stingy that they are painful to consider. Kevin Green, an ex-Marine who spent sixteen years in prison in California, received that state's maximum compensation: $10,000. "Cash in hand, I got sixty-seven hundred dollars because I had to pay the lawyer who helped with the application a third," said Green, who has called numbers in a Utah bingo parlor and worked in a Missouri Wal-Mart since his release. Green's restitution works out to $418 for each year he served. In 1999, the state legislature passed a special bill compensating him.

For the innocent people who serve time in the federal prisons, the compensation is even more miserly. Uncle Sam pays a maximum of $5,000, regardless of how long and how hard the years have been.

Nationally, the Innocence Project study found that only 37 percent of the wrongly convicted received compensation.

Even in states that have exemplary compensation laws, the innocent have a hard time getting paid. The New York saga of Isidore Zimmerman is instructive. Zimmerman was condemned to die in 1937 for murdering a policeman during a candy-store holdup. One afternoon, his hair was shaved for the electrodes. Two hours before the execution, the governor issued a stay, then commuted his sentence to life. He was in prison until 1962, when all parties agreed that he had been railroaded. In his lost years, most of his family and friends had died or moved away. Zimmerman's attempts to get compensation were sympathetically covered in the press, and finally, in 1981, Gov. Hugh Carey signed a private bill granting Zimmerman the right to sue the state. He won a million dollars. Four months later, he dropped dead of a heart attack on the sidewalk. (A few years later, so did his wife. Neither Zimmerman left a will or an obvious heir, so the money they had fought so hard to get was returned to the state.)

In 1984, the state expanded the right granted solely to Zimmerman, which would permit anyone who could prove he or she had been wrongfully convicted to sue the state. A legal doctrine known as "strict liability" was used, which meant that no person or institution had to take the blame for the injustice; if an innocent person was sent to prison, the state would have to provide reasonable compensation.

In design, the law seems fair, humane, and generous. The practice has been miserable. The state attorney general's office has litigated ferociously against compensating people it concedes were wrongfully imprisoned. For instance, three state attorney generals—two Democrats and a Republican—went to court to block any payment to Marion Coakley, the mildly retarded man whose wrongful conviction spurred the creation of the Innocence Project.

The politicians argued correctly that the law requires that the innocent party have done nothing to contribute to his own conviction. Coakley's appointed defense attorney didn't prepare the case thoroughly, the state argued, so in effect, Coakley himself contributed to his conviction—even though, as the attorney general's office conceded, "Mr. Coakley was an innocent man." Mae West could have argued the state's case: goodness had nothing to do with it.

Ultimately, Coakley was awarded $460,000, but he will have to wait before he sees any benefit. On his release from prison, he left New York and moved home to South Carolina. He drank, was depressed, and had no money. He ended up breaking into a home, was arrested, and sentenced to twenty years in jail.

David Shephard had fought his way out of prison on his own, filing a brief to get the evidence retested, a move that proved his innocence. Once outside, he had some help fighting for compensation. He met Barry backstage at a legal affairs TV show in Trenton, New Jersey, and, moved by his story, Barry held a press conference on the spot, vowing action.

"We will go to the state legislature and seek to have a private bill passed, addressing the needs of David Shephard," said Barry.

A reporter from the *New Jersey Law Journal* raised a slight problem.

"Did you know that the state constitution forbids the legislature from passing private bills?" he asked.

"No," said Barry, gulping hard. "I didn't know that."

What that meant is that no one in Shephard's shoes could be taken care of until everyone had been. The law could not be tailored to benefit him, as had been done in New York State for Izzy Zimmerman. New Jersey had to make a new law providing compensation for all the wrongfully convicted. Attorney Casteleiro wrote to every state legislator, sending news clips about Shephard's innocence and explaining that he was now broke. He spoke to key Republicans and Democrats, lining up their support. Barry, meanwhile, escorted Shephard to the virtual town square of *Larry King Live* on CNN. They met up with Jay Monahan, a lawyer-turned-journalist from Fox TV, who was outraged by Shephard's plight.

Monahan took on Shephard as a cause. Not only did he present a week-long series about Shephard, but Monahan spent hours coaching him for the interviews, even replaying footage to show the friendly but shy Shephard how he was coming across. Shephard would say he got far more preparation for his TV appearance from Monahan than he did for the witness stand from his defense lawyer.

In the end, the lobbying campaign by Casteleiro and the exposure paid off. Instead of having to blame someone for the wrongful conviction, innocent people now just have to show that they were sent away for at least eighteen months before being exonerated. The maximum award is $20,000 a year—which, for Shephard, meant a $240,000 payout.

He married the fiancée he had left behind, and another child joined their son. They live now with his wife's mother, and her grandmother, and David works as an investigator for the public defender's office in Newark, with plans to go to work for the Essex County prosecutor. "I want to stop these cases," he explained, "before they become trials."

The state, meanwhile, continued to dun Shephard for the one year of welfare his son received while he was in prison. He finally got a judge to stop the garnishment, after the state had collected $7,000 out of his salary. The judge allowed the state to keep the money it already had lifted from his paycheck. If he ordered the state to give back the money, the judge told Shephard, the public wouldn't understand.

The world does not wait for the wrongly convicted to catch up. Nor does it wait very long for crime victims. When prisoners come home vindicated, the cameras hover for a day or two. Then they are gone. The victim and the freed prisoner are once again alone, and often bereft.

———————

"When I was raped," said Jennifer Thompson, "they billed me for the rape kit." She had been a college student in North Carolina when a man broke into her apartment, attacked her, then left and raped another woman. She has been open, eloquent, possessed of far more wisdom about violent crime than anyone could wish for. She bristles when someone casually utters the word *rape* to describe situations having nothing to do with violence—people saying they got raped in a business deal, or were in some fashion taken advantage of.

"When people use the word *rape* that way, I want to scream, 'You have no idea what it feels like to be raped!'" she said. "It's 'specially cruel for a woman. I'm five feet, one inch, one hundred five pounds. Even when you try to carry on a relationship with your husband, it's a problem. I spend a lifetime confronting it. I'm still afraid of the dark."

The man charged with her rape, and that of the neighbor, was Ronald Cotton. At his trials for both crimes, Jennifer revisited the violence and the awful memories.

"The police, the prosecutor, my friends kept telling me I was a great witness—so strong and courageous. Remember, there were two trials," said Thompson. "So I had to go through it all again on the witness stand. I needed to be infallible and self-righteous."

Cotton maintained his innocence; eventually, DNA tests exonerated him and implicated another man, Bobby Poole. Jennifer Thompson had started to rebuild her life by the time the detective and the prosecutor visited her with the news that Ronald Cotton would go free.

"I felt like someone had punched me in the gut. All the air rushed out of my body, and then they left. I cried for days. It was a hollow, empty feeling. My first fear was, 'I'm going to be sued,'" she said.

The story of the wrongful conviction had a brief life in the national media. Ronald Cotton, it turned out, was a man of infinite grace in his sympathy for Jennifer Thompson. Not so the press, it seemed to her.

"The first publicity made me angry. *Larry King* and *People* magazine perceived it as a white woman against a poor black boy. But the reality is, I *am* a white woman raped by a black man," she said.

She gave a long, thoughtful interview to *Frontline*, the PBS newsmagazine show, in which she acknowledged the strength of the new forensic evidence. Despite that intellectual understanding of his innocence, she said during the broadcast, there was no denying the emotional disruption of Ronald Cotton's release.

"All of a sudden, me as a victim who suffered a horrific crime, a crime that a lot of people can't understand, all of a sudden we are almost like thrown away and the victim then becomes the man who has been released out of prison—and all of a sudden, his victimization is just, it's hailed and everyone feels sorry for him and it is just, it's terrible.

"We took away years of his life, which I am not trying to deny any of those things, but the same amount of years have been taken away from me. His bars were made of metal. My bars are emotional. My bars, I can't ever break them free."

At night, she still fears opening the door to put out the trash. When she is alone, her shudders actually make her bed move. "That is how a part of me was ripped away and I can't ever have back. I mean, he gets restitution. I got nothing. And I am not asking for anything, but the tables turn."

Speaking to *Frontline*, using her own name, allowing her face to be shown, was a way of climbing out of the pain. She agreed to do publicity for the show ahead of its broadcast. "And then this black woman reporter from NPR pinned me: 'Do you dislike African American men?' 'How can you live with yourself?' It made me feel resentful and defensive," said Ms. Thompson.

Following the broadcast, she made another decision. Ever since Ronald Cotton's release, she had wanted to write a letter to him, to make some kind of peace, but her family attorney had advised against it.

"After the *Frontline* show, I asked to meet with Cotton," said Ms. Thompson. "The detective arranged it. I met alone with Cotton and his wife. I didn't even want my husband to be with me. I cried, I felt naked. And Ronald said, 'I am not angry with you, I forgive you.' It was a remarkable gift.

"It's weird, I hated him so much I wanted to watch him die. And now I care a lot about him. He taught me grace and forgiveness."

Even with all that she knows now about the goodness of Ronald Cotton, and even with the real criminal, Poole, locked away, the crime lingers in her mind as unfinished business. "Even today," she said, "when I have nightmares about the rape, I still don't see Bobby Poole."

———————

It is one thing for a DNA test to prove that those bones in the Russian grave since the start of World War I really do belong to Czar Nicholas. It is quite another for the test to release a man from prison or death row as an innocent. For the wrongly convicted, the results are vindication. For those who sent the wrong men away, the tests are repudiation. At the most intimate level of memory, personal history must be rewritten when a guilty verdict is vacated not merely as faulty on legal grounds but as dead wrong. The disowned verdicts had supplied a sense of completion, if not closure, to prosecutors, investigators, jurors, the public, and most of all, crime victims such as Jennifer Thompson. Memories and narratives, long fixed in the heart and mind, are overthrown by the sudden exonerations. Nothing less than a revolution happens, with all the attendant turmoil. Perhaps it is not surprising that the raw truths of this new era have not been absorbed with universal gratitude.

For public policy, the resistance to the upheaval of the DNA exonerations has been shaped by officials who now simply refuse to permit tests. And even in the face of this dramatic record of fallibility, many politicians continue to believe that they must support the ultimate punishment of death.

At the personal level, those faced with mistaken convictions include the people who engineered them, many devoted public servants among them. The detectives who investigated the Jennifer Thompson rape said there was nothing they would do differently.

In Alexandria, Virginia, Investigator Barry Shiftic is without apology for anything that happened to Walter Snyder, the man wrongly sent to prison for raping a neighbor.

"I think he's guilty," said Shiftic. "He confessed. The victim testified it was him." In fact, Snyder's "confession" was not recorded, and he disputed that he ever admitted to the crime. Snyder also ended up with broken ribs.

Shiftic had served eleven years as one of two sex crimes investigators in Alexandria, and the Snyder case was one of his last. He suffered stomach ulcers and other physical ailments, Shiftic said, from the pressures of the job and the stress of the Snyder affair, in which his actions were harshly criticized. "I was tired of the damned case. I just wanted it to go away. Y'all don't know me that well. But if a mistake had been made, I'd be the first to tell you."

In his time with the sex crimes squad, DNA evidence attained a pivotal role in many cases, more so for prosecution than for exoneration. How could Shiftic reconcile his claim that Snyder was guilty with DNA tests that showed he could not have been the source of the semen left by the rapist?

"The evidence just sat out there," he said. "It got moved three times. Who has access to the place? Where is the integrity of the evidence?"

These are good, valid questions, although they are ones that would be expected from a layperson who had no familiarity with forensic DNA tests, not from a professional with eleven years in the business. In fact, Barry, Peter, and Jim faced similar questions when Kerry Kotler, one of the first cases they had championed—Barry and Peter in court, Jim in the newspaper—was rearrested and convicted a few years after his release. Kotler had been cleared in 1992 by DNA of the 1981 rape of a nurse's aide on Long Island. Four years later, DNA tests implicated him in a sexual assault on a college student who had been pulled off a highway by someone with a fake police badge. The rape of the college student was so galling, so calculating, that people instantly assumed that Kotler could not have been innocent in the earlier attack on the nurse's aide, and that his release had been some kind of legal trick or sleight of hand.

The questions seemed at once inevitable and inane. The proofs of guilt and innocence were identical. Their reliability does not depend on the results, but in how the tests are conducted.

Perhaps the most common misconception is that sex crime evidence simply could be swapped, as has happened with urine samples when people are tested for drugs. Substituting counterfeit evidence would not work for one simple reason: The victims' DNA also was contained in the original rape kits and remained there, marks of authenticity. The female and the male cells were bound together like meteorite and planet from the moment of collision. Other schemes that would fail include sprinkling DNA from another male into the mixture. To tamper with the rapist's DNA, which is what Shiftic suggested and some speculated had happened in the Kotler exoneration, would require not simply a fleck of skin or blood from another person to contaminate the evidence, but an actual semen sample from a third party. Even then, the DNA of Kotler or Snyder, if it had been in the rape kit, most likely would have been impossible to hide because the DNA tests would have revealed two male profiles, not one. Shiftic should have known all this. When he was interviewed in 1998, five years after Walter Snyder had been released from prison, the detective simply didn't care.

"If he is innocent, I wish him a good life, but I will have no remorse for him," said Shiftic. "I have no remorse for anyone that I have ever arrested."

On the other hand, Walter Snyder's exoneration was a source of anguish to Joseph McCarthy. A few years after he prosecuted Snyder, McCarthy moved into private practice in northern Virginia, where his business includes defense work. "You feel like hell. It's so upsetting. From my side, the lessons are watch your prosecutors, challenge their assumptions. It was awful. That poor soul lost seven years of his life," said McCarthy.

How did it happen? First, there was the disputed statement made by Snyder in the police station. Then there was the victim's identification. But the psychological process of indicting and convicting a man is far more subtle than just pieces of evidence, McCarthy explained. The prosecutor persuades himself of the suspect's guilt, and then observes facts and evidence only through that prism.

"People say, 'I'll believe it when I see it.' But sometimes we see it once we believe it. When there's a preconceived notion, we build facts into it, to support the notion. Did that happen in this case? It very well could have happened," said McCarthy. He did not understand, though, how the investigators could have misheard Snyder's alleged confession.

"Maybe I was too willing to believe what the law-enforcement officers told me. Maybe I got caught up in the sense that the prosecutor and the investigators are all on the same team. Maybe we ought to be more challenging of their assertions. And in a rape case, there's often a bonding between the victim and the prosecutor, and the investigator. They are going through a bad time. The psychology is that you're the last line of defense between them and the guy's getting out on the street.

"It's difficult to challenge the victim—are you certain you saw him and had a good look? You show her the sheet from the bed, and her voice cracks and she breaks into tears. It's tough when someone points out with the conviction in her heart that you're the person who did this.

"We need to teach young prosecutors to do a critical analysis of your evidence. Typically, we give power to people at the wrong end of their lives."

Lessons

In 1998, the Missouri State Investigators Association held its annual meeting and training program in Kimberling, Missouri, a big lakefront resort a few miles from Branson, the Jerusalem of country music. During the educational portion of the meeting, one lecture consisted of a postmortem on a murder case and how poor write-ups of police reports could have hurt the prosecution.

"We're going to review these reports to see if the investigators could have done a better job and tightened up the case," said Kevin Green, a researcher working with Gold Shield Consultants, the firm providing the training materials.

The crime had been committed in September 1979, nineteen years earlier, in Tustin, then a small company town for Marines and their families in Orange County, California. The police were called before dawn to a ground-floor apartment. A Marine corporal named Kirk Grier stated that upon returning from a late-night munchie run, he discovered his pregnant wife in a pool of blood, unconscious. The victim obviously had been hit with a blunt object. Corporal Grier's double cheeseburger sat on the table, unopened.

His wife, Debbie Grier, was taken to the hospital with critical head injuries. "She was nine months pregnant, and there was concern for her survival as well as the baby's," said Green. Soon afterward, the unborn child died and had to be removed by cesarean section. The woman was in a coma for a month. When she came out of it, she was unable to communicate for weeks.

As Green outlined the case, police initially thought that it was another crime by the "Bedroom Basher," a prowler known for climbing into ground-floor apartments, smashing the heads of women, and then raping them. At the time, California was flush with Hillside Strangler fever, and no one rushed out to draw attention to the Basher. Perhaps it was felt that one serial killer at a time was all the public could handle.

In any case, the Bedroom Basher theory was dropped when Mrs. Grier finally did begin to communicate, first with her husband, then with her mother. "She wanted to know what had happened to her," said Instructor Green. "She had lost much of her hearing, her ability to smell, some of her speech, and couldn't recognize family members other than her mother and her husband. Then came the big news."

Based on a series of hand signals from Debbie, the mother realized that her daughter was trying to tell her something about Kirk—namely, that he had hit her. Debbie apparently waited until Kirk was out of the hospital room to give her mother the message that her attacker had been her husband.

Only then was the husband's alibi seriously scrutinized. On the night of the crime, he told one investigator that he had gone out to the Jack in the Box to get some burgers for himself. But he told a second detective that the food had been for his wife. "He also told the police that he didn't get the food from the Jack in the Box right across the street because it had a big line at one-thirty in the morning," said Green. Corporal Grier's story might have been fishy from the jump if the investigators had just paid attention to their own reports. But they hadn't.

Neighbors said they heard yelling from the apartment that night, a woman screaming "Don't hit me," but the neighbors said the couple often had loud arguments.

"Kirk, who almost had slipped past as another victim, quickly became the lead suspect," said Green. Using an overhead slide projector, he displayed the police reports on the crime. Early on, the victim had said she was struck with a full bottle or can of Coors beer, although there was no beer found around the house that night. As a result, explained Green, they overlooked other property in the room. One item in particular, a key caddy, was not mentioned in the reports and not even dusted for fingerprints.

"Debbie testified at the trial that it was this key caddy that was the last thing she saw before her husband hit her with it," said Green. "She said that he had demanded sex from her, and that she refused, sending him into a rage. She said he had beat her with the key caddy and raped her."

During the trial, the defense argued that Debbie had suffered such serious brain damage that her memory was unreliable. Grier swore he had discovered his beaten wife only when he returned from his food run. He claimed to have seen a black man lurking near a van, both when he was leaving the house and when he returned. The prosecution scoffed at the theory. One would describe it as the "bogey man defense."

Originally charged with first-degree murder in the death of the unborn child, Grier was convicted of second-degree murder, so it was not a capital punishment case. Instead, he was sentenced to fifteen years to life. Grier went to prison, his wife divorced him and struggled to live with the devastating injuries, and the matter vanished from public consciousness. "There were some unusual developments in June 1996, seventeen years later," said Green.

In Tustin, a young detective named Tom Tarpley was investigating the old, unsolved murder of Debora Jean Kennedy. In 1980, at age twenty-four, she had been beaten on the head, then raped after she was dead. Tarpley found the crime-scene evidence in a storage locker and sent it away to be compared with a data bank of DNA samples collected from all convicted state prisoners. There was a match: a man named Gerald Parker, a former Marine, now a homeless drifter, had been the person who raped Debora Kennedy. At the same time, Tarpley heard that detectives in Costa Mesa, the next town from Tustin, also had come up with Parker's name in the investigation of two unsolved murders from the 1970s.

"Parker happened to be in prison on a parole violation but was due to be released on July 6," said Green. "This was in the middle of June." Tarpley, and the two detectives from Costa Mesa, Bill Redmond and Lynda Giesler, drove to Avenal State Prison, a low-security facility in California's Central Valley. For more than an hour, Redmond and Giesler questioned Parker. He toyed with them, and they got nowhere. The two Costa Mesa detectives were about to go home, when they told Tarpley to take a shot with Parker.

Tarpley saw that Parker was cuffed behind his back. "He had the cuffs turned around, so he was showing him respect," said Green. Then Parker began to talk.

He had committed so many murders and beaten so many women that he could not keep track of who had died, and who had survived. But he had something to say about a case that was not even on the list of unsolved crimes.

"First thing," Parker told Tarpley, "you better go get that Marine off death row for killing his wife. I did that one."

That would have been Debbie Grier, and it was not a case that Tarpley or anyone else was investigating because it wasn't "cold"—it had been closed seventeen years earlier with the arrest of Kirk Grier. At the time, Detective Tarpley was in junior high school.

Parker's opening words were the beginning of a long, creepy videotaped recording about the blur of murder and rape, a window into the banal mind of a serial killer. He spoke about the women he had killed with two-by-fours or with hammers, women alone in their homes. He didn't set out to kill them, just knock them out so they would not resist. Before entering, he rarely checked to see if anyone else was in the house, an act that Parker conceded, years later, was reckless. "There could have been a raving lunatic on the other side of that door," said the serial killer. Two decades earlier, he had murdered five women, beaten many others, and was caught only when he kidnapped and raped a thirteen-year-old girl on the way home from her father's funeral. Until June 14, 1996, no one had ever spoken to him about the murders.

By now, the class of Missouri investigators was buzzing. They wanted to hear more about the confession to the Grier attack.

Parker had told the detectives at the prison: "While I was incarcerated,

I was reading the paper about the Marine and his wife, and this one was in Tustin, and ah, I, if I'm not mistaken, they sent him to death row. And so there's a man on death row because of a murder I committed. She was pregnant at the time, and ah, he, they were arguing in the house. I was standing outside the window and then, ah, I didn't know he was coming out, and he got in his car and left. And I didn't actually know that until I entered the home. But I did, I did that murder, the one, the face, I do not recall the actual faces you know. . . ."

Pressed for details, Parker told the detective what he could remember of things done in a drunken stupor years earlier. "She's in the bedroom, okay, first when I opened the door, she's in bed and she sits up. Almost as if in recognition of somebody that she thought that I was, but I wasn't. And she laid back down, as if she recognized me, I guess she thought it was her husband or boyfriend, whichever, whichever the case it was. And then I hit her. I rushed into the room and hit her over the head with the board. Then I raped her."

When they asked for more information about the Grier attack, Parker said that he could not keep track of it all. He told them to check the DNA evidence for proof.

"Sure enough," said Green. "They found the old rape kit. One of the detectives had decided to keep it."

The semen in the seventeen-year-old case matched with Gerald Parker, just as he predicted. Instructor Green had the audience eating out of his hand. "Tom Tarpley went to see Kirk Grier in prison and told him he was getting out," said Green. "He had already been turned down for parole several times because he wouldn't acknowledge responsibility for the crime. One of the district attorneys would come to the hearings and oppose parole.

"Grier had tried to get DNA tests while he was inside, but he couldn't afford them. They brought him out of the prison, down to court, and dismissed the charges."

The instructor picked up the clicker for his last slides. He flashed a newspaper clipping up on the screen: INNOCENT MAN WALKS OUT AFTER 16 YEARS.

"He got on a plane at John Wayne Airport, flew to St. Louis, to meet his family. The papers carried it on the front page. And one other thing."

He clicked the slide tray forward one more time.

"His name isn't Kurt Grier," said Kevin Green. "His name is Kevin Green, and he settled down in Missouri with his family. He works at a Wal-Mart. He also was hired by Gold Shield Consultants to give a lecture in Kimberling this weekend for the Missouri Investigators Association."

On the screen was a newspaper photograph showing Kevin Green arriving home in Missouri. The people in the room played the face in the picture against the man standing in front of them. It was a showstopper.

———

All wrongfully convicted people take the lash of punishment for someone else's crime; that is the very definition of their predicament. Far too often, they are surrogates for serial criminals and killers, as in California, where Kevin Green carried the weight for a crime by Gerald Parker, who for twenty years stood unprosecuted for five murders. In Oklahoma, Robert Miller was condemned to die for murdering and raping two elderly women before DNA testing put a man named Ronnie Lott in their houses, as well as in the homes of several other women who survived his rapes. In Chicago, Rolando Cruz and Alejandro Hernandez were sentenced to death for killing Jeanine Nicarico, although it turned out that Brian Dugan admitted to murdering Jeanine and five others, including children, during sexual assaults. In North Carolina, Ronald Cotton was cleared of two rapes committed by a man tied to eight others. In Virginia, David Vasquez, a borderline mentally retarded man, pleaded guilty to raping a woman and hanging her from a pipe. Vasquez said he was innocent but copped a plea to avoid the death penalty. The time he served belonged to Timothy Spencer, who raped and murdered not only the victim in the Vasquez case, but three other women, all of them hanged. And because Spencer ultimately was sent to death row for the murders, he was not prosecuted for eight other rapes in which he was the prime suspect.

Each year, the technology for linking and solving these kinds of crimes gets faster and cheaper. Computers can sort through data banks of DNA samples with dazzling speed and connect identical profiles among far-flung atrocities. If a genetic profile of a criminal is already lodged in a data bank, identifying him is a no-brainer. Even if a pattern of crimes can't be tagged to a known criminal, prompt testing will prevent the lengthy detention of innocent suspects and immediately put the police back to the task of finding the real perpetrator. The failure to take full advantage of this technology, both for solving crimes and freeing the innocent, is a national scandal. Current investigative approaches must change.

Typically, DNA testing of evidence is done only *after* a suspect has been apprehended—and then takes two or three months. Hundreds of thousands of rape kits from unsolved cases are thrown out or sit in dead storage for years with no effort made by the authorities to run DNA tests, squandering opportunities to identify serial offenders and clear the wrongly convicted, such as Kevin Green. If crime scene materials were tested and catalogued immediately, one case could be linked quickly to others. Since a forensic DNA test can be completed in two or three days, crime laboratories could be given the resources to finish a case within a week. This would speed up apprehension of criminals before they commit additional crimes, and prevent the grotesque detention of thousands of innocent people.

And that goes not only for rapes and homicides but for burglaries, robberies, assaults—any kind of incident in which a criminal may have left a trace of skin, saliva, hair, or any biological evidence.

No matter whose privacy is at stake, data banks full of genetic information can be dangerous, particularly when the samples disproportionately come from black and brown men. Modern-day Mengeles, in search of evidence for master-race theories, would find data bases irresistible in the quest for a genetic link to criminality. A simple reform could slam the door on such eugenic inquiries. Any leftover blood, tissue, or DNA should be discarded once a profile has been stored.

———

Most of the lessons of the DNA era have nothing to do with high-tech gizmos or biotechnical wizardry. "Jurors should get innocence training," says Kevin Green. They need to be told: " 'You're doing this because we have to find the truth. The police haven't necessarily found the truth. The district attorney hasn't found the truth. Only you can.' "

Yet Kevin Green—bright, handsome, articulate, thoughtful—is legally an invisible man. America keeps virtually no records when a conviction is vacated based on new evidence of innocence. Judges typically write one-line orders, not official opinions, meaning that they don't analyze what went wrong. Neither does anyone else. The only place to study innocence is through accounts carried in newspapers and by broadcast news, a most haphazard net. By comparison, after England and Canada were scandalized by wrongful convictions, both countries set up commissions to study what went wrong. England now has an official Criminal Case Review Commission that investigates claims of innocence.

In the United States, there are grave consequences when an airplane falls from the sky; an automobile has a defective part; a patient is the victim of malpractice, a bad drug, or an erroneous lab report. Serious inquiries are made: What went wrong? Was it a systemic breakdown? An individual's mistake? Was there official misconduct? Can anything be done to correct the problem and prevent it from happening again?

In 1999, the Innocence Project reconstructed sixty-two cases in the United States of the sixty-seven exonerations in North America to determine what factors had been prevalent in the wrongful convictions. Mistaken eyewitnesses were a factor in 84 percent of the convictions; snitches or informants in 21 percent; false confessions in 24 percent. Defense lawyers fell down on the job in 27 percent; prosecutorial misconduct played a part in 42 percent, and police misconduct in 50 percent. A third involved tainted or fraudulent science. Among the more troubling findings is that several of these factors are more pronounced in the conviction of innocent black men. These numbers provide but a glimpse of an unexplored, undocumented, and challenging world. A more commanding view awaits further study by legal scholars and journalists of all innocence cases, including ones that do not avail of DNA as a tool in the exoneration process. Every state could use an Innocence Commission. None exist. Only the criminal justice system exempts itself from self-examination. Wrongful convictions are seen not as catastrophes but topics to be avoided.

Ignorance is law. The only two states with statutes that permit DNA tests after conviction, New York and Illinois have the most exonerations. In most states, a convicted prisoner has no right to obtain tests that might prove innocence. In practice, many prosecutors disregard those limits and agree to the tests. But not all.

"Without rules, we would never have finality to any case. It's common sense," said Robert Wayne Holmes, a chief assistant in the Brevard state's attorney's office. Holmes and his associates have persuaded two Florida courts to bar DNA tests for Wilton Allen Dedge, who was convicted in 1982 of a rape. The case against him was built on testimony from a jailhouse snitch, scent "evidence" provided by a police dog, and the victim's identification of Dedge—who was seven inches shorter and fifty pounds lighter than the man she said had stabbed and raped her. Dedge has been unable to obtain a DNA test because prosecutors and judges have strictly enforced Florida's two-year deadline.

"I'm not going to change the law," Holmes told the *St. Petersburg Times*. "Put yourselves in the shoes of the victim. Do you want that reopened?"

Finality is a doctrine that can be explained in two words when it comes to innocence tests: willful ignorance. In dozens of states, particularly Florida, Missouri, and Louisiana, the Innocence Project and other advocates have spent hundreds of hours just arguing against "finality" doctrines that are used to block inquiries that no fair person would resist. While several state courts have not budged, one did, memorably.

Once a year, the South Dakota Supreme Court moves its sessions to the farming town of Vermillion, home of the University of South Dakota School of Law. The court saves a few high-profile cases for the benefit of students in the audience. On March 24, 1998, the matter of *Davi v. Warden* was argued at the law school in front of Chief Justice Robert Miller and four other members of the court. The issue was simple. Once a convicted defendant has lost his appeals, does he still have the right to DNA testing? Peter presented the case for access. Ann Meyer advocated the case for the attorney general of South Dakota. Like the prosecutor in Florida, she warned the court about a flood of demands from people claiming to be innocent. Peter put forward the same position that he and Barry have taken around the country for the Innocence Project: what should govern on these questions is not legal precedent, not factual loopholes, but the fundamental obligation of everyone in the criminal justice system to ensure that only the factually guilty suffer in prison. As he spoke on that day in March 1998, Peter noted, fifty-five people had been exonerated by DNA. Five had been on death row.

Ms. Meyer attacked Peter's reference to the fifty-five exonerations. It's not in the record; the number hasn't been verified, she thundered. Mr. Neufeld is testifying as an expert rather than as an advocate.

The justice wondered what difference it made if there had been fifty-five exonerations or twenty-five. Wasn't the critical question how the attorney general would have answered if those same fifty-five or twenty-five men sought DNA testing in South Dakota?

Meyer responded: We would not allow them to be tested.

Chief Justice Miller reddened. He leaned over and his eyeglasses slid forward. At that moment, the case was as good as decided. Perhaps for the sake of the idealism of the young students in the room, Justice Miller chose not to ask the assistant attorney general if the state's position would have been the same for the people DNA tests showed had been wrongly sentenced to death. On April 15, 1998, the Supreme Court of South Dakota ordered the case remanded for DNA testing. The decision was unanimous. That day, willful ignorance lost, five to zero.

———

Even after definitive exonerations, authorities rarely try to find the real criminal, much less examine what went wrong. Among some prosecutors, the belief that even discredited convictions must be protected from challenge has forced them to take bizarre positions. They cling to the original verdicts by contriving new theories to explain why the semen of another man, not the convicted party, was discovered in the rape kit. Perhaps, they say, two men participated in the rape, or three, even though the victim only noticed one man. The foreign semen is explained by these new parties to the crime, first mentioned years after the fact: the unindicted co-ejaculator.

A Justice Department task force reported in late 1999 that the appellate process was poorly equipped to handle requests for new tests. But it said that prosecutors and judges should make every effort to help prisoners get the tests. The reason was clear: The DNA era had shaken the foundations of the system.

"The strong presumption that verdicts are correct has been weakened," wrote the National Commission on the Future of DNA Evidence.

Attention for the innocent person imprisoned or executed has burst in flashes through this century, before DNA even had a name. In the 1930s, the district attorney of Worcester County, Massachusetts, provocatively challenged Edwin Borchard, a professor of law at Yale University. "Innocent men are never convicted," the D.A. told the professor. "Don't worry about it. It is a physical impossibility." Professor Borchard proceeded to compile narratives of sixty-five cases in which innocent people were convicted, and in 1932 published his classic text, *Convicting the Innocent.*

Erle Stanley Gardner was most famous as the creator of the Perry Mason legal potboilers. In 1948, after a magazine profile mentioned that he had been a crusading lawyer in his younger days, Gardner was deluged with mail from mothers begging him to take up the causes of sons they believed to have been wrongly convicted. The writer set up a highly unofficial "Court of Last Resort" in *Argosy* magazine, investigating and publicizing a few of these. One involved a man who had been convicted of murder by strangulation after the bruises from ten fingers were found around the neck of the victim. However, the convict only had nine fingers.

In more recent years, Jim McCloskey and Kate Hill of the Centurion Ministries have taken on the causes of wrongly convicted. In Chicago, students, lawyers, and reporters led by professors at Northwestern University's law and journalism schools—Larry Marshall and David Protess—have saved the lives of innocent people condemned to die. At the now-defunded Alabama Capital Representation Resource Center, attorneys Bryan Stevenson and Michael O'Connor saved the life of Walter McMillan, an innocent man sentenced to die for a murder in the small Alabama town that was the setting for Harper Lee's classic *To Kill a Mockingbird.* In Queens County, New York, eighteen people locked up for crimes they had not committed were freed after investigations by a tough prosecutor, Gregory Lasak, and two former police officers, Stan Carpenter and Ted Wess. And in Canada, the wrongly convicted are represented by AIDYCK, an organization formed by the ex-boxer Rubin "Hurricane" Carter and attorney James Lockyer. There are many others.

In a few years, the era of DNA exonerations will come to an end. The population of prisoners who can be helped by DNA testing is shrinking, because the technology has been used widely since the early 1990s, clearing thousands of innocent suspects before trial. Yet blameless people will remain in prison, stranded because their cases don't involve biological evidence. The debt of justice will remain unpaid to innocent people accused of crimes in which the criminal did not ejaculate, spit, bleed, or shed tissue. For this reason, North American law schools, led by Cardozo and Northwestern, are forming an innocence network to handle cases of the wrongly convicted, whether or not the magic bullet of DNA testing is possible.

From Borchard's review of cases stretching back to the dawn of the American republic, all the way to the dawn of the twenty-first century, the causes of wrongful convictions remain the same. Clarity is manufactured about moments of inherent confusion. Witnesses swear they can identify the man who held the gun or knife. Police officers then coax or force confessions from suspects they believe guilty. Prosecutors bury exculpatory evidence and defense lawyers sleep on the job. Forensic scientists shade their conclusions or skip the tests altogether, to accommodate a presumption of guilt. Racism and bigotry, written out of the books, still shadow some police precincts, courtrooms, and jury boxes. And a nation, fed up with the coddling of criminals, grudgingly provides defense lawyers a $2,500 stipend, even with an execution at stake. Not many today would take up with Thomas Sharkie, who proclaimed in 1830: "The maxim of the law is . . . that it is better that ninety-nine . . . offenders shall escape than that one innocent man shall be condemned."

To ignore the possibilities of fixing the causes of unjust convictions is to render invisible the living witnesses, the fugitives from the unreal dream of wrongful incarceration.

Marion Coakley, back in the Bronx and broken by prison, fell to drinking; he returned home to South Carolina, couldn't keep a job, and burglarized a home. He went back to prison. In Virginia, Walter Snyder installs car radios and his parents still live on the street where Faye Treatser once saw him washing his car and decided he was a rapist. Walter has found new uses for DNA tests. Two women accused him of fathering children; in both cases,

DNA tests proved that he was not the father. "DNA is God," joked his mother Edith. "Three times we've rolled the dice with DNA, and we won every time."

Rob Miller left Oklahoma City after he was proven innocent of murdering the two elderly ladies. He married Kim Ogg, who never stopped fighting for him, and they moved to Utah, where he installs heating and air-conditioning systems. Glen Dale Woodall, liberated from a cell when Fred Zain's frauds were uncovered in West Virginia, became a father with Teresa, the wife who saw her new husband carried away in chains. He works barges that ply the Ohio and Mississippi rivers, loading cargo. Rather than serving out his sentence of 3,120 years, Tim Durham runs his family's electronics business in Tulsa.

Home, and just down the road from the mythical Tara in Georgia, Calvin Johnson works in the shipping and receiving department for a manufacturer of vinyl railing systems. He is much in demand as a Sunday preacher and was invited on a missionary trip to Uganda. He was brought back to Dooly State Prison by the Hope Prison Ministries and told the inmates of his rage and anger. Guilty or innocent, to change their lives they needed God, he told them. He was greeted with much affection.

Freed from death row, Kirk Bloodsworth remarried and moved back to the Chesapeake Bay, where he bought a boat and works in a fishing business. David Shephard, the airport employee who could get no help when he was released, does investigations for the public defender's office in Newark, New Jersy. The former Marine, Kevin Green, besides giving talks and lectures to law enforcement, has a job with Wal-Mart in Missouri.

Ringing through all these lives are the words of a conservative federal judge in Oklahoma. U.S. District Court Judge Frank H. Seay reviewed the trial of Ronald Williamson and decided it had been unworthy of the constitution. He wrote an epilogue to his order vacating Williamson's conviction.

"While considering my decision in this case, I told a friend, a layman, I believed the facts and law dictated that I must grant a new trial to a defendant who had been convicted and sentenced to death.

"My friend asked, 'Is he a murderer?'

"I replied simply, 'We won't know until he receives a fair trial.'

"God help us, if ever in this great country we turn our heads while people who have not had fair trials are executed. That almost happened in this case.

"Accordingly, the Writ of Habeas Corpus shall issue . . ."

———————

In April 1999, a few days after Dennis Fritz and Ron Williamson were freed from a life sentence and death row in Oklahoma, they appeared briefly on national TV. Footage of their release struck a nerve with the public. Their story was national news, after all. One of the big networks decided that it could stand one more story of people who were actually innocent. So the two men flew to New York and appeared on a morning talk show with Barry. Before they went back home, they took a tour of Yankee Stadium, the place that inhabited the dreams of many little kids in Oklahoma. They were joined by Tim Durham and Greg Wilhoit, two other men wrongly convicted in Oklahoma.

Dennis had aged since that spring night in Kansas City when the phone rang and the SWAT team descended on his mother's house. His hair had grayed. The daughter who had been twelve when he left home was now twenty-four. Still, his schoolteacher's inquisitive mind was sharp and intact as he followed the tour guide around the old ballpark. Dennis relished every free breath, whether drawn in the Bronx or on Lister Avenue in Kansas City.

Even squinting, it was hard to glimpse any trace of the Ron Williamson who once came roaring out of high school in small-town Oklahoma, a second-round draft choice full of promise and brains. Maybe there was a touch of the old Bull Durham character, the man who played a thousand nights in little parks where the mosquitoes buzzed and the lights hummed and the beer got warm if you didn't drink it fast.

"I just got a taste of how much fun they were having up here," said Ron, one foot on the Yankee dugout.

As remote as the old athlete was the condemned man, the one who stood in a cell on death row in Oklahoma, five days before his execution date, hands on the bars, yelling, "I'm innocent! I'm innocent! I'm innocent!" Yelling it over and over until he had no voice left to yell with.

All that raw anguish was veiled and inaudible on that beautiful April morning. Ron Williamson was visiting the life he thought he might have had, not the one he lived. The ballpark was empty. The sun was high in a clear sky, soft on the skin. The tour guide made a remark about Mickey Mantle's longest home run in Yankee Stadium. Ron immediately chimed in that Mickey had hit a longer one in Washington. He even told a baseball story of his own.

Because he had gone in a high draft round to the Oakland A's, Ron was allowed to dress with the regular major-league team one day in his first spring training.

"Catfish Hunter, Gene Tenace, Reggie Jackson—they had Dick Green playing second base, he was out of Oklahoma, he knew about me," said Williamson. "He called Reggie Jackson over."

He recited the twenty-year-old conversation.

"This is our second-round pick, another Oklahoma boy," Green said.

"What position you play?" Jackson asked.

"I'm not too sure," said Williamson, who could pitch, hit, and catch, and would gladly stand anywhere on a baseball field.

"Nah, Reggie, he's a right fielder," Green teased.

Jackson, who prowled right field like a lion, glared.

"Boy," Jackson snarled, "you're gonna die in the minor leagues."

Williamson cackled. He left out the next part, when the small-town hero came back home, broken; the part when he had been tapped for the big leagues but went mad with illness; and the time he was sent away to be executed. Also, how he ended up twelve years later as the seventy-eighth American to leave death row, exonerated.

For one moment, Williamson stood alone in center field, looming over the sparkling grass, his lumpy old athlete's body visible through an arc of water from the sprinklers.

"Don't feel too much," he said bluntly. "This all washed out of me over the years. Tell you the truth, I am more interested in a cold beer these days."

They drove out to the airport for the flight home. Traveling with Ron were his sister, Annette Hudson, who served as his guardian, and Mark Barrett, his public defender from Oklahoma.

For Ron and Dennis, nothing was simple in negotiating a world they had not seen for more than a decade.

"Photo ID, please," the gate agent said.

"I don't have one," Ron said.

"A driver's license with your picture?" she suggested.

"I don't have any ID," said Ron.

"I'm sorry," the gate agent said, "federal regulations require a photo identification for all passengers."

Then they all began to explain the places that Ron Williamson and Dennis Fritz had been, and that, once again, they had places to go.

Appendix 1

A Short List of Reforms to Protect the Innocent

DNA Testing

Pass statutes on the state and federal level modeled after legislation in New York and Illinois that allow postconviction DNA testing if it could establish a reasonable probability that inmate was wrongfully convicted. Until these laws are passed, follow the 1999 Justice Department report *Post Conviction DNA Testing: Recommendations for Handling Requests*.

DNA testing should be done within seven to fourteen days of a crime to make sure innocent suspects are not incarcerated and to improve the chances of catching the guilty. Do DNA tests on unsolved crimes, including more than 100,000 untested rape kits.

Mistaken Eyewitness Identification

Implement the recommendations from the 1999 National Institute of Justice report *Eyewitness Evidence: A Guide for Law Enforcement*. These measures all can be implemented by changes in police policies; legislation is not necessary:

> All lineups, photo spreads, and other identification processes should be video-taped.

An independent, trained identification examiner should run the lineups and photo spreads. The examiner should not know the suspect—avoiding the possibility of hints or reactions that would steer the witness.

Witnesses should be always be instructed prior to viewing that the actual perpetrator might not be in the lineup or photo spread.

Lineups and photo spreads should use the sequential presentation method rather than the simultaneous presentation method. With the sequential procedure, witnesses must decide on each person before seeing the next one. This prevents relative judgments and makes witnesses "dig deeper" to make the determination, and studies show such sequential presentations are more reliable.

Show-ups should be used only in rare occasions, such as when the person was detained near the scene of the crime and the witness can be shown the suspect within sixty minutes (or less) of the offense. Beyond this, proper lineups or photo spreads (using fillers) should be conducted.

The witness should be asked to rate his or her certainty at the time of the identification.

Police and prosecutors should be trained about the risks of providing corroborating details that may disguise doubts a witness may hold.

False Confessions

One simple rule: Videotape, or at least audiotape, all interrogations so there is an objective record. Alaska has such legislation, and it has long been the rule in the United Kingdom.

Jailhouse Snitches and Informants

Following the lead of Canada's Guy Paul Morin Commission recommendations, jurisdictions should set up a high-level screening committee of prosecutors to vet the jailhouse snitch/informant's testimony and all the attendant circumstances before permitting it to be used at trial. There are fourteen factors that must be considered, including:

- Can the statement be confirmed by extrinsic evidence, i.e., not by another snitch?
- Does it contain details or leads to the discovery of evidence known only to the perpetrator?

- Does the statement contain details that could reasonably be accessed by the in-custody informer, other than through inculpatory statements by the accused—e.g., press accounts or legal pleadings?
- What is the snitch/informer's general character—e.g., criminal record or other disreputable or dishonest conduct known to the authorities?
- Is the snitch/informer a recidivist snitch/informer?

Trial judges should presume that a jailhouse informant's testimony is unreliable and require the prosecutor to overcome that presumption before a jury can hear the evidence.

All deals with snitch/informants must be in writing and all communications between the snitch and the police or prosecutor should be videotaped or at least audiotaped.

Forensic Fraud

Forensic scientists should formally agree, as standard of practice, that crime laboratories function as an independent third force within the criminal justice system, unbeholden to prosecutors or defense lawyers, operated by professionals who will not misrepresent or slant data for either side.

Crime laboratory budgets should be independent from the police, and police officials should not be able to exercise supervisory responsibility over the scientists.

Complete discovery of underlying data from forensic tests should be provided in criminal cases. Reports from forensic tests should be comprehensible explanations of the work performed, not conclusory assertions, and must describe all potentially exculpatory inferences that could be drawn from the results.

There should be whistle-blower protection for forensic scientists in government who question the reliability of work, and experienced omsbudpersons who can be called in to mediate disputes between scientists.

State and local governments should establish an independent inspector general–type lawyer who is authorized to investigate allegations of misconduct in crime laboratories the same way that Michael Bromwich investigated the FBI laboratory.

First-rate postgraduate forensic science programs should be established in leading American universities; they are desperately needed, and there are plenty of jobs in the field for highly qualified personnel. Law schools and medical schools should become active sponsors of these programs.

Junk Science, Sloppy Science

The underlying scientific basis for many forensic tests must be objectively reevaluated under the standards enunciated in recent Supreme Court decisions designed to keep junk science out of court.

Microscopic hair-comparison evidence should be abandoned. Instead, mitochondrial DNA testing of hairs should be conducted in any hair evaluation involving a matter of importance.

Like medical labs, all the disciplines in crime labs should be subjected to regulatory oversight and should meet standards of professional organizations. States should create agencies modeled after New York's Forensic Science Review Commission—an independent panel composed of scientists, prosecutors, defense counsel, crime lab directors, police, and judges—that have real authority to provide effective regulation of laboratories.

All crime laboratories must be accredited. This is not a panacea but a good first step. Accreditation should involve rigorous quality-control and quality-assurance review, periodic inspections, and spot checking of technicians' data.

Laboratories must submit to a rigorous proficiency-testing program, including blind proficiency testings, in which samples would be sent in and analyzed as though they were part of an ordinary case. Labs should be rated on their ability to come up with valid results.

In court, the scientists should provide, as a matter of course, information about "controls" and whether they failed; and what the error rate is for a procedure.

Defense lawyers should have all material scientific evidence independently scrutinized, if not retested, by a competent expert. Public defenders and court-appointed lawyers must have funds to retain qualified independent experts.

Every public defender's office should have at least one lawyer who acts as a full time forensic science specialist, helping other lawyers on their cases.

Bad Prosecutors, Bad Cops

Create specialized, blue ribbon disciplinary committees to deal exclusively with misconduct by criminal defense attorneys and prosecutors.

Enhance federal involvement in prosecution of misconduct by state police officers.

Bad Defense Lawyers

Fees for court-appointed lawyers must be raised to a level that will attract competent lawyers to take cases. Public defender salaries should be the same as prosecutors in each jurisdiction to ensure adequate pay levels.

Public defender caseloads should not exceed the generally accepted standards of the National Legal Aid and Defenders Association. Ethical complaints should be filed with the state bar when lawyers are forced to proceed with too many cases.

To ensure high-quality defense services for the poor, there must be performance standards enforced in every jurisdiction—standards that apply both to defender organizations and to individual court-appointed counsel. The standards serve three purposes: educating a skeptical public about what it takes to provide capable lawyers, promoting an understanding of why greater funding is essential, and providing notice to the lawyers themselves of what is expected.

Federal money to assist defense services should be roughly comparable to prosecutorial funding.

Compensation and Victims

Victim services experts should be assigned to assist victims whose mistaken identification testimony turns out to have convicted an innocent defendant.

Each state should pass no-fault compensation statutes to provide decent relief to those who can prove they were wrongly convicted by clear and convincing evidence. New York's no-fault statute, which permits recovery for past and future pain and suffering and lost wages, should be the model.

Appendix 1

The Death Penalty

At the very least, follow the American Bar Association recommendations that call for a moratorium on the death penalty and other affirmative reforms, including adequate compensation and resources for death penalty counsel.

Innocence Commissions

Form state and federal institutions modeled after the Criminal Case Review Commission in the United Kingdom to investigate wrongful convictions. Require the official collection and reporting of data on cases where newly discovered evidence of innocence is the basis for overturning a conviction.

Create and fund Innocence Projects at law schools that will represent clients in DNA and non-DNA cases.

Fund teaching and research on wrongful convictions, causes, and remedies.

An Innocence Network at Law Schools

Appendix 2

DNA Exonerations
At a Glance

DNA Exonerations by State

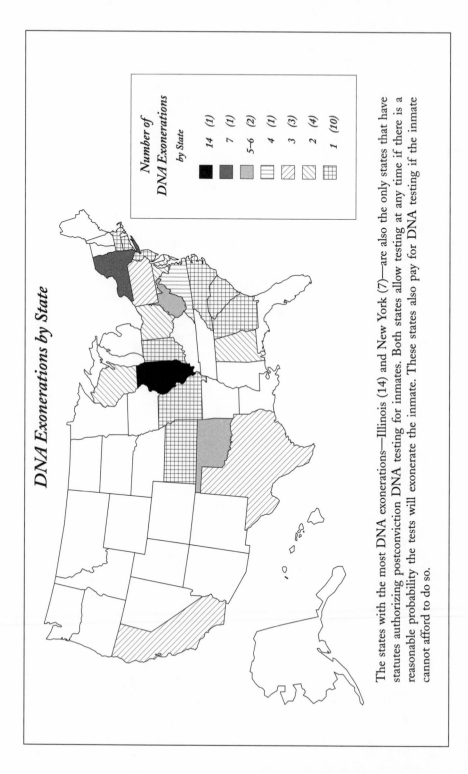

Number of DNA Exonerations by State

■	14 (1)
▦	7 (1)
▨	5–6 (2)
▥	4 (1)
▧	3 (3)
▨	2 (4)
▦	1 (10)

The states with the most DNA exonerations—Illinois (14) and New York (7)—are also the only states that have statutes authorizing postconviction DNA testing for inmates. Both states allow testing at any time if there is a reasonable probability the tests will exonerate the inmate. These states also pay for DNA testing if the inmate cannot afford to do so.

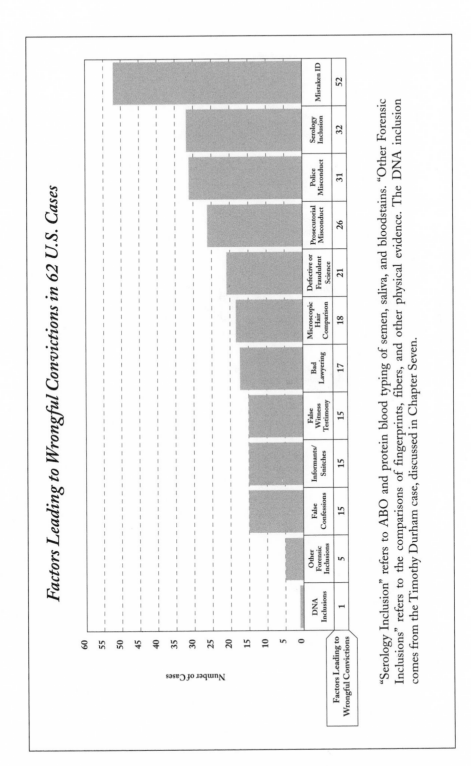

Factors Leading to Wrongful Convictions in 62 U.S. Cases

	DNA Inclusions	Other Forensic Inclusions	False Confessions	Informants/ Snitches	False Witness Testimony	Bad Lawyering	Microscopic Hair Comparison	Defective or Fraudulent Science	Prosecutorial Misconduct	Police Misconduct	Serology Inclusion	Mistaken ID
Factors Leading to Wrongful Convictions	1	5	15	15	15	17	18	21	26	31	32	52

"Serology Inclusion" refers to ABO and protein blood typing of semen, saliva, and bloodstains. "Other Forensic Inclusions" refers to the comparisons of fingerprints, fibers, and other physical evidence. The DNA inclusion comes from the Timothy Durham case, discussed in Chapter Seven.

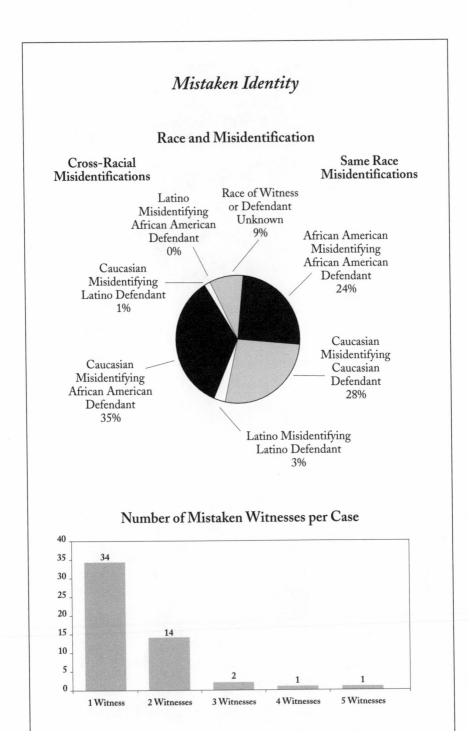

Mistaken Identity

Race and Misidentification

Cross-Racial Misidentifications

Same Race Misidentifications

Latino Misidentifying African American Defendant
0%

Race of Witness or Defendant Unknown
9%

African American Misidentifying African American Defendant
24%

Caucasian Misidentifying Latino Defendant
1%

Caucasian Misidentifying Caucasian Defendant
28%

Caucasian Misidentifying African American Defendant
35%

Latino Misidentifying Latino Defendant
3%

Number of Mistaken Witnesses per Case

	1 Witness	2 Witnesses	3 Witnesses	4 Witnesses	5 Witnesses
	34	14	2	1	1

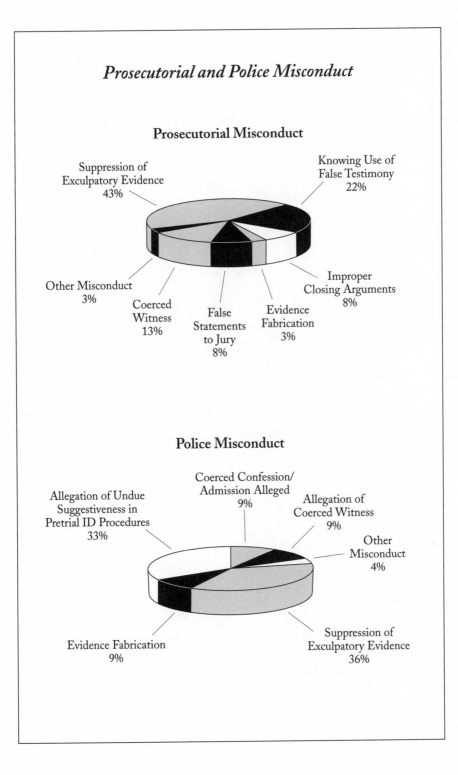

Prosecutorial and Police Misconduct

Prosecutorial Misconduct

Suppression of
Exculpatory Evidence
43%

Knowing Use of
False Testimony
22%

Other Misconduct
3%

Coerced
Witness
13%

False
Statements
to Jury
8%

Evidence
Fabrication
3%

Improper
Closing Arguments
8%

Police Misconduct

Coerced Confession/
Admission Alleged
9%

Allegation of Undue
Suggestiveness in
Pretrial ID Procedures
33%

Allegation of
Coerced Witness
9%

Other
Misconduct
4%

Evidence Fabrication
9%

Suppression of
Exculpatory Evidence
36%

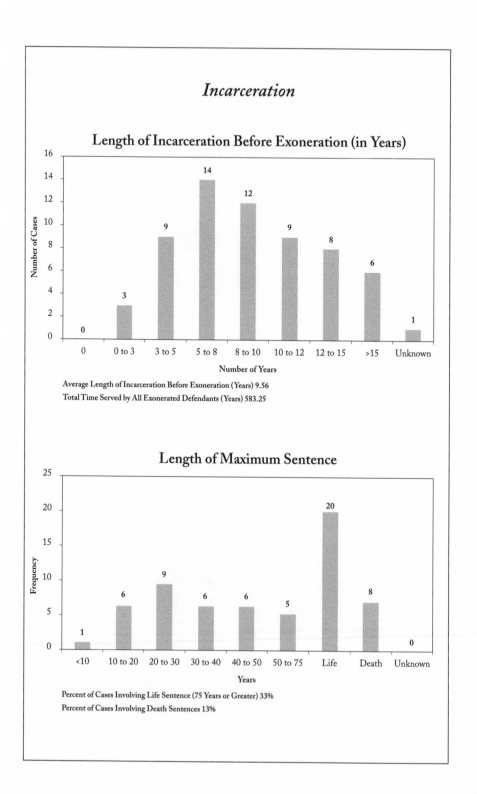

Incarceration

Length of Incarceration Before Exoneration (in Years)

Number of Cases

0	0
0 to 3	3
3 to 5	9
5 to 8	14
8 to 10	12
10 to 12	9
12 to 15	8
>15	6
Unknown	1

Number of Years

Average Length of Incarceration Before Exoneration (Years) 9.56
Total Time Served by All Exonerated Defendants (Years) 583.25

Length of Maximum Sentence

Frequency

<10	1
10 to 20	6
20 to 30	9
30 to 40	6
40 to 50	6
50 to 75	5
Life	20
Death	8
Unknown	0

Years

Percent of Cases Involving Life Sentence (75 Years or Greater) 33%
Percent of Cases Involving Death Sentences 13%

Race

Race of Victim

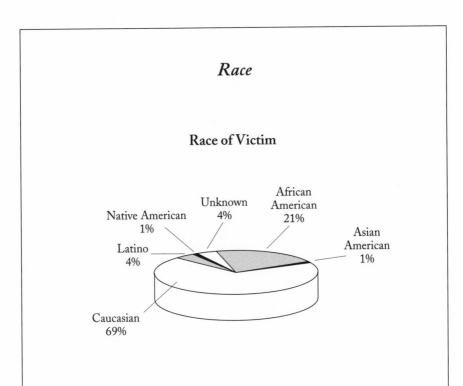

Race of Exonerated Defendant

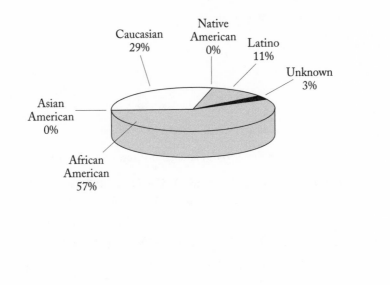

Sources

Preface: Wrong Numbers

CASES

Herrera v. *Collins*, 506 U.S. 390 (1993)

INTERVIEWS

Kevin M. Doyle
Dennis Fritz

BOOKS

Convicted by Juries, Exonerated by Science, National Institute of Justice, 1996

Convicting the Innocent, Edwin M. Borchard, Da Capo Press, 1970 (c. 1932)

JOURNALS

"Meaningless Acquittals, Meaningful Convictions: Do We Reliably Acquit the Innocent?," Daniel Givelber, *Rutgers Law Review* 49: 1317

Chapter One: An Innocence Project

CASES

People of State of New York against Marion Coakley, Ind. No. 816 (1983)

Marion Coakley against the State of New York, Claim No. 77025 (1991)

INTERVIEWS

Donald duBoulay
Ed King
Candace Reid

Chapter Two: An Invention

INTERVIEWS

Ed Blake
Kary Mullis

BOOKS

Dancing Naked in the Mind Field, Kary Mullis, Pantheon Books, 1998

NEWSPAPERS AND MAGAZINES

Gannett News Service, July 1, 1994, "Cases That Have Hinged on DNA Evidence"
Laura Frank and John Hanchette

OTHER SOURCES

Nobel Prize address, Kary Mullis, November 1993

Chapter Three: Seeing Things

CASES

Commonwealth of Virginia v. Walter T. Snyder, No. F8118 (1995)

Snyder v. City of Alexandria, Federal District Court of Virginia

U.S. v. Wade, 388 U.S. 218 (1967)

Gilbert v. California, 388 U.S. 263 (1967)

Actual innocence

Neil v. Biggers, 409 U.S. 188 (1967)

Manson v. Brathwaite, 432 U.S. 98 (1977)

INTERVIEWS

Nina Ginzberg
Elizabeth Loftus
Joseph McCarthy
Barry Shiftic
Edith Snyder
Walter Snyder, Sr.
Walter Snyder, Jr.

BOOKS

On the Witness Stand: Essays on Psychology and Crime, Hugo Munsterberg, Fred B. Rothman & Co., 1926, 1981

Eyewitness Testimony, Gary Wells, Carswell Legal Publications, 1988

Mistaken Identification: The Eyewitness, Psychology, and the Law, Brian L. Cutler and Steven D. Penrod, Cambridge University Press, 1995

Eyewitness Testimony, Elizabeth Loftus, Harvard University Press, 1996

Eyewitness Evidence: A Guide for Law Enforcement, U.S. Department of Justice, 1999

JOURNALS

"Eyewitness Testimony," Robert Buckhout, *Scientific American,* 231, no. 6 (December 1974)

"Nearly 2000 Witnesses Can Be Wrong," Robert Buckhout, *Social Action and the Law,* 2, no. 3 (May 1975)

"External Validity of Research in Legal Psychology," Vladimir J. Konecai and Ebbe B. Ebbesen, *Law and Human Behavior* 3, nos. 1 and 2 (1979)

"Loss of Innocence: Eyewitness Identification and Proof of Guilt," Samuel Gross, *Journal of Legal Studies* 395 (1987)

"Eyewitness Identification: What Can a Psychologist Tell a Jury?," M. McCloskey and H. Egeth, *American Psychologist* 38:550–563

"A Time to Speak, or a Time to Keep Silence," M. McCloskey and H. Egeth, *American Psychologist* 38:573–577

"Process and Outcome Considerations in Juror Evaluation of Eyewitness Testimony," M. McCloskey and H. Egeth, *American Psychologist* 39:1065–1066

NEWSPAPERS AND MAGAZINES

Washington Post, March 16, 1993, "DNA Testing and Judicial System's Flaws," Colman McCarthy

Washington Times, April 22, 1993, "Innocent Man Waits for Word from Wilder," Kristan Metzler

Washington Post, April 24, 1993, "DNA Evidence Frees Prisoner," Patricia Davis

Washington Times, April 24, 1993, "Truth, Via DNA, Sets Virginia Man Free," Kristan Metzler

New York Times, April 25, 1993, "DNA Testing Frees Man Jailed in Rape" (no byline)

New York Newsday, April 26, 1993, "Justice from a Lab Instead of a Court," Jim Dwyer

Washington Post, April 29, 1993, "DNA Test Helps Unlock Prison Cell," Patricia Davis

Washington Post, May 3, 1993, "Trials and Errors," Steve Twomey

Washington Post, July 4, 1993, "Prisoners Play the DNA Card for High Stakes; for Some, It Can Mean Freedom," David Montgomery

Chapter Four: False Confessions

CASES

Oklahoma v. Robert Lee Miller (CRF-87-963)

Robert Lee Miller v. Oklahoma (F-88-593)

INTERVIEWS

Ray Elliot
Garvin Isaacs
Kim Ogg Miller
Rob Miller
Lee Ann Peters

JOURNALS

"The Decision to Confess Falsely: Rational Choice and Irrational Action," Richard J. Ofshe and Richard A. Leo, *Denver University Law Review* 74, no. 4, p. 979 (1997)

Actual innocence

"False Confessions and Fundamental Fairness: The Need for Electronic Recording of Custodial Interrogations," by Gail Johnson, *Boston University Public Interest Law Journal* 6:719 (1997)

"The Social Psychology of Police Interrogation: The Theory and Classification of True and False Confessions," Richard J. Ofshe and Richard A. Leo, *Studies in Law, Politics & Society* 16 (JAI Press, 1997)

NEWSPAPERS AND MAGAZINES

Daily Oklahoman, February 11, 1987, "Police Add Detectives to Murder Task Force," Anthony Thornton

Daily Oklahoman, February 26, 1987, "Death Penalty Sought in Killings" (no byline)

Phoenix New Times, January 8, 1992, "The Ultimate True-or-False Test: You Wouldn't Confess to Murder If You Didn't Do It," Philip Martin

Daily Oklahoman, January 23, 1995, "DNA Results Lead to Second Suspect, New Trial in Deaths," Ed Godfrey

Daily Oklahoman, February 2, 1996, "Charges Dropped in Deaths," Ed Godfrey

Daily Oklahoman, August 29, 1996, "Judge to Rely on Videotape to Decide Inmate's Trial Fate," Ed Godfrey

Daily Oklahoman, February 8, 1997, "Charges Against Inmate Dropped in 2 Slayings," Ed Godfrey

Daily Oklahoman, March 1, 1997, "Judge to Mull Charge Reinstatement," Ed Godfrey

Daily Oklahoman, March 14, 1997, "Retrial Ordered in Deaths of 2 Elderly City Women. Dismissal of Charges on DNA Evidence Overturned," Ed Godfrey

Daily Oklahoman, March 20, 1997, "Charges Refiled in '80s Slayings," Ed Godfrey

Daily Oklahoman, January 23, 1998, "After 11 Years, Former Death Row Inmate Gains Freedom," Ed Godfrey

Daily Oklahoman, March 21, 1998, "DNA Tests Link Inmate to Murders; Judge Orders Trial," Ed Godfrey

Tulsa World, "State Urged to End Death Penalty, Group Hears *Dead Man Walking* Author," Ashley Parrish

Chicago Tribune, January 10, 1999, "'Cowboy Bob' Wins but at Considerable Cost," Ken Armstrong

Chapter Five: White Coat Fraud

CASES

State of West Virginia v. Glen Dale Woodall (Ind. No. 87-F-46)

Glen Dale Woodall v. Carl Logursky, Warden, Civil Action No. 89-C-1332

State of West Virginia v. William Harris (Ind. No. 86-F-442)

Robert Carl Crain, et al., v. Donald E. Bordenkircher, Warden, No. 16646, Supreme Court of Appeals of West Virginia

State ex rel. William Harris, Jr., petitioner v. George Trent, Warden, No. 93-W-43

OTHER DOCUMENTS

Letter, July 29, 1992, from Steven P. McGowan, Attorney, Steptoe & Johnson, Charleston, W. Va., to Bruce Harding, CNA Insurance Companies, Charleston

In re: An Investigation of the West Virginia State Police Crime Laboratory, Serology Division, 190 W. Va. 321, 323, 438, S.E.2d 501, 503 (1993)

"The FBI Laboratory: An Investigation into Laboratory Practices and Alleged Misconduct in Explosives-Related and Other Cases," Michael R. Bromwich, Inspector General, U.S. Department of Justice, 1997

"Lab Fraud, Wrongful Convictions, and Freeing the Innocent: The Lessons Learned from the 'Fred Zain' Affair," George Castelle (in manuscript)

INTERVIEWS

George Castelle (1998, 1999)
Lonnie Simmons (1992, 1999)
Glen Dale Woodall (1992)

JOURNALS

"The Abuse of Scientific Evidence in Criminal Cases: The Need for Independent Crime Laboratories," Paul Gianelli, *Virginia Journal of Social Policy and Law* 4:439 (1997)

NEWSPAPERS AND MAGAZINES

From 1992 to 1999, scores of articles from the *Charleston Daily Mail* and the *Charleston Gazette,* including:

Daily Mail, September 23, 1992, "One Million Explanation Needed," editorial

Gazette, September 24, 1992, "Woodall Settlement Concerns Legislators," Associated Press (no byline)

Daily Mail, January 6, 1997, "Zain Just Didn't Make the Grade: Chemistry Was Never Strong Suit for Serologist," Kay Michael

Daily Mail, January 8, 1997, "Mall Rapist Case Just the Beginning of Troubles: Zain's Testimony in Case Earned Him Praise from His Boss," Kay Michael

Daily Mail, January 9, 1997, "Co-Workers Say They Reported Mistakes," Kay Michael

Gazette, September 27, 1997, "Settlement Reached in Harris Suit," Kay Michael

Other publications consulted include:

Houston Chronicle, March 8, 1992, "Autopsy Record of Pathologist Who Quit Raises Many Eyebrows," Roy Bragg

Gannett News Service, July 16, 1994, "A Look at Some Folks Who Put Up False Evidence," Laura Frank and John Hanchette

Gannett News Service, July 16, 1994, "Defendants in False Evidence Cases at Clear Disadvantage," Stacey McKenzie

Gannett News Service, July 19, 1994, "Convicted on False Evidence," Laura Frank and John Hanchette

Associated Press, June 8, 1995, "Bodies Have Come Back to Haunt Rogue Pathologist," Jean Pagel

Chicago Tribune, February 25, 1999, "Man Cleared in Rape Revels in His Freedom," Anthony Colarossi and Terry Wilson

TV BROADCASTS

48 Hours, January 28, 1999, "Fighting the System," Susan Spencer and Peter Van Sant, reporters

Chapter Six: Snitch

CASES

State of Oklahoma v. Ronald Keith Williamson and Dennis Leon Fritz, CRF87-90

In the U.S. District Court for the Eastern District of Oklahoma: *Ronald Keith Williamson v. Dan Reynolds,* No. CIV 94-539-S Order Granting Writ of Habeas Corpus

INTERVIEWS

Mark Barrett

Sara Bonnell

Janet Chesley

Dennis Fritz

Terri Holland

Ben Hudson

Alex Obelin

Bill Peterson

Chris Ross

Mike Tenney

Ron Williamson

BOOKS

The Dreams of Ada, Robert Mayer, Signet, 1991

JOURNALS

"The Informant Trap," Mark Corriden, *National Law Journal,* March 20, 1995

NEWSPAPERS AND MAGAZINES

Los Angeles Times, November 3, 1988, "Jail Informer First Told of Scam in '87," Ted Rohrlich

Los Angeles Times, November 13, 1988, "Jailhouse Infomants: The DA's Ethical Bind," Kevin Cody

Los Angeles Times, December 7, 1988, "Early Checks on Use of Jail Informants Were Rejected," Ted Rohrlich and Robert W. Stewart

Time, December 12, 1988, "A Snitch's Story" (no byline)

Los Angeles Times, April 16, 1989, "Jailhouse Snitches: Trading Lies for Freedom," Ted Rohrlich and Robert W. Stewart

Los Angeles Times, October 20, 1989, "Informant-Aided Convictions Going Unchallenged," Ted Rohrlich

St. Louis Post-Dispatch, April 12, 1998, "A Sheriff's Belief in Him Led to His Freedom, Despite Implications of Jailhouse Snitch," Terry L. Nelson

Norman Transcript, April 16, 1999, "Escapee Suspect in 1982 Murder," Jane Glenn Cannon

Kansas City Star, April 18, 1999, "A Fateful Friendship Led to Prison and Pain," Malcolm Garcia

New York Daily News, April 18, 1999, "Death Row Lacks Prime Candidate," Jim Dwyer

Ada Evening News, April 21, 1999, "Prosecutor Defends His Work in High Profile Case," Ann Kelley

Daily Oklahoman, April 21, 1999, "Escapee Surrenders to Prison Officials," Associated Press (no byline)

Ada Evening News, April 24, 1999, "Gore Surrenders to Prison Officials," Ann Kelley

Purcell (Oklahoma) Register, April 24, 1999, "Escapee and Murder Suspect Turns Himself in Tuesday Night" (no byline)

New York Daily News, May 2, 1999, "Ex-Death Row Inmate Finally Sees the Stadium," Jim Dwyer

Chapter Seven: Junk Science

CASES

State of Oklahoma v. Timothy Edward Durham (CF-91-4922)

Timothy Edward Durham v. State of Oklahoma (F-93-913)

In the U.S. District Court for the Eastern District of Oklahoma: *Ronald Keith Williamson v. Dan Reynolds,* No. CIV 94-539-S Order Granting Writ of Habeas Corpus

INTERVIEWS

Tim Durham
Richard O'Carroll
Sharisse O'Carroll

JOURNALS

"Out of the Blue" Mark Hansen, *ABA Journal,* February 1996

"The Abuse of Scientific Evidence in Criminal Cases: The Need for Independent Crime Laboratories," Paul Gianelli, *Virginia Journal of Social Policy and Law* 4:439 (1997)

NEWSPAPERS AND MAGAZINES

Gannett News Service, July 16, 1994, "Defendants in False Evidence Cases at Clear Disadvantage," Stacey McKenzie

Gannett News Service, July 19, 1994, "Convicted on False Evidence," Laura Frank and John Hanchette

Chapter Eight: Broken Oaths

CASES

Commonwealth of Massachusetts v. Cornish, 28 Mass. App. Ct. 173 (1989)

People of State of New York v. Kerry Kotler, 2480-81

Glen Dale Woodall v. Carl Logursky, Warden, Civil Action No. 89-C-1332

Timothy Edward Durham v. State of Oklahoma (F-93-913)

Billy Wardell v. City of Chicago, 98 C 8002

Marvin Mitchell v. City of Boston, Trent Holland, and Robin DeMarco, 98-3693

INTERVIEWS

Tom Breen
Larry Marshall
Noah Rosmarin
Randy Schaffer
Lonnie Simmons
Flint Taylor
Rob Warden

JOURNALS

"The New Prosecutors," Bennett L. Gershman, *University of Pittsburgh Law Review* 53:393 (1992)

"Just the Facts, Ma'am: Lying and Omission of Exculpatory Evidence in Police Reports," Stanley Z. Fisher, *New England Law Review* 28:1 (1993)

NEWSPAPERS AND MAGAZINES

Chicago Tribune, Eric Zorn columns, including 1994: February 6, 8, 15, 17, 22, 24; March 1, 3, 6, 8, 10, 13, 15, 17, 20; July 14, 15, 19, 31; October 27

Vanity Fair, October 1996, "Presumed Guilty," M. A. Farber

New York Times, December 13, 1996 "Ex-prosecutors and Deputies in Death Row Case Are Charged with Framing Defendant," Don Terry

Boston Globe, May 7, 1997, "Officers Defend Actions in Raid of Wrong Home," Patricia Nealon

Actual innocence

Houston Chronicle, July 29, 1997, "After 12 years, DNA Clears Inmate in Rape Case," John Makeig

Chicago Tribune Magazine, August 10, 1997, "Nine Lives," David Protess and Rob Warden

Houston Chronicle, September 11, 1997, "Cleared Man Loses a Bid for Pardon," John Makeig

Dallas Morning News, October 3, 1997, "Attorney Seeking Pardon Says Bush Asked for Gift," Wayne Slater

Fort Worth Star-Telegram, October 9, 1997, "Bush Will Pardon Byrd, Based on Court Ruling," Jay Root

Chicago Tribune, January 22, 1998, "Perjury Charge Dropped Against Key Cruz Witness," Art Barnum and Ted Gregory

Chicago Tribune, January 8, 1999–January 12, 1999, "Trial and Error," series by Ken Armstrong and Maurice Possley

Chicago Tribune, June 5, 1999, "Dupage 5 Win Acquittal," Maurice Possley and Ted Gregory

Chicago Tribune, June 6, 1999, "Cruz, Lack of Evidence Hurt Case, Jurors Say," Jeff Coen and Lynn Van Matre

Chapter Nine: Sleeping Lawyers

CASES

Illinois v. Dennis Williams, 93 Ill.2d 309 1982

In re: Archie Benjamin Weston, 92 Ill.2d 431 1982

INTERVIEWS

Stephen Bright
Kate Hill
Rev. Jim McCloskey
Rob Miller
Kim Ogg
Lee Ann Peters
David Shephard
Carmela Simoncini

Rebecca Stith
Rob Warden
Stormy White

BOOKS

Gideon's Trumpet, Anthony Lewis, Vintage Books, 1966

A Promise of Justice: The Eighteen Year Fight to Save Four Innocent Men, David Protess and Rob Warden, Hyperion, 1998

No Equal Justice: Race and Class in the American Criminal Justice System, David Cole, New Press, 1999

JOURNALS

"Neither Equal Nor Just: The Rationing and Denial of Legal Services to the Poor When Life and Liberty Are at Stake," Stephen B. Bright, New York University School of Law, *Annual Survey of American Law,* 1997, no. 4

"Rates of Compensation Paid to Court-Appointed Counsel in Non-Capital Felony Cases at Trial: A State-by-State Overview, 1997," Marea Beeman and David Carroll for the Spangenberg Group. The American Bar Association Bar Program

NEWSPAPERS AND MAGAZINES

Los Angeles Times, September 24, 1994, "DNA Test Frees Inmate After 10 Years," Tony Perry

San Diego Tribune, December 11, 1994, "Innocence Lost and Found," Mark Sauer and Uri Berliner

Chapter Ten: Race

CASES

The State of Georgia v. Calvin Crawford Johnson, Jr., Criminal Action No. 83 Cr. 12-22011-3

McClesky v. Kemp, 481 U.S. 279 (1987)

OTHER DOCUMENTS

"Interim Report of the State Police Review Team Regarding Allegations of Racial Profiling," Peter Verniero, Attorney General, State of New Jersey, April 20, 1999

Actual innocence

INTERVIEWS

Stephen Bright
Calvin Johnson, Sr.
Calvin Johnson, Jr.
Tara Johnson
Robert Keller

BOOKS

Among the Lowest of the Dead: The Culture of Death Row, David Von Drehle, Times Books, 1995

Legal Lynching: Racism, Injustice & the Death Penalty, Rev. Jesse Jackson, Marlowe & Co, in association with National Press Books, 1996

No Equal Justice: Race and Class in the American Criminal Justice System, David Cole, New Press, 1999

JOURNALS

"Discrimination, Death and Denial: The Tolerance of Racial Discrimination in Infliction of the Death Penalty," Stephen B. Bright, *Santa Clara Law Review* 35, no. 2 (1995)

NEWSPAPERS AND MAGAZINES

Atlanta Journal-Constitution, February 8, 1998, "Whites More Apt to Get Probation," Bill Rankin

New York Times, June 16, 1999, "DNA Test Brings Freedom, 16 Years After Conviction," David Firestone

New York Daily News, June 17, 1999, "Freed After 16-year Error," Jim Dwyer

Atlanta Journal-Constitution, June 20, 1999, "From Inmate to Celebrity" (no byline)

Chapter Eleven: The Death of Innocents

CASES

State of Maryland v. Kirk Bloodsworth, Case No. 84-CR-3138 (two trials: March 1985; retrial, April 1987)

OTHER DOCUMENTS

"Innocence and the Death Penalty: The Increasing Danger of Executing the Innocent," Richard C. Dieter, Esq., Death Penalty Information Center, July 1997

"Post-conviction DNA Testing: Recommendations for Handling Requests," Commission on the Future of DNA Evidence, National Institute of Justice, September 1999

Other reports on the World Wide Web, http://www.essential.org/dpic

INTERVIEWS

Kirk Bloodsworth

BOOKS

Among the Lowest of the Dead: The Culture of Death Row, David Von Drehle, Times Books, 1995

Legal Lynching: Racism, Injustice & the Death Penalty, Rev. Jesse Jackson, Marlowe & Co., in association with National Press Books, 1996

A Promise of Justice, David Protess and Rob Warden, Hyperion, 1998

JOURNALS

"Miscarriages of Justice in Potentially Capital Cases," Hugo Bedau and Michael Rodelet, *Stanford Law Review* 40:21 (1987)

"Protecting the Innocent: A Response to the Bedau Radelet Study," Steven Markman and Paul Cassell, *Stanford Law Review* 41:121 (1988)

"Responding to *Herrera* v. *Collins:* Ensuring That Innocents Are Not Executed," Tara Swafford, *Case Western Reserve Law Review* 45:603 (1995)

NEWSPAPERS AND MAGAZINES

Baltimore Evening Sun, July 26, 1984, "Man Hunted in Killing of Area Girl," Anthony Pipitone and Jenny Abdo

Baltimore Sun, July 27, 1984, "No Solid Leads Found in Girl's Killing," Milton Kent

Baltimore Evening Sun, July 27, 1984, "Drawing Issued of Slaying Suspect" (no byline)

Baltimore Sun, August 10, 1984, "Psychological Profile of Suspect Drawn by FBI," Ann LoLordo

Actual innocence

Baltimore Evening Sun, August 10, 1984, "Man Arrested in Girl's Death in Rosedale" (no byline); "Slaying Suspect a 'Nice Guy,'" Anthony Pipitone

Boston Globe, July 24, 1993, "Ex-Death Row Inmates Hit Plan to Curb Appeals," Joel Engardio

Baltimore Sun, January 9, 1994, "Innocent Man's Ordeal Raises Many Questions," Glenn Small

Chapter Twelve: Starting Over

CASES

People of the State of New York against Kerry Kotler, 2480-81

INTERVIEWS

Paul Casteleiro
Kevin Green
Joseph McCarthy
David Shephard
Barry Shiftic
Jennifer Thompson

JOURNALS

"Tough Luck for the Innocent Man," Michael Higgins, *ABA Journal,* March 1999

"When Justice Fails: Indemnification for Unjust Conviction," Adele Bernhard, University of Chicago, *The Roundtable,* Fall 1999

NEWSPAPERS AND MAGAZINES

Newark Star Ledger, April 29, 1995, "DNA Evidence Exonerates Man of Kidnap-Rape," Robert Misseck

Newark Star Ledger, February 8, 1997, "Costly Mistake Haunts an Innocent Man," Robert Schwanberg

Newark Star Ledger, March 16, 1997, "If Time Is Money, the State Owes This Man 11 Years' Worth," Fran Wood

Newark Star Ledger, March 25, 1997, "Bill Allows Suit for Wrongful Conviction," Robert Schwanberg

TV BROADCASTS

Frontline (Show #1508) February 25, 1997, "What Jennifer Saw"

Chapter Thirteen: Lessons

CASES

Interview of Gerald Parker by Tustin Investigator Tom Tarpley, CMPD Detectives Giesler and Redmond (Case 79-34249)

In the U.S. District Court for the Eastern District of Oklahoma: *Ronald Keith Williamson v. Dan Reynolds*, No. CIV 94-539-S Order Granting Writ of Habeas Corpus

INTERVIEWS

Mark Barrett
Kirk Bloodsworth
Tim Durham
Dennis Fritz
Kevin Green
Annette Hudson
Calvin Johnson
Gregory Lasak
Robert Miller
Walter Snyder
Tom Tarpley
Greg Wilhoit
Ron Williamson
Glen Dale Woodall

JOURNALS

"Miscarriages of Justice in Potentially Capital Cases," Hugo Bedau and Michael Radelet, *Stanford Law Review* 40:21 (1987)

"Protecting the Innocent: A Response to the Bedau Radelet Study," Steven Markman and Paul Cassell, *Stanford Law Review* 41:121 (1988)

"Responding to *Herrera* v. *Collins:* Ensuring That Innocents Are Not Executed," Tara Swafford, *Case Western Reserve Law Review* 45:603 (1995)

Actual innocence

NEWSPAPERS AND MAGAZINES

United Press International, April 30, 1988, "Suspect Linked to Serial Rapes," (no byline; dateline, Richmond, Virginia)

United Press International, November 30, 1988, "Spencer Gets Second Death Sentence," Lori K. Weinraub

United Press International, January 4, 1989, "Governor Pardons Man Wrongly Convicted of Murder," Carolyn Click

Washington Post, February 14, 1990, "Virginia Senate Allows Compensation for Innocent Man," Donald P. Baker and Dana Priest

New York Times, March 3, 1993, "Alabama Releases Man Held on Death Row for Six Years," Peter Applebome

Orange County Register, June 22, 1996, "Falsely Jailed: What Happened?," Anne C. Mulkern, Bryon MacWilliams, and Tony Saavedra

Los Angeles Times, June 26, 1996, "Green's Ex-Wife Insists He Beat Her," Rene Lynch and Dexter Filkins

Orange County Register, June 27, 1996, "Alibis Didn't Wash with Jury," John McDonald

Orange County Register, January 2, 1997, "Tustin Police Honor Their Finest," George Stewart

Orange County Register, March 1, 1998, "State DNA Database Lacks 200,000 Samples," Stuart Pfeifer

Los Angeles Times, January 22, 1999, "Another Bizarre Twist in a Macabre Tale," Mike Downey

Los Angeles Times, January 22, 1999. "Man Sentenced to Death in Killings," Daniel Yi

New York Daily News, May 2, 1999, "Ex-Death Row Inmate Finally Sees the Stadium," Jim Dwyer

St. Petersburg Times, June 21, 1999, "DNA Testing Denied to Inmates Seeking Justice," Sydney P. Freedberg

OTHER SOURCES

"The Walter McMillian Case," Equal Justice Initiative, Montgomery, Alabama

Acknowledgments

The work on this book began long before we realized it, early in 1992, when Barry passed along the legal papers for one of the early innocence cases to Rich Esposito, then an editor at *New York Newsday*, who handed it off to Jim. Before long, Peter was pulling up in a station wagon to drive all three of us to prison. After a few polite hellos, we commenced the arguments. The breadth of revelations from the DNA era can, but need not, rest on any single case. Though we record the experiences of only a few here, our prime debt is to dozens of wrongfully convicted men, some still imprisoned, and their loved ones. Their grace and hard-earned wisdom have made this book possible. We are grateful to them all. One can only be inspired by all those who have left prison to lead lives of honor and dignity.

In particular, we acknowledge Walter Snyder and his family, Rob Miller and Kim Ogg, Glen Dale Woodall, Dennis Fritz and Elizabeth Fritz, Ron Williamson and Annette Hudson, Tim Durham, Calvin Johnson, Jr., Calvin Johnson, Sr., and other members of the Johnson family, Kirk Bloodsworth, David Shephard, and Kevin Green.

Acknowledgments

Our own families have been patient, tolerant, and loving beyond measure. For this, and much else, Peter thanks his wife, Adele Bernhard, and their children, Shane and Lena, as well as his mother, Muriel Neufeld, who always knows right from wrong, and his brother, Russell, whose passion for social and economic justice is infectious. Barry thanks his wife, Dorothy Rick. Their children, Gabe and Olivia, have grown up while this book was written. Jim's younger daughter, Catherine, born not long after this effort began, spurred its completion by observing: "I always know where to find you: sleeping or working on the book." Jim's older daughter, Maura, and his wife, Cathy, helped bring a third book in for its landing.

We thank Flip Brophy, our literary agent and friend. At Doubleday, Pat Mulcahy made sure this project got going, and Bill Thomas insured that it was finished. We also thank Linda Steinman, Deborah Cowell, Harold Grabau, Maria Carella, and Michelle Paolella.

From Jim:

Jim has been fortunate to have as friends and teachers Raymond A. Schroth, S.J., and Kevin M. Doyle. Editors and the talented librarians at two newspapers, the late *New York Newsday* and the *New York Daily News,* have supported the reporting on these subjects. They include Don Forst, Rich Galant, Martin Dunn, Pete Hamill, Debbie Krenek, Bill Boyle, Karen Von-Rossen, Christine Baird, Donna Mendes, Karen Magruder, Caroline Brooks, Faigi Rosenthal, Pete Edelman, Alan DeLaqueriere, Ellen Locker, Scott Browne, Scott Widener, Shirley Wong, Jimmy Converso, Dawn Jackson, Matt Silverman, among others. He thanks Dee Lyons of the *Baltimore Sun* library, and Alexandra Pelosi of NBC's *Dateline.*

Kirsten Hamilton was a tremendous help to Jim at several stages of this book, and he benefited from the moral support of two great friends, Kevin P. Hayes and the late Mike McAlary. Other friends who helped were Jenny Avecillas, Tom Curran, Dave Hunt, Peter Walsh, and Niall O'Dowd. His brothers, Pat, Philip, and John, and their families, as well as Julia and Dennis Sullivan, Bob and Cassie Muir, and Sheila Carmody, all contributed wisdom, support, and love. Jim also thanks R by honoring his wish for invisibility.

Jim is particularly grateful for guidance on DNA testing provided by Ed Blake, and the insights of Steve Bright into the experiences of the poor in the American legal system.

For helping to round out the picture of these cases, Jim thanks Ed King, Candace Reid, Bob Thompson, Jim Catterson, Joseph McCarthy, Barry Shiftic, Ray Elliott, Bill Peterson, Robert Keller, Tom Tarpley, Stormy White, Kerry Kotler, Burton Roberts, Jennifer Thompson, and Mike Downey.

From Peter and Barry:

Writing a book such as this presents many of the same problems as reopening old convictions. The years passed, witnesses and principals sometimes died or moved away, and evidence was often lost or destroyed. This book was eight years in the making; the Innocence Project is almost as old, and over so long a period there are many people who contributed and must be thanked.

Dozens of law students from Cardozo and other schools (lawyers, doctors, high school students, scientists) make the Innocence Project work. We mention only a few here who must stand for many others. The heart and soul of the Project over the years are the full-time staff: Jane Siegel Greene, Huy Dao, Gille Ann Rabbin, Elena Aviles, Elizabeth Vaca—without whom nothing at Cardozo could happen—Jonas Kant, Jeremy Manning, Sara Miller, and Jill Smith.

The entire faculty and staff of Cardozo Law School deserve special thanks, particularly Ellen Yaroshefsky, Jonathan Oberman, Louise Hochberg, Mira Gurari, Larry Vogelman, Myriam Gilles, Peter Lushing, Kyron Higgins, who helped on cases; deans Paul Verkuil, Frank Macchiarola, Monroe Price, and Lester Brickman; administrators Susan Ebersole, Debby Niederhoffer, Dan Forman, and Matt Levine. And from Columbia University School of Law, Ellen Chapnick, Director of the Center for Public Interest Law, has attracted her students as well. Special thanks to the people at Open Society Institute: Catherine Samuels, Nancy Mahon, and Tanya Coke.

We thank the scientists, including Ed Blake, Bill Thompson, Eric Lan-

Acknowledgments

der, David Page, Lorraine Flaherty, Conrad Gilliam, Bill Shields, Paul Hagerman, Terry Speed, Peter D'Eustachio, Richard Lewontin, Dan Hartl, Larry Mueller, Simon Ford, Jay Koehler, Paul Ferrera, Alan Kheel, David Werrett, Mike Barber, Pam Newell, Brian Wraxall, Peter Barnett, Dave Bing, Henry Lee, Michael Baden, Cyril Wecht, Mark Taylor, Elizabeth Johnson, Marcia Eisenberg, Larry Ragle, Fred Whitehurst, Michael Baird, Robin Cotton, Mark Stolorow, Charlotte Word, George Herrin, Fred Drummond, Stephen Penrod, Sam Gross, Bruce Budowle, Dwight Adams, John Simich, Jennifer Mihalovich, Gary Sims, Bradley Popovich, Kary Mullis, Mary Long, Robert Shaler, Howard Baum, Terri Melton, Phil Reilly, Jennifer Lindsay Smith, and Jan Bashinski.

Our appreciation also to the lawyers, advocates, and academics who are working on innocence projects, doing cases, and helping form an Innocence Network: Larry Marshall, David Protess, Rob Warden, and Jim McCloskey and Kate Hill of the Centurion Ministries, James Lockyer, Peter Meier, and Rubin "Hurricane" Carter of AIDWIC, Locke Bowman, Matthew Kennelly, Catherine Arcabascio, Milton Hirsch, Carol Henderson, Jacqueline McMurtrie, Fred Leatherman, Richard Rosen, Jim Coleman, Diane Martin, Sheila Berry, Darryl Brown, Len Cavise, Keith Findly, Stanley Fisher, Lionel Frankel, Paul Giannelli, Sally Frank, Lionel Frankel, Dan Givelber, Roberta Harding, Fran Hardy, Johann Herklotz, Michelle Jacobs, Ellen Kreitzberg, Carolyn Kubota, Bill Summers, Gerald Uelmen, David Gottlieb, Bruce Lyons, the Testa & Hurwitz firm, Ron Weich, Eric Freedman, Larry Yackle, Michael Avery, Steven Wisotsky, Kenneth Margolis, Thomas Kaczka, Kay Anderson, Scott Turow, Stephen Schulhofer, Noah Rosmarin, David Kelston, Kathleen Zelner, Bennett Gershman, Rebecca Stith, Flint Taylor, Bob Morin, Richard Ofshe, Richard Leo, Gary Wells, Elizabeth Loftus, Hugo Bedeau, Michael Radelet, Richard Huff, Dick Dieter, George Kendall, Steve Bright, Bryan Stevenson, Charles Ogletree, Phil Cormier, Gia Baresi, Jeff Fagan, Chris Stone, Jo Ann Harris, Paul Shechtman, Carl Slevaka, Bob Byman, Mark Ter Molen, William Murphy, Jeffrey Urdangen, Daniel Sanders, and Roger Appell.

We were helped by a remarkable group of public and capital defenders, including George Castelle, Alan Sincox, Greg O'Reilly, Mark Barrett, Sara

Bonnell, Marty McClain, Rita Fry, Jonathan Gradess, Jeff Thoma, Carmela Simoncini, Janet Chesley, Lee Ann Peters, Lisa Schwind, and Michelle Fox. We are grateful to the staff at the National Institute of Justice: Jeremy Travis, Dick Rau, Chris Asplan, Lisa Forman, Robin Wilson, their boss, Attorney General Janet Reno, and the entire subcommittee that wrote the NIJ's *Post-conviction DNA Testing: Recommendations for Handling Requests*.

The National Association of Criminal Defense Lawyers has been an indispensable resource to the Innocence Project. Special mention must go to cooperating attorneys who worked on cases including Paul Casteleiro, Garvin Isaacs, Gerry Goldstein, Stanley Schneider, Cynthia Orr, Randy Schaffer, Bob Glass, John Holdridge, Jim Boren, Gene Mauer, Anthony Bertucci, Murray Janus, Bill Rittenberg, Kemper Durand, Jerry Zirinsky, Jeralyn Merritt, Cristina Gutierrez, David Ruhnke, Jean Barret, Terry Gilbert, Steve Riggs, Jerry Buting, Cheryl Pilate, Sean O'Brien, Burt Shostak, Pat Conrad, Richard Friedman, Andrea Lyon, Erika Kreisman, Sharisse and Richard O'Carroll, Jim Jenkins, Wendy Jenkins, Rebecca Gwinn, Joe Johnson, Tom Breen, Nan Nolan, Andy Good, Harvey Silverglate, Dick Cunningham, Gary Pritchard, Steve Riggs, Nick Trentacosta, Lisa Kemler.

Peter and Barry wish to thank their colleagues at work who supported this undertaking: Richard Finkelstein, John Lewis, Eric Saltzman, and Manuel Quintana. Naomi Fein, a brilliant writer, masks as Peter's assistant. Finally, Peter and Barry thank their special friend and partner, Johnnie Cochran, Jr.

Index

Index

Index

Index

Index